AMERICA IN THE THIRTIES

AMERICA IN THE TWENTIETH CENTURY

John Robert Greene, *Series Editor*

Other titles from America in the Twentieth Century

America in the Twenties
Ronald Allen Goldberg

America in the Forties
Ronald Allen Goldberg

America in the Fifties
Andrew J. Dunar

America in the Sixties
John Robert Greene

America in the Seventies
Stephanie A. Slocum-Schaffer

AMERICA IN THE THIRTIES

John Olszowka
Marnie M. Sullivan
Brian R. Sheridan
Dennis Hickey

With a Foreword by John Robert Greene

SYRACUSE UNIVERSITY PRESS

First Edition 2014
14 15 16 17 18 19 6 5 4 3 2 1

∞ The paper used in this publication meets the minimum requirements of the American National Standard for Information Sciences—Permanence of Paper for Printed Library Materials, ANSI Z39.48-1992.

For a listing of books published and distributed by Syracuse University Press, visit www.SyracuseUniversityPress.syr.edu.

ISBN: 978-0-8156-3380-8 (cloth)
978-0-8156-3378-5 (paper)
978-0-8156-5285-4 (e-book)

Library of Congress Cataloging-in-Publication Data

Olszowka, John.

America in the thirties / John Olszowka, Marnie M. Sullivan, Brian R. Sheridan, Dennis Hickey ; with a foreword by John Robert Greene.

pages cm. — (America in the twentieth century)

Includes index.

ISBN 978-0-8156-3380-8 (cloth : alk. paper) — ISBN 978-0-8156-3378-5 (pbk. : alk. paper) — ISBN 978-0-8156-5285-4 (ebook) 1. United States—History—1933–1945. 2. United States—History—1919–1933. 3. Nineteen thirties. I. Title.

E806.O54 2014

909.82'3—dc23 2014029024

Manufactured in the United States of America

To All Our Families and Friends

Dr. John Olszowka is associate professor in the History Department at Mercyhurst University and specializes in labor and working-class history, with a focus on the 1930s. He has written several articles, including "The UAW's Struggle to Organize the Aircraft Industry, 1937–1942" and "The Niagara Frontier Defense Leagues Patriotic War on Labor, 1917–1919." He is completing a manuscript tentatively titled *"I Am the Curtiss Man": Work and Labor at the Curtiss Aeroplane and Motor Company, 1908–1945*, which looks at the rise of organized labor in the aircraft industry. In addition he is working on a project exploring the anti-communist movement in Buffalo, New York. Dr. Olszowka earned a PhD in history from Binghamton University. His teaching interests include immigration, African American history, the Progressive Era, and interwar America, 1919–1939.

Dr. Marnie M. Sullivan is an assistant professor of English at Mercyhurst University. She has interdisciplinary interests that include the creative expressions of traditionally underrepresented groups such as women, people of color, immigrants, LGBTQ, and those among the working class. In addition, she studies literature of the environment and science writing, and these interests collectively inform her scholarship of the 1930s. She has also conducted research and presented papers on feminist pedagogy and teaching practices, service learning, and learning communities, and has published articles on Rachel Carson and teaching Native American literature. Dr. Sullivan earned a PhD in literature from Bowling Green State University in 2004 with a dissertation that examined both the scientific and literary aspects of Rachel Carson's three sea books.

Brian R. Sheridan, MA, is a faculty member in the communication department at Mercyhurst University. He teaches new media, journalism, and film, with emphasis on broadcast news and the Golden Age of Hollywood. Sheridan also works as a freelance journalist for a variety of publications. He previously spent more than twenty years in broadcast news as an award-winning reporter and anchor.

Dennis Hickey is an associate professor in the Department of History, Anthropology, and World Languages at Edinboro University of Pennsylvania. He received his BA and MA from Michigan State University and his PhD in history from Northwestern University. He is co-author, with Kenneth C. Wylie, of *An Enchanting Darkness: The American Vision of Africa in the Twentieth Century*, and the editor of volume 5 (*Sub-Saharan Africa*) of the *Greenwood Encyclopedia of World Popular Cultures*. His most recent publication is "From Marginal to Mainstream: Barack Hussein Obama and the Enigma of American Identity," in *Obama, U.S. Politics, and Transatlantic Relations*, ed. Giles Scott-Smith (Brussels: Peter Lang, 2012).

Contents

Foreword, *John Robert Greene* *ix*

Preface *xi*

Acknowledgments *xv*

Introduction *1*

1. The Coming of the Great Depression *4*
2. The Rise of Franklin Roosevelt *28*
3. The Environment and Science *51*
4. African Americans *77*
5. The Second New Deal, 1933–1940 *101*
6. Workers and the Labor Movement *134*
7. Gender *166*
8. Media *202*
9. Isolationism Interrupted *245*

Conclusion *278*

Index *283*

Foreword

JOHN ROBERT GREENE

"THERE JUST NEVER SEEMS TO BE ENOUGH TIME." "The textbook is so bland, the students won't read it." "Don't *teachers* ever write?" "If I could only find more than one book that I feel good about assigning."

These complaints are endemic to those of us who teach survey American history courses. The book series America in the Twentieth Century was designed to address these issues in a novel fashion that attempts to meet the needs of both student and instructor alike. It uses decades for its organizational schema (admittedly a debatable choice, but it is our experience that chronology, not theme, makes for a better survey course), and each book tackles the main issues of a particular decade in a fashion at once readable and scholarly in nature. The series editor has chosen authors primarily for their teaching skills—indeed, each book proposal was accompanied by syllabi that show the prospective author's course pedagogy. In fact, contributors have been urged to write these books from their lecture notes and to limit footnote references, which can often distract or intimidate the student reader. In a departure from virtually every textbook series of note, one member of our editorial board is a presently sitting college student, whose comments on the manuscript may well be the most helpful of all. Each chapter ends with a recommended reading list of the authors' favorite books. The list is, admittedly, not exhaustive, but no list of our favorite works ever *is.*

The result is a readable, concise, and scholarly series of books from master teachers who know what works in the college classroom. We offer it to college instructors and their students in hopes that they will, in the words of the Latin maxim, do the one thing that we all in the academy hope that professor and student will do together: "Tolle et lege" (Take and read).

Preface

WHAT MAKES A DECADE? The word "decade" itself derives from the Greek word *dekas*, which means ten. Based on a standard definition, the ten-year decade of the 1930s begins on January 1, 1930 and ends on December 31, 1939. Yet, as anyone who studies history and culture knows, that is simply too restrictive a definition when examining the decade of the thirties. One has to only look at "Black Tuesday," the pivotal event that set in motion the economic catastrophe of the Great Depression. The stock market crash that impacted every aspect of American life from Wall Street to Main Street did not even occur in the 1930s but began on October 29, 1929. Similarly, the economic fallout produced by the Great Depression pressed on into the next decade, the impact still being felt by Americans well into the early 1940s. The conventional way of looking at decades chronologically just does not apply neatly to the period.

Rather than recount the decade chronologically, this book explores the themes of the 1930s topically. It explores some of the key events and conditions unique to the era. The authors place particular emphasis on the Great Depression, the Dust Bowl, a popular president who would serve an unprecedented four terms (another storyline lasting until well into the following decade), African Americans, industrial workers, a series of media golden ages, and America's role in the world. Still, the book makes no claim to be all inclusive. There are events, people, and trends from the 1930s that are not covered. Some of the significant figures and important events that are unfortunately left out include Joe Louis, Walt Disney, Richard Wright, Dorothy Day, Aimee Semple McPherson, Babe Didrikson, Sidney Hillman, the World's Fairs in New York and Chicago, sports, theater, and architecture, just to name a few. The decision to leave out such topics is in part editorial. Rather than try to cover everything, the intent is to introduce students to a fuller, more balanced view of the 1930s—one that explores politics, society, culture, and technology. A thematic approach allows us to feature tales that reach amazing heights of creativity and imagination and descend to the lowest depths of human misery. Readers learn of the conditions faced by workers and farmers, the political and economic climate that caused the crash, and the emerging role of the media in private and public life. Each chapter opens with the lyrics of popular 1930s songs that entertained listeners of the period. The lyrics reflect the ideas contained in the chapter.

In examining the thirties, the book takes as its focus the significant shift in the political and social landscape that occurred during the decade when once disparate groups in society were brought together by shared economic suffering. The great transformations in politics, media, gender, and race were made by people who probably had less of an eye on changing history and predicting long-term legacies than on taking advantage of an opportunity or attempting to solve a pressing problem. Yet, from the experiences of the period, these groups formed coalitions that have endured into the twenty-first century and continue to shape America's political, social, economic, and cultural institutions.

This book grew out of a freshman interdisciplinary course, "American Life in the 1930s," team taught at Mercyhurst University by three of the authors. Teaching the course, it quickly became apparent that most college freshmen had only a passing knowledge of the 1930s. They had learned about the New Deal, the Dust Bowl, and the Great Depression in high school. Some recognized the names of famous movie stars from the thirties, though even fewer had watched a film from the period with the exception of *The Wizard of Oz* (1939), which airs frequently on television. They had also read *The Grapes of Wrath* (1939) by John Steinbeck but never connected the story of the Joads to the bigger reality of the decade. Worse yet, what the students often claimed to know about the 1930s was colored by the social, cultural, or political ideologies of today. The decade certainly helped shape modern life, but conclusions drawn now about the period must be based on an understanding of the world in which those decisions and creations occurred.

The goal was to move students beyond their cursory knowledge of the decade and allow them to focus on the period in greater depth. The authors also sought to advance students' understanding of the thirties going forward, considering how the events of the decade shaped American well after December 31, 1939.

Acknowledgments

NUMEROUS PEOPLE played a role in helping bring this book to fruition. We are especially grateful to Deanna McCay of Syracuse University Press and John Robert Greene, the editor of this series, for graciously giving us the opportunity and for showing enormous patience and support as we worked to complete the book. Mercyhurst University provided vital support and encouragement. In particular we wish to thank Phil Belfiore, Brian Reed, and the University's Office of Academic Affairs for allowing us the latitude to create the freshman interdisciplinary course "American Life in the 1930s," which served as the genesis for this book. Most of all we wish to thank our family members for their unwavering love and support—Nancy, Ed, and Mark Seidel; Jennifer, Brian, Adeline, and Charley McCloskey; Edward Kruszewicz; Katherine and Bennett Sheridan; and Lisa, Evan, and Eli Olszowka.

AMERICA IN THE THIRTIES

Introduction

ON NEW YEAR'S DAY, 1933, Charles Andrews paid a visit to his old Amherst College classmate Calvin Coolidge. The two New Englanders entered the Massachusetts school together in 1891. Much of the world had changed since they graduated from the quaint liberal arts school nearly thirty-eight years earlier. Now in the twilight of their lives, the visit was an occasion to recollect about their youth and better days. For Andrews, a successful businessman and onetime member of the Massachusetts House of Representatives, the visit also provided one last opportunity to see his increasingly sick and frail friend—in fact, the aging Coolidge would die from coronary thrombosis just four days later. As the two men reminisced, the conversation invariably turned to the recent presidential election that saw Americans turn out of office Coolidge's Republican successor, Herbert Hoover. Coolidge, who had supported Hoover's failed reelection bid, was bothered by the shift politics had taken in the wake of the Great Depression. A true advocate of laissez-faire capitalism, Coolidge was deeply troubled by the activist path his former commerce secretary charted in trying to combat the economic collapse. Just days earlier in a conversation with the newspaper publisher Henry Stoddard, the former president expressed disdain for such so-called socialistic notions of government. Yet the stoic Coolidge could offer no solutions. As he admitted to Andrews, the depth of the struggle was beyond his realm of comprehension. For a man who prided himself on upholding traditional values of hard work and self-sacrifice, the Great Depression had washed away Coolidge's neatly ordered society. His ideas no longer fit the times.

Like many Americans in the 1930s, Coolidge struggled to make sense of the chaos and tumult that engulfed the nation. The decade stood in stark contrast to the carefree, happy-go-lucky days of the Roaring Twenties, when prosperity appeared endless. The stock market crash in October 1929 and the economic collapse it unleashed threatened the very foundations of America's economic, political, and social institutions. The ecological disaster produced by the Dust Bowl ravaging the Great Plains only added to the suffering and misery. Yet the decade was not just one mired in complete disorder. The 1930s was also a vibrant period of innovation, transformation, and in some cases even optimism. Politics, beginning with Herbert Hoover and continuing with Franklin Roosevelt, underwent a fundamental transformation, ushering in an activist state and firmly establishing the idea that through prudent federal policies it was not only possible to orchestrate an economic recovery but also to prevent future economic downturns. Workers, African Americans, ethnic Americans, and women responded to the era's challenges through their newfound political voice in Roosevelt's New Deal and through the institutions and communities they created to alleviate their suffering. Culturally the 1930s also proved to be a boon to America, ushering in the Golden Age of Hollywood as millions of Americans looked to movies as a momentary refuge from their daily plight. For all the hardship and despair of the 1930s, there was also a vitality that defined the decade. The great transformations in politics, media, gender, and race that this book examines were made by pragmatic people who had to solve pressing problems.

One of the central themes examined is how Americans were affected differently by the 1930s. Although a set of shared circumstances drove the 1930s—poverty, unemployment, and homelessness—the experiences of people living at the time was far from universally felt. Men experienced the decade's tribulations differently than women. Whites confronted circumstances dissimilar to that of blacks. Immigrant experiences with the Depression Era stood in contrast to those of native-born Americans. And the conditions confronting industrial workers were different from those encountered by the upper class or even farmers.

The second theme explored is the ways in which people tried to reestablish order over their lives. Workers turned to strikes and labor unions—most notably the Congress of Industrial Organizations—as a way to readdress declining conditions. Farmers, particularly those in the environmentally ravaged Midwest, packed their bags and headed West, inspired by the ballads of Woody Guthrie, who implored Okie migrants to do it themselves. African Americans found sanctuary within their communities, taking a comfort in a growing sense of cultural pride and a nascent civil rights movement. Media also played a key role in the efforts of Americans to shape their world. Films such as *The Awful Truth* not only delighted audiences and provided momentary respite from the daily struggles of the Depression, but they also became important cultural vehicles to poke fun at those less effected by the economic calamity. Writers such as Rachel Carson used literature to inform the public and encourage action. And perhaps the most visible effort of Americans to gain control over their lives was the election of Franklin Roosevelt, which signaled a new age in politics. With the shift toward the second New Deal in 1935, Roosevelt effectively empowered Americans once on the periphery of the political spectrum to stand up and have their voices heard. Even in foreign affairs, Americans looked for control, eschewing an insular approach that placed the nation's self-interests firmly ahead of the growing conflagrations raging in Europe and the Pacific.

By working to establish control over their lives people were looking to find comfort, or even provide themselves with purpose, in one of the most tumultuous times in American history. The results, as described in the chapters that follow, were mixed. At times the efforts ran counter to one another—as evidenced by the ideological battle waged by the adherents of Huey Long or the American Liberty League against Franklin Roosevelt. In some cases the results could be long lasting, particularly in the expanding influence of the mass media. And in some cases the results failed or were barely visible, as demonstrated by the economic struggles women, minorities, and others continued to endure throughout the decade.

1

The Coming of the Great Depression

"Brother, Can You Spare A Dime?"
—Yip Harburg and Jay Gorney, 1930

ON AUGUST 11, 1928, over seventy thousand people packed into the football stadium at Stanford University. The occasion was not to watch a sporting event, but rather to hear the acceptance speech of the Republican Party presidential nominee Herbert Hoover. For Hoover it was a moment rich with symbolism. In 1891, this orphaned son of a Quaker blacksmith and Iowa schoolteacher wandered on to the newly built Palo Alto campus with little more than the clothes on his back. He was part of Stanford's inaugural class. Now, thirty-eight years later, a far different Hoover stood before throngs of gazing onlookers, former classmates, and fellow alums. He was the epitome of the American success story, a self-made businessman and millionaire who found untold financial success by the early 1900s. Then in a dramatic shift, for much of the past decade Hoover put aside the pursuit of personal wealth and dedicated his life to national service. He was "the Great Humanitarian," the man who fed millions in war-ravaged Europe and provided relief to famine-stricken Russia in 1921. He was "the Great Engineer," a self-styled efficiency expert, who as secretary of commerce worked to rationalize and standardize industry, blazing a trail of unprecedented cooperation between business and government. He was the "Boy Genius," a Washington bureaucrat who captured the imagination of the American public while providing relief for millions displaced by the Great Mississippi Flood of 1927. He was the "Wonder Boy," a political innovator and reformer who won the adulation of both businessmen and Teddy Roosevelt Progressives while earning the suspicion of the Old Republican Guard. And now, in 1928, he was the Republican presidential nominee asking the American people to let him lead the nation for the next four years.

Given the circumstances of Hoover's past and the conditions surrounding his return to the Stanford campus, one could hardly blame Hoover for getting caught up in the euphoria of the evening. Standing at the dais, the presidential hopeful spoke in glowing terms of the virtues of American individualism. To Hoover, the American way of life was far superior to any other in the world and possessed endless, transformative opportunities. He closed his address to the audience by declaring, "We in America today are nearer to the final triumph over poverty than ever before in the history of any land. . . . We have not yet reached the goal, but . . . we shall soon with he help of God be in sight of the day when poverty will be banished from this nation."

Without a doubt, the message of Hoover's nomination speech was buoyed by his personal achievements. His was a life that would make Horatio Alger envious. Yet Hoover was not prone to misplaced emotion or vague sentimentality. That evening Hoover was also celebrating the exploits of the Republican Party. For Hoover, the success, wealth, and prosperity that seemed to envelope the 1920s were as much a product of Republican rule as American individualism. Rather than restrict business, Hoover pledged to continue the Republican Party's laissez-faire economic policies, an approach he believed encouraged American individualism and allowed for personal and national prosperity. By doing so, Hoover believed, America could continue its march to end poverty, a march that began in 1920 with the election of the GOP presidential candidate Warren Harding and continued with his successor Calvin Coolidge.

Ironically, Hoover's prophetic call to end poverty ultimately came back to haunt America's thirty-first president. A little over fourteen months after the speech, Hoover stood at the head of a nation on the cusp of an economic crisis that brought untold misery to tens of millions of Americans. By January 1930, poverty was less an abstract political concept and more a personal reality for Americans as the economy plummeted in the wake of the stock market crash. Ever the rugged individualist, Hoover responded the only way he knew how. He called on the American people to dig deep and persevere in the face of the hardship. Direct government intervention was anathema to the Republican stalwart, at least during the earliest days of the crisis. Instead, recalling America's experience in World War I, Hoover called on business leaders to embrace a form of economic volunteerism. By working together, they could alleviate the suffering caused by the crisis. Unfortunately, the strategy failed miserably. Businesses felt no compulsion to enact policies that worked against their own economic interests and Hoover had no stomach to compel them to act. By 1931, the economic crisis was spinning out of control and Americans were growing increasingly angry and frustrated. In desperation, Hoover turned to government policy to try to jump-start the economy. The approach did little to salvage Hoover's tarnished reputation. Nor did it end the Great Depression. But the strategy laid the groundwork for his successor Franklin Roosevelt, who built on Hoover's ideas in crafting his New Deal.

The aftermath of World War I marked the end of the Progressive Era, a period of dynamic social, political, and economic reform that in the simplest terms sought to curtail the excesses caused by unrestrained industrial capitalism. By 1920, Americans had grown weary of idealistic calls for reform and sacrifice. Disillusionment over the Great War and stalled peace negotiations contributed to the nation's growing frustration with progressivism. However, internal issues were the determining factor behind the demise of the Progressive Era. With rising industrial conflict, escalating racial tensions, and a looming economic recession, many Americans wondered whether progressivism had changed anything. The spirit of sacrifice that inspired progressivism and fueled the war movement simply petered out. Coming out of the war, the public looked to return to a simpler, less confrontational climate. They found both in the candidacy of Warren Harding, a modestly talented yet affable Republican governor from Ohio.

Grabbing control of the White House with a near landslide victory in 1920, Harding prepared to bring the nation—and with it the Republican Party—back to what he termed "normalcy." There was no confusing the president-elect with fellow Republican Teddy Roosevelt, in either substance or style. Rather than using the presidency as a bully pulpit, Harding sought to restore the oval office to the hands-off days of William McKinley and Benjamin Harrison, all the while letting his "Ohio Gang" rule the roost. Philosophically, Harding's plan centered on ending business regulation, once a hallmark of progressivism. By crafting economic policy that increased wealth at the top of the economic spectrum, Harding and his staff believed prosperity would filter down to the rest of society. Signaling this philosophical shift, Harding tabbed Andrew Mellon to serve as his secretary of the treasury. Mellon, an aging financier, counted the likes of J. P. Morgan, Andrew Carnegie, and John Rockefeller as his contemporaries in the business world. Having made a fortune in the aluminum industry, Mellon was considered to be the third richest man in the United States by 1920. An appointment of such magnitude would have been unthinkable during the Progressive Era, the equivalent of putting the fox in charge of the hen house. But what was unthinkable then was embraced in 1920, illustrating the intellectual break with progressivism and marking the pro-business tenor reestablished by Republicans.

Andrew Mellon stood as the central figure and key architect behind Republican economic policy throughout the 1920s, serving first Harding, then Calvin Coolidge, and eventually Herbert Hoover. Starting in 1921, Mellon worked to drastically cut tax rates across the board. Estate taxes were reduced, gift taxes abolished, and excess-profit taxes eliminated. Meanwhile, the income tax—the bane of businessmen—was significantly slashed. From a top rate of 77 percent on anyone making over $1 million during World War I, the rate steadily declined during Republican rule, dropping to 24 percent per $1 million by 1929. The rationale was that by increasing wealth at the top, prosperity would eventually trickle down to all other classes of people across the nation. The shift in economic philosophy was significant. Whereas business had been the whipping boy of the Progressive Era, both Harding and later Coolidge embraced it. Republicans also worked to create a more favorable climate for business to operate. Federal regulation was drastically curtailed throughout the 1920s. Anti-trust prosecution came to a virtual standstill. Instead of prosecuting companies for engaging in monopolistic practices, Republican administrations encouraged business cooperation, as evidenced by the policies coming out of the Commerce Department under Herbert Hoover. Cooperation became the watchword for creating greater industrial and economic efficiency, and thereby promoting national economic prosperity. As Coolidge remarked, "the business of government is business," signaling a clear departure from Republican and Democratic policies over the past twenty years.

Republican economic policies produced their desired effect, at least in the short run. The postwar economic recession subsided by 1922. With the exception of a few minor economic downturns, the economy appeared strong throughout the decade and many enjoyed the benefits of an emerging large-scale consumer culture. Cameras, cigarette lighters, wristwatches, and a host of personal luxury items were common purchases during the decade. Once seen as extravagant indulgences, many Americans came to view these products as necessities during the Roaring Twenties. Installment purchasing plans further fueled the growing appetite for mass-produced consumer goods. Radios, washing machines, vacuum cleaners, phonographs, refrigerators, and other electric appliances became household staples with a small deposit followed by weekly or monthly payments. Perhaps no product symbolized the growing consumer culture in the 1920s more than the automobile. Once a symbol of wealth and extravagance, advances in industrial production gave millions of ordinary Americans access to cars in the postwar era. Henry Ford's Model T, a vehicle that transformed automobile manufacturing, could be had for $240 in 1924. At the start of the decade over eight million automobiles were registered in the United States. By 1929, that number had grown to over twenty-three million, a testament to the industry's explosive growth.

The motion picture industry further illustrates the 1920s themes of mass consumerism and individualism. Throughout the decade films steadily gained an influence on an American public that looked to the silver screen for examples of "Roaring Twenties" glamour and extravagant style. Perhaps no actor represented the decade's idea of individualism on the big screen better than Douglas Fairbanks. The "King of Hollywood's" on-screen devil-may-care style captured the fun and upbeat attitude of the decade. The film historian Scott Curtis called him the "icon of Americanism." By the end of 1919, Fairbanks was already a bona fide movie star, having appeared in nearly thirty films. He was also a budding industry mogul in charge of his own production company. During the 1920s, Fairbanks's stature continued to grow as he starred in blockbusters such as *The Mark of Zorro* (1920), *The Three Musketeers* (1921), *Robin Hood* (1922), and *The Black Pirate* (1926). Whether playing a suave swashbuckler exuberantly swinging from chandeliers or a heroic rogue leaping from balconies, his characters brimmed with optimism, vigor, and youthfulness as they conquered all obstacles. Fairbanks was a visible representative of what was possible for Americans who remained positive and were willing to work hard.

While audiences admired Fairbanks's wealth, glamour, and success, they identified with another popular actor who offered a more modest version of rugged individualism, the comedian Harold Lloyd. Lloyd did not portray larger-than-life dramatic (and mostly historical) heroes like Fairbanks's characters. Instead, he played a likable "everyman" who aspired for popularity, love, and riches. Lloyd's first role was a character dubbed "Lonesome Luke," a knock-off of Charlie Chaplin's "Little Tramp." Then, in a stroke of genius, Lloyd put on a pair of round spectacles and a straw boater hat that resembled what young people of the day wore. This character became affectionately known as "Glasses" and earned Lloyd lasting success. "Glasses" was a youthful striver who never gave up the idea that success was close if only he kept working hard. The character worked to be a big-man-on-campus in *The Freshman* (1925) and an indispensable jack-of-all-trades in *Speedy* (1928). In his most famous comedy, *Safety Last* (1923), Lloyd played an upwardly mobile worker who climbs a Los Angeles skyscraper to win money and fame. Though Lloyd's popularity began to decline after 1927 when the industry began to make the transition to sound, his always positive "Glasses" character inspired an emerging middle class during the halcyon days of the 1920s with the idea that perseverance and hard work led to prosperity.

Fairbanks's and Lloyd's characters reinforced the growing attitude that individual achievement was a matter of personal responsibility and that everyone had an equal ability to succeed. These attitudes in turn reflected larger social and political changes encompassing the 1920s. Herbert Hoover's election in 1928 further affirmed the individualistic mood of the American public. During the campaign, Republican and Hoover operatives were quick to remind voters that the economic growth and the expanding array of consumer goods were all a product of their policies. Reluctant to remove a party from office in good times, Americans turned out in droves to cast their votes for the two-term commerce secretary. Despite having never run for public office, Hoover handily defeated his Democratic opponent, New York Governor Al Smith. Internal divisions within the Democratic Party, along with Smith's personal political baggage, doomed the "Happy Warrior's" chances from the start. But the Democrats' failures only go a portion of the way in explaining Hoover's success. In the end, Hoover and the GOP won the election because they successfully cast themselves as the party of prosperity. When the polls closed, Hoover polled over 58 percent of the popular vote, besting Smith by over 17 percent. He also won forty of forty-eight states, including Smith's home state of New York. The popular Hoover took five southern states—Texas, Florida, Tennessee, North Carolina, and Virginia—the first Republican to do so since the Reconstruction Era.

Hoover entered the White House exuding hope and optimism. As he declared in his inaugural address, "I have no fears for the future of our country. It is bright with hope." Hope, however, soon faded. By mid-1929, leading economic indicators began showing signs of an economic slowdown. Production rates dropped, particularly in steel, a bellwether industry. Several banks failed during the same period. Still, the stock market continued to chug upward. On September 3, the Dow Jones reached a high of 381.17, an increase of 27 percent over the previous year. Days later the first signs of trouble began to appear. Rapid fluctuations occurred as investors began to unload overinflated stocks, causing prices to plummet. The downturns, though, were quickly followed by rallies, leading the market to rebound and offset any losses. Conservative business leaders expressed concerns about the volatile market and urged investors to exercise caution. Distressed that speculative investment practices seemed to be overtaking sound financial judgment in America's financial districts, Hoover conveyed similar apprehensions. The president went as far as to urge the Federal Reserve to actively discourage such dangerous practices. Yet the fears of Hoover and others were quickly dismissed. Instead investors preferred to believe in the naïve optimism of endless economic growth.

Late in the day on Wednesday, October 23, stock values dropped suddenly. The downward decent continued the next day. Over thirteen million shares of stock swapped hands that day, marking the highest volume of trading in the history of the market until that point. As investors tried to make sense of the frenzy, political and business leaders stepped forward to try to bolster confidence in the stock market. On the nation's airwaves that evening, Hoover declared that the economy was "sound" and "prosperous," and therefore investors had nothing to fear. Several leading bankers joined together to purchase stocks in the hopes their actions would inspire confidence and prop up the sagging market. A rally followed on Friday, but it was brief. Heading in to the next week, prices continued to drop. Investor confidence was clearly shaken. Industry giants like US Steel and General Electric, once viewed as immune to market whims, saw their values decline.

The floodgates opened on Tuesday, October 29. With the sound of the opening bell, a massive stock sell-off began and swiftly drove prices down. Over 3 million shares of stock changed hands in the first thirty minutes of business, resulting in a loss of over $2 million. By midday, the turmoil reached such proportions that investment houses, fearing that they would be left holding the bag for clients for whom they purchased stocks, began issuing "margin" calls. They demanded immediate payment from investors for whom they purchased stocks on credit. When clients could not cover their debt, brokers started unleashing enormous amounts of stocks onto the market, only adding to the chaos. Trading occurred at such a feverish pace on the New York Stock Exchange that no one seemed to have any clue as to what was going on. Fistfights broke out on the floor between brokers. At least one broker collapsed, only to be revived so he could return to work. By the time the market closed on Black Tuesday, 16.4 million shares of stock had been sold, many of them at rock-bottom prices. Over the next two weeks the steady swoon continued. By mid-November, the stock market bottomed out. By that point stocks had dropped in value by an average of 37 percent. All told, an estimated $25 billion was lost in the great crash of 1929.

Black Tuesday signaled the start of the Great Depression, a prolonged economic crisis that crippled the nation. Many Americans blamed the stock market crash for the economic crisis that engulfed the 1930s. However, the crash did not cause the Depression so much as it exposed structural problems rooted in the so-called prosperity of the 1920s. By the late 1920s, the American economy was showing significant signs of wear, crushed under the weight of untenable Republican economic policies. Businesses plowed the added revenue from Mellon's tax cuts back into production, modernizing facilities to create greater efficiency, improve output, and increase profits. As a result, companies produced more goods at lower costs than ever before. But the plan never worked as Mellon and the Republican leaders envisioned. The money brought by tax cuts and production improvements rarely trickled down, as wage increases and wage levels stagnated by 1923. Even worse, the availability of cheap credit and installment purchasing plans allowed consumers to live beyond their means, masking the growing problems of overproduction and declining wages. Finally, corporate profits steadily found their way back to an already bloated stock market on Wall Street. When the stock market crashed in late October 1929, financial leaders responded in typical fashion. Faced with mounting losses, businesses tightened their belts by laying off workers and slashing wages. Meanwhile, workers confronting rising unemployment and declining wages quickly cut back on spending, further adding to the economic decline.

Compounding the economic problem for businesses, the safety valve of foreign trade was virtually shut off by the end of the 1920s. With the European economy struggling throughout much of the decade, the likelihood of foreign trade offsetting America's overproduction appeared improbable. America's foreign-trade policies further contributed to the problem. During the 1920s the Republican Party fell back on its old mantra of creating protectionist trade policies to safeguard American business against foreign competition. Mellon and the Republicans increased restrictive tariffs on goods entering the United States throughout the decade. In the short run, the policy helped American business by eliminating competition from low-cost foreign goods. It also helped make up for revenue lost by the tax cuts. In the long run, though, the policy proved disastrous. By limiting access to the American market throughout the 1920s, Mellon and the Republicans contributed to Europe's sluggish postwar economy. As European nations struggled to get out from under the debt of World War I, foreign manufacturers found themselves increasingly shut out from one of the largest markets in the world. Unable to compete, the situation slowed Europe's economic recovery. European nations responded in kind, initiating their own protective measures designed to close out American competition. Thus by the end of the decade, as American manufacturers dealt with the effects of overproduction, the one market that might have absorbed some of the excess production was closed off to them.

Manufacturing was not the only industry struggling with the effects of overproduction. So too was agriculture. World War I provided a boon to American farmers as the warring European nations created a growing overseas demand for US agricultural products. Farmers experienced record profits during the war. However, the prosperity proved to be short-lived when foreign agricultural production returned to its prewar levels in the early 1920s. Rather than scale back production, farmers responded to the crisis by increasing output in an effort to recoup their losses. Adding to the problem, they followed the prevailing wisdom of the day by modernizing agricultural processes to improve efficiency and increase production. Mechanical harvesters, plows, combines, and other technological innovations were readily available with easy credit. New chemical fertilizers and advances in animal husbandry also improved agricultural yields.

Altogether, agricultural production growth was significant throughout the 1920s. An acre of land that once produced 40 bushels of corn per acre now produced 100–120 bushels. Wheat production also increased, though not as dramatically, from around 19 to over 23 bushels per acre. As production increased and demand declined, prices plummeted. Corn that sold for $.70 a bushel at the start of the decade went for $.10 a bushel by decade's end. Hogs, which had once fetched $.09 per pound, sold for $.03 a pound. Cotton, long the staple of the southern economy, saw a similar decline, going from $.40 per pound in 1920 to $.10 per pound just one year later, and continuing to decline for the remainder of the decade. Wheat went from a high of $2.50 a bushel during the war to less than $1.00 in the span of just eighteen months. Rather than prosperity, the Roaring Twenties was a time of struggle and hardship for most farmers. Many felt the effects of a depression well before 1929. When the collapse hit, it only exacerbated an already perilous economic situation for a large percentage of American farmers.

As the crisis unfolded, America's banking system soon teetered on the precipice of collapse. Heading into the Depression, a multitude of structural problems plagued America's banking industry. Perhaps the biggest issue centered on the overabundance of small, poorly financed community banks.

As of 1920, over 30,000 banks operated nationwide, a total higher than all other nations combined. Many of these institutions were locally based and capitalized at less than $1 million. Primarily serving the communities in which they operated, when the local economy went south, so too did the banks. On average, approximately 70 banks failed each year throughout the 1920s. When the Depression hit, small banks proved particularly vulnerable. Of the more than 1,300 banks that failed in the first year of the Depression, many of them were small local financial institutions.

Another problem confronting the nation's bank system was its connection to the inflated stock market. Just as investors poured personal profits into the stock market during the 1920s, so too did America's banks. In the 1920s, "buying on margin" afforded investors opportunities to gamble on the stock market. For a modest down payment, or "margin," brokerage houses purchased and then held stocks for investors. The investor essentially "borrowed" the remainder of the funds from the brokerage house, which in turn borrowed the money from a bank. The brokerage house made its money when the investor sold the stock, charging a fee for the transaction and loan. Banks profited as well by charging interest for the money lent to the brokerage house. The so-called safeguard of the system was that the loan could be called in at any time for immediate payment, thereby dissuading investors from borrowing beyond their means. The precaution ultimately failed. By 1929, it was estimated that two out of every five dollars loaned out by banks was used to purchase stocks. Too much money was tied to the stock market, further inflating the value of stocks. As the stock market bubble grew, investor money stood at risk. Not surprisingly, when the stock market collapsed it brought down America's banking structure with it. Banks lost millions, forcing many institutions to shut their doors, taking investors' deposits with them.

Finally, banks also suffered from self-serving business practices and mismanagement. The lack of regulation and oversight during the 1920s allowed bankers to engage in reckless—and at times unethical—activities that placed in jeopardy the stability of their institutions. Perhaps no bank symbolized the failings of financial mismanagement more than the Bank of the United States in New York City. Joseph Marcus, a Jewish immigrant who had worked his way up from tailor to bank owner, established the bank in 1913. The bank began with a modest $100,000 working capital and catered primarily to the local Jewish immigrant community. Slowly, Marcus built up the bank, eventually adding four branch offices in the city by 1925. Following Marcus's death two years later, his son Bernard began acquiring additional banks to serve as branches in other New York neighborhoods. By 1930, the Bank of the United States controlled sixty-two branches. With over 440,000 investors and $300 million in assets, it stood as the largest retail bank in New York. But on December 10, 1930 it all unraveled.

The crisis began with a bank run at a branch office in the Bronx. Nervous investors lined up to withdraw their money when rumors began circulating in the community that the bank was insolvent. Soon, tens of thousands gathered outside the bank's doors and local police were called in to maintain order. By midday, nearly three thousand investors had withdrawn over $2 million from the bank. The panic grew and spread to other branches in the Bronx and Brooklyn. Bank of the United States officials had little choice but to close their doors. Once news of the closing hit Wall Street, it led to a massive sell-off of the bank's stock, whose value quickly dropped. The stock, which had been trading at over $91 per share just a year earlier, plunged to under $3 per share. Bank officials tried to calm public fears. Marcus predicted the bank would reopen in a couple weeks pending the finalization of a merger with another financial institution. When the merger failed to materialize, local authorities launched an investigation. The inquiry revealed that Marcus and his vice president, Saul Singer, had been purchasing the bank's stock with the bank's funds in order to drive up the value. Making matters worse, they had loaned out over $37 million in dubious dealings. Additionally, the pair had raided the bank's reserve, using that money to finance their own real estate investments.

The collapse of the Bank of the United States marked the largest bank failure to date. It symbolized the reckless and often self-serving practices that became rampant in the 1920s with the lack of federal regulation and oversight. Marcus and Singer were convicted of fraud and sent to prison for three years for their role in the debacle. The penalty for many investors was far more severe. Thousands lost their life savings, including over forty-four thousand investors who had accounts totaling less than $400 at the time of the collapse.

Though less than 1 percent of the population invested in the stock market, the sting of the Depression touched nearly everyone by 1930. Americans found themselves trapped in a vicious cycle with no apparent way out. By 1930, nearly 10 percent of the population was without work, more than triple the pre-Depression unemployment rate of 3.2 percent. Many more workers dealt with wage cuts as companies scaled back production costs. Unemployed or underemployed workers soon became reluctant consumers. Employers responded by reducing operations even more, thereby adding to the nation's rising unemployment rolls. To add insult to injury, bank closures destroyed what little savings people had amassed. With no safety net beyond local charities, millions of Americans became crushed under the weight of the Depression, struggling to live day-to-day.

Farmers were among the hardest hit following the stock market crash. By 1932, agricultural prices were about 40 percent of their already low pre-Depression levels. With falling prices, many farmers found it difficult to maintain their farms. Farm mortgages amounted to over $9 billion by 1929. Anxious for their money, struggling banks pushed for payment. Foreclosures rose as many farmers found themselves unable to pay their first and sometimes second mortgages. By the time Franklin Roosevelt took office, an estimated two hundred out of every thousand farms in the Midwest, the South, and the Great Plains had fallen to foreclosure. Adding to the midwestern and plains farmers' woes, lurking around the corner in 1930 was the onset of the Dust Bowl, an ecological disaster of epic proportions.

The initial response to the stock market crash in Washington political circles was to do nothing. Economic downturns were nothing new to the American financial landscape. Panics, recessions, and depressions had occurred before 1929 in a variety of forms and to varying degrees of magnitude. For example, the Panic of 1837 resulted in over six hundred bank failures and an estimated unemployment rate as high as 25 percent in some locales. The Long Depression that lasted from 1873 to 1896 saw nearly eighteen thousand businesses close and unemployment peak at an estimated 14 percent nationwide. As recently as 1920, Americans struggled with the effects of a postwar recession when production dropped significantly across the board and unemployment rose to almost 10 percent—more than triple the rate during the Great War. To policymakers these events were accepted as inevitable episodes in the economy. Slumps were how the market corrected itself by allowing the economy to purge itself of its excesses. Any redress by policymakers was unnecessary, perhaps even detrimental. The nation merely needed to ride out the crisis.

Within Hoover's administration, Treasury Secretary Andrew Mellon was one of the most vocal advocates for inaction. Mellon advised the president that it was time to "liquidate labor, liquidate stocks, liquidate farmers, liquidate real estate." He urged Hoover to cut government spending and remain steadfast in working to balance the budget. Mellon believed the bank failures should be allowed to continue without government interference. Indeed, Mellon argued that bank closings ultimately helped the economy by weeding out nonviable financial institutions. The hands-off approach, he believed, also benefited the American people by allowing for values to adjust. People would be forced to work harder, Mellon reasoned. Enterprising people would rise to the occasion and overcome the hardship produced by the economic crisis. Government aid and relief only threatened cherished American individualism and fostered dependency by destroying peoples' will to work.

Hoover shared Mellon's economic philosophy, at least at first. Like many Americans in 1930, the president saw the crash as a short-term financial crisis rather than the start of a decade-long national catastrophe. Hoover remained convinced that the American economy was fundamentally sound and that the crisis was driven largely by irrational fears. Hoover was also reluctant to act because he shared Mellon's concern that government initiative could be disastrous, risking America's long-term economic health. Ever the rugged individualist, Hoover understood the value of hard work and sacrifice. These qualities defined every aspect of his life. Creating programs that aided the public during the crisis, though noble in the short run, threatened the self-determination that made Americans unique. Like Mellon, he saw the value in pulling oneself up by the bootstraps. Still, even though Hoover gravitated toward the traditional views held by Mellon and other officials within his cabinet, he also saw himself as a progressive. He rejected the complete laissez-faire approach embraced by Mellon and Republican traditionalists, believing government action had a role in society. The challenge for Hoover was to balance his philosophical fears and worries against the need to help those who were suffering.

Hoover took to the nation's airwaves as the crisis unfolded. In speech after speech, he tried to calm public fears and build confidence. He spoke of how the economy was sound and the downturn was merely a temporary setback. Rather than use the terms "panic" and "crisis" to describe the situation, he referred to it as a "depression," believing it carried fewer negative connotations. At the same time, he reminded Americans again and again that prosperity remained just around the corner. By bolstering confidence in the economy, Hoover was convinced he could restore hope for Americans and jump-start the economy. Though the president loathed initiating formal federal policies to combat the crisis, indirectly he used the White House to help push the economy forward. Following the path blazed during World War I, Hoover turned to volunteerism to try to combat the Depression. Starting in late 1929, he organized a series of conferences that drew together representatives from business, labor, and government. The purpose was to discuss the economy and come up with voluntary strategies to help arrest the crisis. Hoover asked business leaders to pledge not to lay off workers or cut wages for the duration. Similarly, he exhorted labor unions to promise to refrain from engaging in strikes, to put aside their wage grievances and criticisms during the crisis, and to keep working until the economy improved. Voluntary cooperation became the watchword for Hoover's administration.

Hoover was neither apathetic to the suffering of citizens nor passive in his response to the crisis. As Hoover employed his top-down voluntary approach, he also worked to ease the suffering for struggling Americans. In a dramatic departure from past presidential policy, Hoover hastily pushed through government construction projects designed to provide jobs for the growing ranks of unemployed. He called on state and local governments to do the same. Such programs were not providing direct assistance, Hoover reasoned. Instead, they provided jobs that helped bolster America's work ethic and resiliency in the midst of crisis and despair. Finally, in October 1930 he created the President's Emergency Committee for Employment, a nonfunded government initiative that coordinated the efforts of private charities and local relief agencies in aiding the unemployed. Doing so, the president believed, allowed for greater efficiency and better use of resources.

Hoover's voluntary approach in dealing with the Great Depression marked a significant change in federal economic policy. Although unprecedented, the measures he took were not enough. Like many, Hoover failed to appreciate the magnitude of the economic downturn. In a June 1930 meeting with bankers, the president announced that the Depression was over. The statement reveals a limited understanding of the depth of the economic crisis. Far from being over, the Depression continued to grow. In March, the unemployment rate had nearly doubled since Black Tuesday and it continued to rise with each passing month in 1930. By fall, nearly one year after the stock market crash, the number of business failures reached twenty-five thousand. In the Midwest, farmers began confronting the effects of the Dust Bowl. The collapse of the European economy in 1931 added to the despair and accelerated the crisis in America. There was no end in sight.

As the intensity of the Depression reverberated across the nation, Hoover's strategy of volunteerism collapsed. Businessmen, although observing Hoover's request to preserve wage levels, began reducing work rolls and cutting back on work hours to insulate themselves from the economic crisis and preserve profits. With no mechanisms to ensure compliance, Hoover's volunteerism proved impractical for combating a long-term economic crisis. Equally problematic, the direct action Hoover advocated in response to the crisis proved counterproductive. The government construction projects he facilitated failed to produce their desired effect, as states and local governments often cut their financial contributions for the projects. Thus any added revenue Hoover committed from Washington was often offset by the loss of state and local resources, thereby minimizing the impact the works programs might have had on helping local economies and the unemployed.

Similarly futile was Hoover's approval of the Smoot-Hawley Tariff in June 1930. Pushed by congressional Republicans, the measure raised tariffs on over twenty thousand goods entering American markets, many of which were among the highest rates in the history of the United States. Supporters argued that high tariffs would aid domestic production and protect American jobs. Opponents, however, expressed concerns as to the long-range implications of the tariff restrictions. They feared reprisals from foreign nations, upset over being further excluded from the American market. The automobile manufacturer Henry Ford labeled the tariff "economic stupidity." Over one thousand economists from across the United States petitioned Hoover to veto it. Even Hoover was opposed to the tariff increases, calling them "vicious, extortionate, and obnoxious." Nevertheless, he passed the measure rather than risk alienating the GOP in Congress. As it turned out, the Smoot-Hawley Tariff plunged the economy into further disarray by precipitating drastic drops in both United States imports and exports.

Despite the problems emanating from White House policy, during the initial months of the Depression Hoover demonstrated an ability to break from traditional practices. By using the office of the presidency to try to jump-start the economy, the Great Engineer went where no president had gone before. Yet, for all the boldness, there were clear boundaries for Hoover. His capacity for bold innovation could not overcome his commitment to self-reliance. Calls to establish programs to provide direct relief for the poor too often fell on deaf ears. In protest, Colonel Arthur Woods, head of Hoover's Emergency Committee for Employment, resigned in April 1931, after the president refused his requests to initiate a broad-base work relief program that included slum clearance, a massive public works initiative, and the creation of low-cost housing. In rejecting the plan Hoover remained convinced that relief needs could be best meet by local communities and private charities. The problem was that local relief agencies and private charities soon found their limited resources stretched to the breaking point.

In March 1931, sixteen months after the stock market crash, America's unemployed population swelled to over eight million people, double the rate from the previous year. In June, Pennsylvania's Department of Labor reported a statewide unemployment rate of nearly 25 percent. In Toledo, Ohio, the unemployment rate for men reached 30 to 40 percent. For those fortunate enough to still be working, the situation was not necessarily better. In September, US Steel quietly instituted a 10 percent wage cut affecting all workers. Other companies, including Ford Motor, followed suit, thus ending Hoover's call for employers to voluntarily preserve wages. It did not take long for underpaid and underemployed workers to join the breadlines and soup kitchens, further taxing perilously underfunded relief agencies.

Growing numbers of Americans found it increasingly difficult, if not impossible, to make ends meet. What savings people had amassed during the twenties was quickly exhausted, either used to pay a growing number of bills or, worse, lost in the wave of bank closings. With little or no cushion to soften the blow, homelessness soared. In countless back alleys across the nation, the poor could be seen rummaging through garbage looking for the smallest morsels of food. In New York, thousands of unemployed citizens peddled apples to passersby for 5 cents each. Families struggled with the psychological burdens of the Depression. Often pushed beyond the breaking point, husbands and fathers aimlessly wandered city streets in search of any job they could find. Some simply gave up and abandoned their families. Taking to the road or leaving to ride the rails, they went in search of jobs elsewhere, promising one day to return. Women were suddenly forced to take on the dual roles of housewife and breadwinner, searching for any means possible to help tide the family over. Children dropped out of school and teens delayed college in order to find jobs to help contribute to the family income. In the Northeast, children could be seen walking along railroad lines looking for spare pieces of coal to be used to keep the family warm during cold winter months. Young adults postponed marriage, while married couples avoided adding to their family size. For a nation that had seemed so prosperous in the 1920s, the start of the new decade was defined by poverty, hunger, and despair.

By early 1931 a collective anger started to overtake a desperate public as the magnitude of the Depression intensified. Across America's heartland farmers banded together at foreclosure auctions threatening violence against anyone who dared bid on the property of a struggling neighbor. In Iowa, tensions escalated until Governor Daniel Turner called out the National Guard after a mob dragged a judge out of a courthouse with a noose around his neck, threatening to lynch him if he refused to stop carrying out farm foreclosure proceedings. Mobs of tenant farmers broke into the Red Cross facility in England, Arkansas, and compelled staff to dispense provisions to the needy. Nebraska farmers burned their corn for fuel rather than selling it after prices dropped so low that it was pointless to harvest their crop. In New York City, people standing in a breadline, overcome with hunger, attacked two bakery cars making a delivery to the hotel across the street. In Henryetta, Oklahoma, over three hundred jobless men attacked local merchants demanding food. Many more incidents simply went unreported as merchants, newspapers, and local authorities feared that publicity might encourage further lawlessness. By 1931, people found themselves pushed to lengths they had never imagined. Still, Hoover refused to act.

As volunteerism failed and public frustrations grew, the president dug in and refused to adjust his policies. In part, Hoover remained convinced that local and private charities could meet the needs of the suffering. He also believed the situation was not as bad as the press made it out to be, at one point declaring that nobody was "actually starving." In the end, Hoover retreated into old dictates that hard work and self-reliance could get anyone through the toughest of times. The president simply doubled down, sternly refusing to back away from his core beliefs even as local and private charities floundered.

Hoover soon became the focal point of public outrage. Shantytowns filled with growing throngs of homeless people began springing up on the outskirts of towns or along city railway lines; they became known sarcastically as "Hoovervilles." Empty pockets turned inside out, showing that the bearer was penniless, were referred to as "Hoover flags." "Hoover hogs" were jackrabbits killed by the poor to feed their families. A "Hoover blanket" was a newspaper used by the poor to keep warm as they faced the elements. Hoover, the man whom the public once embraced as a symbol of the American Dream, was now seen as a callous villain, a heartless soul who played a duplicitous role in the sustained suffering of countless Americans. With the Depression lasting three years into Hoover's presidential term, it was clear the situation could not last. Something had to give.

In January 1932, Hoover finally yielded. Confronting mounting pressure from fellow Republicans facing fall elections, Hoover signed into law a measure to create the Reconstruction Finance Corporation (RFC). The RFC received an initial budget of $500 million, with the authority to borrow up to $2 billion more. RFC officials were to use the money to grant loans to banks, railroads, farm mortgage associations, building and loan agencies, and life insurance companies. The underlying premise was to help resuscitate the economy by making government funds available to banks and other lending institutions. Hoover and RFC supporters believed that by increasing the availability of credit, the program would stimulate economic activity and help bring about an end to the Depression. To head the RFC, Hoover tabbed Charles Dawes, former vice president to Calvin Coolidge and current head of the Central Republic Bank of Chicago.

The RFC marked a dramatic departure from Hoover's faith in individualism and preference for volunteerism. It also marked another bold step away from how past politicians dealt with economic crises. In creating the RFC, Hoover harnessed federal authority to promote recovery, an approach that would become the hallmark of his successor, Franklin Roosevelt. Still, the RFC was not without its problems. The underlying philosophy guiding the RFC was wrong. It failed to recognize that the fundamental problem during the Depression was over production, not a lack of credit. The purpose of the RFC was to make resources available to lending agencies that in turn would provide funds to businesses looking to increase production. Opponents also were quick to point out that the RFC neither addressed the growing problems of unemployment and poverty nor offered provisions for establishing relief programs. In the end, the RFC did little but temporarily stave off the collapse of the American banking system.

For critics the RFC amounted to little more than a "breadline for big business." They charged that the RFC represented the same old stale Republican policies that catered to those at the top of the economic ladder in the 1920s. Fueling the criticism was a scandal that broke over the Central Republic Bank of Chicago. In June 1932 it looked as though Central Republic was about to go under. Many observers feared the failure of the bank would take all other Chicago lending institutions with it, spawning a massive economic crisis. To prevent the collapse, the RFC injected $90 million into the bank. Dawes immediately resigned his post as head of the RFC and returned to take charge of his bank. The relationship between Dawes, the RFC, and the Central Republic Bank became public fodder for critics of the agency and Hoover. Making the situation worse, just weeks earlier Chicago Mayor Anton Cermak requested a loan from the RFC to help pay the salaries of city teachers and municipal workers. The request was quickly rejected, as the RFC possessed no authority to grant such a loan. To detractors, however, the incident illustrated the hypocrisy of the RFC and the Hoover administration. Aid was available for banks and the wealthy, while poor and hardworking Americans were expected to go it alone. The black eye given to the RFC added fuel to the growing chorus of critics who saw the president as cold and out of touch with the plight of the poor.

In July 1932, Hoover's reputation suffered another devastating blow, just as he was gearing up to battle Franklin Roosevelt for the presidency. The controversy pitted Hoover against the veterans from the Great War, a clash he was destined to lose. Overcome by the exuberance of a strong economy in 1924, Congress voted to grant World War I veterans a "bonus" as a reward for serving their country. The plan passed in spite of strenuous opposition by Calvin Coolidge, who vetoed the measure, declaring, "Patriotism . . . bought and paid for is not patriotism." The plan called for veterans to receive $1 for each day they served stateside, up to a maximum of $500, and $1.25 for each day overseas, the sum not to exceed $650. The cost for the program came to just over $3.6 billion, the bonuses to be paid in 1945. If a veteran died before that time, his bonus would be paid to his estate.

Struggling veterans became anxious as the Depression took hold. Calls came for Congress to release the bonuses ahead of schedule. In May 1932, former Army Sergeant Walter Waters announced plans to lead a group of disgruntled veterans from Portland, Oregon, to the nation's capital. Waters wanted to impress on Congress the need to grant early payment of the bonuses. Others picked up on the plan and a massive march ensued. By June, over fifteen thousand poor and homeless veterans descended on Washington DC. The press dubbed it the march of the "Bonus Expeditionary Force," a play on the term "American Expeditionary Force," which had been used to describe the soldiers during the Great War. With military precision the veterans erected a giant Hooverville on Anacostia Flats, a low marshy flatland overlooking the nation's capital. They organized food details, constructed sanitation facilities, and coordinated daily marches. Only veterans who were honorably discharged from the armed forces and their family members were permitted to reside in the camp.

On June 15, the House of Representatives took up the matter and eventually agreed to advance the payment date of the veterans' bonuses. The victory was short lived when two days later the Senate voted down the bill by a resounding margin of sixty-two to eighteen. Some opponents expressed concern over the financial ramifications of the $3.6 billion price tag. Others saw the protest as little more than blackmail and simply refused to buckle under to the threat of disgruntled ex-soldiers. Still other Senators opposed the legislation out of fear that the government ran the risk of setting a dangerous precedent that might encourage more discontented citizens to rally in protest. For many of these politicians, the memory of the demonstration by Cox's Army just five months earlier still hung heavy in the air.

In January 1932 the massive protest of nearly twenty-five thousand jobless men took to the streets of Washington DC. Led by Father James Cox, a Catholic priest from Pittsburgh, the group presented a petition to Hoover requesting the creation of a massive $5 billion works program to be paid for by increasing the inheritance tax in the United States to 70 percent. The protest was the largest in Washington history to date and sparked immediate concern. Thoroughly embarrassed by the situation, Hoover launched an investigation, fearing that perhaps some sinister forces might be behind the protest—the Communist Party, the Vatican, or worse, the Democratic Party looking to further discredit his administration. Much to Hoover's dismay, he learned that a major contributor to the protest was none other than his treasury secretary, Andrew Mellon. Mellon had ordered all Gulf Oil gasoline stations that he owned in Pennsylvania to provide fuel for the protesters free of charge as they marched through the state on their journey to Washington. The discovery shocked Hoover, who immediately demanded and received Mellon's resignation.

Following the defeat of the bonus bill, many somber veterans left Washington and returned to their hometowns. Others lingered behind. Unemployed, homeless, and with nowhere else to turn, they settled in to their shantytown in Anacostia Flats. Many took up residence outside government offices and in abandoned buildings. Daily "death marches" were conducted outside the capital, serving as a vivid reminder of the disillusionment veterans felt for the nation they had served. To help diffuse the situation, Hoover persuaded Congress to pay for the veterans to return to their homes, as many lacked the financial means to do so. Still, with no homes to return to, many chose to stay in Washington. In late July, local law enforcement officials ordered veterans to vacate the vacant buildings and government facilities they occupied. A confrontation followed with police shooting into a crowd and killing two veterans. Hours later, a second confrontation occurred when US General Douglas McArthur led a contingent of seven hundred soldiers—including the future military icons Dwight Eisenhower and George Patton—into the camp. Armed with tanks, fixed bayonets, and adamsite gas, a sickening agent, the soldiers quickly routed the remaining bonus marchers and their families. A twelve-week-old infant died in the ensuing melee. For Hoover, the incident was a public-relations nightmare. Whereas the press had sided with the government's refusal to grant the bonuses, turning the military on America's "heroes" from World War I was an altogether different matter. The incident solidified Hoover's image as a coldhearted, uncaring leader who failed the nation in its darkest hour.

The Bonus Army returned to Washington the following year in May 1933. This time the results were strikingly different. Hoover was out of office, replaced by Franklin Roosevelt. When Roosevelt received word that the veterans were coming to Washington, he ordered officials to set up a facility for them at Fort Hunt in Virginia. Far from the shantytown in Anacostia Flats, the camp came with electricity and running water. As veterans began to arrive, Roosevelt toured the campsite and tipped his cap to the former soldiers as his car passed by. Following his visit, he sent the first lady to greet the men and their families. Always a favorite among the people, Eleanor lunched with the veterans, spoke of her experiences in France, and sang camp songs with them. As one veteran remarked to a reporter, "Hoover sent the army, Roosevelt sent his wife."

Roosevelt's response to the situation spoke volumes to the contrast in leadership styles between the current and former presidents. Whereas Roosevelt exuded compassion and confidence, Hoover seemed detached and aloof. In spite of obvious differences in style, however, the two men were tied together. Hoover in confronting the Great Depression went to lengths beyond anything his predecessors ever attempted in trying to combat an economic crisis. Hoover used the office of the presidency to try to end the Depression, initially turning to volunteerism before embracing government spending as a means to jump-start the economy. His failure to end the crisis had more to do with his limited understanding of the problem and his reservations in fully utilizing the forces of Washington to meet the challenge. His inability to convey strong leadership to the American people during its darkest hour only exacerbated his policy limitations. Yet for all his failing, Hoover's presidency opened the door for Roosevelt's success. The New Deal that lay on the horizon blazed a path built by Hoover.

Suggested Readings

Several writers offer detailed general studies of the Great Depression. A good entry to the causes of and responses to the economic crisis are Robert S. McElvaine's *The Great Depression: America, 1929–1941* (New York: Times Books, 1984) and David M. Kennedy's *Freedom From Fear: The American People in Depression and War, 1929–1945* (New York: Oxford University Press, 2001). For a more specialized exploration of the economic forces leading to the crisis, readers should consult John Kenneth Galbraith's *The Great Crash, 1929* (Boston: Houghton Mifflin, 1961). Joan Hoff Wilson's *Herbert Hoover: The Forgotten Progressive* (Boston: Little, Brown, 1975) remains one of the best studies exploring the ideology and philosophy of the thirty-first president. For a more recent study, see Glen Jeansonne's *The Life of Herbert Hoover: Fighting Quaker, 1928–1933* (New York: Palgrave Macmillan, 2013). *In the Bonus Army: An American Epic* (New York: Walker & Company, 2006), by Paul Dickson and Thomas B. Allen, offers the most comprehensive study of the veterans' protest.

2

The Rise of Franklin Roosevelt

"Happy Days Are Here Again"
—Milton Ager and Jack Yellen, 1929

IN LATE JUNE 1928, as delegates for the Democratic National Convention gathered in Houston, Texas, an uncertainty hung over the start of the proceedings. Just four years earlier, the convention had disintegrated into utter chaos as party leaders struggled to agree on a candidate. Finally, after sixteen sweltering days and 103 ballots, delegates settled on the uninspiring choice of John Davis, a little-known West Virginian whose strongest attribute was that he had few political enemies. Now as Democrats headed into the Houston convention, many delegates feared that the deep-seated political divisions that had ripped apart the party in 1924 would reappear in the Magnolia City. The anxieties proved misplaced. Unity became the watchword of the convention as delegates rallied behind the candidacy of four-term New York Governor Al Smith, nominating the "Happy Warrior" on the second ballot.

The unity that the Democrats exhibited in 1928 was not the only distinction to come out of the Houston convention. The other was the political reemergence of Franklin Delano Roosevelt. Once a rising star in the Democratic Party, Roosevelt's political career waned after the New York politician contracted polio in 1921. Although Roosevelt retreated from public life, he continued to pursue his political aspirations by serving as an unofficial adviser to New York politicians, chiefly Al Smith, his mentor and close personal friend. With the 1928 nomination assured, Smith called on Roosevelt to give an acceptance speech on his behalf. In the most memorable moment of the convention, Roosevelt appeared to walk across the dais with the aid of his son. By all accounts the speech was a rousing success and a vivid reminder to Democrats of the cool, charming, and inspiring confidence that set Roosevelt apart from his fellows. Following the convention, as the dust settled, Smith convinced his protégé to cast aside his reservations and run for New York governor, a seat that Smith expected to vacate with his upcoming presidential bid.

Looking back on Roosevelt's political career, it is evident that his speech at the 1928 Democratic convention proved to be a pivotal event. One could also argue that the speech proved to be a major turning point in the nation's political course, signaling the political ascendency of one of the most influential politicians of the twentieth century, if not in all of American history. Whether revered or reviled, few politicians have had as much impact on American life. Roosevelt refashioned the Democratic Party and established an influential political coalition that reigned for a generation and beyond. Of greater significance, he changed the very nature of American politics. Heading into the 1930s, few Americans expressed an outward desire for a strong federal government to play a role in their everyday lives. By the end of the 1930s, most expected it. In tackling the challenges of the Great Depression, Roosevelt built on ideas articulated by his political predecessors and firmly established the notion that the president and the federal government have a responsibility to protect the interests and promote the well-being of its citizens.

Few politicians were better equipped to understand the inner workings and personal challenges of the presidency than Franklin Roosevelt. Having witnessed the presidency through Theodore Roosevelt, his fifth cousin, Roosevelt possessed clearer insight into the demands of the Oval Office than any other politician, with the exception of John Quincy Adams. Coming in contact with the energetic and fearless Teddy Roosevelt during his political heyday had far-reaching consequences on young Franklin. When Teddy Roosevelt assumed the presidency in 1901, Franklin was an impressionable nineteen-year-old. Until that point, he appeared destined to live out the leisurely patrician lifestyle accorded to someone of his economic and social status. Political careers were out of the question for someone of Roosevelt's pedigree. His peers associated politics with the lower elements of American society. Instead, Roosevelt was expected to follow in the footsteps of his father, James Roosevelt, a lawyer and financier, managing the family's wealth. His mother, Sara Delano, a strong-willed and domineering woman, was determined to fulfill that prophecy, raising her son to be the perfect little gentleman.

Roosevelt's mother focused on instilling in young Franklin the social etiquette and niceties of the privileged elite. His earliest education came from private tutors. Traveling with the family through Europe, Roosevelt became conversant in French and German. While at the family estates, he learned to sail and ride horses, play polo, lawn tennis, and golf. The expectations placed on him by his family and his rank carried through when he finally began attending school at age fourteen. Though Roosevelt went to some of the finest schools in America, the family placed little emphasis on academic achievement and intellectual fulfillment. Instead, school for the Roosevelts meant exploiting social experiences and extending the family's sphere of influence. Attending the prestigious Groton School and Harvard University, Franklin Roosevelt was expected to cultivate social and business connections that would ensure the continuity of his and his family's status. Academic subjects pursued for the sake of intellectual fulfillment were frowned on for making one "bookish" rather than producing well-rounded elite men.

For much of his early life, young Roosevelt seemed perfectly content to live out the life defined by his privilege, showing no signs of rebelling against the expectations placed on him by his mother, his family, or his rank. Experiencing the Teddy Roosevelt White House changed all that. In Teddy Roosevelt, Franklin saw a politician with power and prestige. During the Progressive Era, Teddy Roosevelt redefined the meaning of the executive branch, viewing the presidency as a bully pulpit from which to forcefully address the social, economic, and political problems emerging out of America's industrial transformation. Coming of age in this era, the impressionable Franklin Roosevelt embraced the presidency of Teddy Roosevelt. Roosevelt came to see politics as a means to alter the world in which he lived and rejected the view held by his parents and peers that it was a tawdry profession for society's undesirables. In 1910, determined to follow the path blazed by his older cousin, Franklin Roosevelt set aside the expectations placed on him and entered the political arena.

Roosevelt's privileged life stands in stark contrast to the image American held of him in the 1930s: a humble fatherly figure concerned for the well-being of the "forgotten man." Nothing about Roosevelt's background made him ordinary. He lived a world apart from the vast majority of Americans. And yet Roosevelt successfully connected with the lower elements of American society, cultivating ideas and programs that resonated deeply in their consciousness and inspired reverence across social boundaries. No doubt part of Roosevelt's ability to connect with the masses rested with his outgoing personality and effective communication skills. The charming and jovial Roosevelt disarmed critics and engaged the public, effortlessly cultivating the image of someone who genuinely cared. Yet Roosevelt's ability to forge bonds with the American people went beyond his personality and speaking skills. Roosevelt was able to project the image of someone who cared because he genuinely did care, at a time when the American people craved just such a leader.

One of the driving forces shaping Roosevelt's social outlook was his wife, Eleanor. The niece of Teddy Roosevelt and Franklin's fifth cousin, once-removed, Eleanor was the polar opposite of her husband in many ways. Whereas Franklin was dashing, handsome, and confident, Eleanor was awkward, shy, and insecure. Her mother even called her "Granny," in reference to her serious, introverted, and at times dour ways. Yet she would prove to have irresistible appeal to both Franklin and the American people. The couple met in 1902 during a reception at the White House. They began courting soon after and were married two years later. Roosevelt's mother vehemently opposed the union, early on going so far as to whisk her son away on an extended trip to Europe, hoping that time and distance would extinguish the budding relationship. Despite the family connection, Sara Delano saw in Eleanor a young, immature, and unrefined girl who was poorly equipped to marry a man of her son's stature. Eleanor, however, ultimately proved to be the perfect complement to Franklin Roosevelt.

Eleanor provided balance to her husband's sheltered life of privilege that had been confined to the habits and tastes of his class. She introduced

Roosevelt to a world that he had never seen. When they began their courtship, Eleanor was employed as a social worker in New York City's East Side slums. Roosevelt, who was attending Columbia University Law School at the time, traveled into some of the city's worst neighborhoods to see his future bride. He saw up close the squalor, poverty, and hardship that plagued the area. With Eleanor at his side, he also came to recognize the perseverance and dignity with which residents quietly labored as they tried to eek out a daily living and improve their simple lives. Rather than looking at them with disdain or derision, Eleanor helped Roosevelt see the poor with compassion. In later years, Eleanor would continue to serve as the moral compass guiding her husband, always quick to remind him of the human dimension of his policies.

Roosevelt's worldview and politics were also shaped by his personal battle with polio. In August 1921, Roosevelt traveled to the family's summer home on Campobello Island in New Brunswick, Canada. After a stinging defeat in the 1920 presidential election, where he had been the Democrat's vice presidential candidate, Roosevelt intended to relax, regroup, and plan his next political move. Following a day of sailing, he went to sleep only to wake in the morning with chills. Family members chalked up Roosevelt's symptoms to the flu and prescribed rest. As his condition worsened, a family physician was summoned to the estate. Weeks later, doctors determined that it was not the flu, but polio, an infectious viral disease that left Roosevelt paralyzed from the waist down. Until that moment, the charming and outgoing New York aristocrat had never endured great hardship or faced adversity that challenged his mettle. Polio humbled Roosevelt. He became determined to overcome his paralysis and tried a number of remedies, including hydrotherapy at Warm Springs, Georgia. Roosevelt built up enormous upper-body strength and with the aide of leg braces he learned to balance his body on canes while dragging his legs. It gave onlookers the impression that he could walk, which Roosevelt believed was essential for resuming his political career. Though polio robbed Roosevelt of his ability walk, the disease was not his master. From the experience, Roosevelt learned about hardship, perseverance, compassion, and above all else the need for hope—traits that served him well later in life.

By June 1932, when the Grand Old Republican Party gathered for its presidential convention in Chicago, Herbert Hoover was the proverbial man without a country. His lack of bold and decisive leadership in the early years of the Great Depression ensconced an image in the public mind of a callous and coldhearted leader. Sensing the rising tide against Hoover, Republicans privately explored the possibility of jettisoning the incumbent for the upcoming fall election. The problem was that no one wanted to step forward and take on the unenviable task of assuming the helm of the GOP ticket and possibly imperil their own political career. Calvin Coolidge seemed like a logical choice, given his continued public popularity. Unfortunately, the former president had little taste in risking his favorable reputation among the American public and made it clear he intended to resist any efforts to draft him as the party's candidate. With no alternative, Republicans reluctantly cast their lot behind Hoover's reelection bid. Six weeks later, the fiasco with the Bonus Army exhausted what little good will remained for the nation's leader. Hoover was a dead man walking.

For the Democrats the task at hand appeared much simpler, at least on paper. That summer they had merely to settle on a candidate, stand squarely behind him, and then ride the anti-Hoover wave of anger into the White House. But, given the acrimonious divisions between Democrats, unity was not necessarily easy to achieve. The memories of the debacle at the 1924 Democratic convention continued to linger, creating a sense of discomfort for party leaders. The fact was that diverse economic, geographical, and social interests within the Democratic Party made unity a difficult, if not impossible, proposition. Southern conservatives battled northern liberals, urban and rural forces competed against one another, Protestants stood in opposition to Catholics, and vice versa, nativists and immigrants clashed, and through it all "drys," who advocated prohibition, brawled with "wets," who favored repealing the law. Internal factionalism was one of the primary reasons why only two Democratic candidates succeeded in capturing the White House in seventy-two years since the start of the Civil War. Even four years earlier, when the party tried mightily to project an image of harmony at its 1928 convention, bitter internal divisions threatened to ruin the façade of unity and unhinge the candidacy of Al Smith. Clearly, party harmony was not to be taken for granted among Democrats.

In January 1932, Roosevelt threw his hat into the ring, announcing his intention to seek the Democratic Party nomination. The two-term New York governor carved out a name for himself with his handling of the Depression in the Empire State, establishing public works projects and providing relief for the unemployed. He also benefitted from the fact that New York represented the largest state in the Electoral College, giving him a significant foundation on which to build his campaign. Over the weeks and months that followed, Roosevelt built strong internal party support, lining up delegate commitments. He won the Democratic primaries in eleven of the seventeen states where such elections were held. Meanwhile, he and his staffers carefully cultivated support among local and state leaders. As the convention neared Roosevelt looked like a shoo-in for the nomination. All that remained for Roosevelt was to secure the support of about one hundred more delegates to attain the requisite two-thirds majority needed to guarantee a place at the top of the Democratic ticket. Still, winning another hundred delegates was no small order, as history showed. Once conventioneers took the floor, anything was possible. Chicago proved no different.

Despite Roosevelt's formidable lead, by the eve of the convention it looked suddenly as though the Democrats were destined yet again to travel down the path of self-destruction. The main obstacle facing Roosevelt's candidacy proved to be his old political friend and ally, Al Smith. Heading into the convention, the affable Smith grew increasingly disenchanted over Roosevelt's presidential bid. At a March meeting of the Democratic National Committee (DNC), Roosevelt refused to come out in favor of the repeal of prohibition. While Roosevelt was by no means a "dry," he recognized that throwing his support behind the repeal of the Eighteenth Amendment threatened to alienate conservative Southerners, a base he needed if he wanted to win the party's nomination in June. Smith favored repeal and saw Roosevelt's stance as tantamount to treason. Friction between the men only grew after that. In an April radio address weeks later, Roosevelt laid clear his plan to remedy the Great Depression should he win the election. In his famed "Forgotten Man Speech," the New York governor announced his belief that any economic recovery program needed to help small farmers, workers, and homeowners rather than banks and businesses. As Roosevelt told listeners, defeating the Depression could only be achieved by building from the "bottom up," not the top down, and by restoring faith in "the forgotten man at the bottom of the economic pyramid." Roosevelt's words infuriated Smith, who felt his fellow Democrat was inciting class warfare for personal gain. "I will take off my coat and fight to the end against any candidate who persists in . . . setting class against class and rich against poor," Smith told reporters. Increasingly, Smith viewed his former protégé as a dangerous demagogue, one who should not be afforded the privilege of the Democratic nomination. However, neither issues nor principles fully accounted for Smith's opposition to Roosevelt. Smith was also motivated by his own political ambitions. The former three-time New York governor sensed the tremendous opportunity presented to the Democrats in 1932, and he wanted the nomination. In fact, Smith believed the party owed it to him for all the personal abuse and scorn endured four years earlier when he stepped forward and challenged Hoover and the incumbent GOP. Now, with the presidency in sight for any viable Democratic nominee, Smith believed his time had come.

Smith held several important cards heading into the convention, even though Roosevelt had worked hard to stack the deck. First and foremost, Smith controlled the powerful New York delegation. Though Roosevelt was a two-term governor, the Empire State's democratic political forces maintained their allegiance to Smith. This rang particularly true of the influential Tammany Hall, which had never warmed up to Roosevelt during his tenure in New York. Second, Smith could count on the continued support of several powerful political allies in New Jersey and Massachusetts. Finally, Smith held sway over the DNC. With these cards in hand, Smith and his supporters worked busily behind the scenes to push the party's nomination to the man Roosevelt once dubbed "the Happy Warrior of the political battlefield." But in the end, Smith's stubbornness proved his undoing. Though some party members were less than enthusiastic about Roosevelt's candidacy, the prospect of another Smith campaign was even less appealing. When Smith refused to back out and support an alternative third candidate, Democratic delegates swung toward Roosevelt, giving him the nomination on the fourth vote. The man whose political career seemed dead only ten years earlier now appeared on the cusp of securing the nation's highest elected office.

The presidential contest between Hoover and Roosevelt painted stark contrasts. Roosevelt undertook a vigorous campaign, determined to show Americans that he had overcome polio and was up to the rigorous challenges of the presidency. On the campaign trail, he spoke of bringing America a "new deal," but what exactly that meant remained unclear. He promised to help farmers and workers and provide relief for the poor and suffering, all while balancing the federal budget. He pledged to help business and industry, even indicating a willingness to continue Hoover's Reconstruction Finance Corporation. Most important, he tried to instill a positive message of hope, as evidenced by the song that played before each campaign stop, "Happy Days Are Here Again." In essence, he strove to be all things to all voters.

Meanwhile, Hoover's campaign floundered. Initially, the GOP strategy was to run a traditional "front-porch campaign," with Hoover giving a couple of speeches before retreating from the campaign trail and having surrogates stump across the nation for him. The strategy had worked successfully for McKinley, Harding, Coolidge, and other former Republican presidents. However, none of those men had faced the calamities of the Great Depression. When the campaign failed to gather support, Hoover reluctantly expanded his role. In a series of public radio addresses, he unapologetically defended his administration and its response to the economic crisis. Furthermore, he told Americans that the end of the crisis was in sight and that the economy was already exhibiting signs of a recovery. To voters, Hoover's words rang like more of the same hollow platitudes that had characterized his response to the Depression. They wanted results and Hoover offered them nothing. The depth of the public's animosity came to light on the campaign trail. Hoover was heckled in speech after speech. Onlookers pelted his train and motorcade with tomatoes and rotten eggs as the president passed through towns. When Hoover's presidential train arrived in Detroit, crowds chanting "Hang Hoover" greeted him. No other presidential candidate in modern history faced such public hatred and scorn.

By November, the election was all but a forgone conclusion. When Americans went to the polls, they gave Roosevelt and the Democrats a resounding victory. The New York governor polled over 57 percent of the vote, the first Democrat to win a majority of the popular vote since 1876. Even more impressive, Roosevelt garnered 472 electoral votes compared with Hoover's 59. Hoover had won all but seven states only four years earlier. This time, he claimed only six: Pennsylvania, Delaware, Vermont, Maine, New Hampshire, and Connecticut. Equally important, the election gave Roosevelt a strong

Democratic base with which to work. Showing the public's disgust toward Republican policies, the GOP lost 12 seats in the Senate, giving Democrats a majority, and another 101 seats in the House of Representatives. Heading to Washington in March 1933, Roosevelt did so with the full backing of the American people and majorities in both the House and the Senate.

Roosevelt entered the White House with high expectations, perhaps higher than any president since Abraham Lincoln. The public wanted swift action. Unfortunately, Roosevelt could offer no immediate assistance. Though he claimed victory in November, Roosevelt could not officially take over the office of the presidency until his inauguration on March 4, 1933. Until then, Hoover would continue to run the nation. Epitomizing the very definition of a lame duck president, "the Great Humanitarian" sat in the Oval Office with no mandate to lead and no one willing to support legislation if he had any. For the next four months political inertia engulfed Washington, DC, with millions of Americans in limbo, struggling under the weight of the Great Depression. The only significant piece of legislation that did passed was ratification of the Twentieth Amendment, which moved future presidential inaugurations to January 20. Never again would a president-elect have to wait as long to assume the Executive Office. But for Americans suffering through the winter of 1932–1933, they could find no solace in the changes to come.

Leading up to the inauguration, Roosevelt and his staff worked busily to define the "new deal" he pledged to the electorate during the campaign. Many political pundits doubted Roosevelt was up to the task of leading the nation out of its economic morass. Walter Lippmann, a celebrated political commentator, counted among the unimpressed, doubting that Roosevelt possessed the intellectual capabilities to lead the nation through this bleak period. H. L. Mencken, another journalist of note, agreed, seeing the president-elect as an amiable opportunist unprepared for the challenges of the presidency. However, the criticisms missed the mark. By 1932, Roosevelt had developed into a skilled politician under the tutelage of Louis Howe. The former newspaperman had met Roosevelt in 1911. The two forged a strong bond and Howe became Roosevelt's right-hand man. Referred to as "the king maker," Howe proved invaluable in cultivating Roosevelt's political acumen and is seen as the instrumental figure behind his rise to the

White House. Ever present by his side, Howe turned Roosevelt into a savvy, talented, and skilled politician.

Behind the scenes Roosevelt also drew heavily on a group of trusted and highly capable advisers. Although Roosevelt's academic record would never lead anyone to confuse him with an intellectual, he possessed a keen appreciation for the abilities of others and surrounded his administration with scholars and intellectuals. Dubbed the "brain trust" by the press, the group gave ideological form and practical function to many of Roosevelt's broad ideas. Among the initial group were the Columbia University law professors Raymond Moley and Adolph Berle, the agricultural economist Rexford Tugwell, retired Brigadier General Hugh Johnson, the social reformers Frances Perkins and Harry Hopkins, and the banker James Warburg. To this group, Roosevelt bestowed the mighty task of defining the mechanics of his New Deal. His leadership style allowed the group tremendous latitude. He did not want staffers to be held prisoner by past practices and customs. Nor did he want them to be paralyzed by the fear of failure. Instead, he looked to the brain trust to find bold and imaginative solutions to the complex, multifaceted problems facing the nation. If a program failed to work, they would simply scrap it and move on. The importance, for Roosevelt, lay in finding a solution to the dire conditions of the day for a public that demanded action. In the months leading up to the inauguration, the brain trust feverishly set to work on solving the Great Depression and curing the public's suffering.

When Roosevelt's inauguration finally arrived on Saturday, March 4, 1933, it brought great anticipation and fanfare. Millions sat eagerly by their radios to listen to Roosevelt's speech, which was carried live on several networks. Hidden from the public, a palpable tension between Hoover and Roosevelt hung over the cool, cloudy, late-winter day. What remained of their once amicable relationship collapsed in the weeks leading up to the inaugural ceremony as Hoover tried to lure Roosevelt into supporting several last-minute political measures. The president-elect steadily refused, not wishing to be associated with the failures of the outgoing commander in chief. Now, as the two men rode together from the White House to the inaugural site, barely a word was uttered. After being sworn in by Chief Justice Charles Evans Hughes, himself a one-time Republican presidential candidate in 1916, Roosevelt proceeded to give a brief twenty-minute address that calmed public anxieties. As he explained in a much-quoted phrase, "the only thing we have to fear is fear itself." "This great nation will endure as it has endured," Roosevelt confidently declared, "[it] will revive and will prosper." The president-elect went on to explain that he intended to vigorously fight the economic crisis, using all powers afforded him under the Constitution. Should that approach fail, he would ask Congress for "broad executive authority" to confront the Depression head-on as if it were a war.

Immediately after taking the oath of office, Roosevelt began to act. Calling Congress back into action in a special session, the new administration began the onerous task of putting America on the road to recovery. The challenge was daunting. By March, unemployment had reached an estimated 25 percent nationwide. Farm prices had dropped nearly 60 percent below their pre-Depression value. Meanwhile, industrial output had declined by half. Homelessness was on the rise, with estimates placing the figure at nearly two million people coast-to-coast. Still, the biggest problem facing the new administration centered on the looming banking crisis.

By the time Roosevelt took office over nine thousand banks had shuttered their doors. With the closings, tens of thousands of people saw their life savings vanish almost overnight. The banking system looked poised to collapse and potentially bring down the entire nation's financial system. Adding to the chaos was the prospect of further closings in the days, weeks, and months ahead. In February, fearing the collapse of the Union Guardian Trust Company, one of Detroit's most powerful financial institutions, Michigan Governor William Comstock announced the temporary closing of all banks across the state. The shutdown was to last approximately eight days, allowing Michigan's banks to secure stronger fiscal footing. Rather than calming investor fears, Comstock's announcement escalated an already delicate situation. The eight-day time frame came and went. Michigan banks remained closed nearly thirty days. In desperate need of funds, Michigan businessmen turned to financial institutions in Chicago and New York for help, straining already depleted reserves in those states. Panic ensued. By the end of February, bank closings were declared in Arkansas, Indiana, and Maryland. Other states quickly followed suit. In the early morning hours of March 4, New York Governor Herbert Lehman, Roosevelt's successor, announced the immediate closure of all banks in the Empire State. Less than 45 minutes later, Illinois Governor Henry Horner issued a proclamation doing the same in his state. As Roosevelt readied to take the oath of office, banks in thirty-four out of forty-eight states were closed.

Closing the remaining banks was a clear priority for Roosevelt and his staffers. Keeping the banks open would have been madness, exposing the remaining institutions to tremendous financial strain as nervous patrons and creditors, fearing the possibility of similar closings in their states, would look to secure their funds. The closings also threatened the status of the banks that remained open, as businesses in the affected states would invariably look to the open institutions for assistance, straining already limited reserves. On March 6, invoking the Trading with the Enemy Act of 1917, Roosevelt issued a proclamation declaring the immediate closure of all remaining banks. With typical Roosevelt flair, he explained to a reporter that he was not closing the banks, but rather initiating a "bank holiday," preferring the light, positive connotations associated with the latter phrase.

Roosevelt staffers worked franticly to figure out how to stabilize the banking system and reopen America's banks. Oddly, among the key architects behind Roosevelt's solution were several holdovers from the Hoover administration, including Ogden Mills, the outgoing secretary of the treasury, who would later become a fervent critic of Roosevelt and the New Deal. It was Mills who came up with the overall structure for the administration's Emergency Banking Relief Act. The plan called for financial institutions on a sound economic footing to be reopened quickly once it was determined they were financially stable. Unstable banks, meanwhile, would be divided into two categories. The first were banks that, although at risk, could be reopened in a short period of time pending modest financial assistance or reorganization. The second were banks deemed at risk or unstable that could not be reopened without significant reorganization. For these banks, government resources would be tapped to help get them back on a firm financial footing before reopening. Three days later the formal legislation was drafted by Arthur Ballantine and Walter Wyatt, Treasury officials from Hoover's staff, and put before Congress. Congress, summoned hastily back to the nation's capital by Roosevelt, offered virtually no resistance to his plan. The bill flew through the House, passing by a 302 to 110 vote, even though hard copies had not been distributed to House members. The Senate approved it by a margin of 73 to 7. In just over seven hours, Roosevelt secured passage of the first piece of New Deal legislation, a measure that ironically had the fingerprints of the Hoover administration all over it.

The Emergency Banking Relief Act's success ultimately hinged on the public's willingness to buy into Roosevelt's banking plan. The president had to convince the American people that when the banks reopened, their money would be secure and they need not fear losing their life savings. If the public failed to buy into the plan, a strong possibility existed that the bank runs would resume, thereby imperiling the banking system. This was no small task for Roosevelt. Many Americans had grown cynical of banks and had taken to keeping their money under mattresses. On the evening of Sunday, March 12, just eight days after taking the oath of office, Roosevelt took to the nation's airwaves and gave the first of what came to be known as his fireside chats. In a very plain and direct way, Roosevelt explained the legislation to listeners with a prose and delivery that disarmed concerns. In a straightforward and convincing manner, he assured listeners that the government was "straightening the situation out." And while he could not "promise . . . that every bank will be reopened or that individual losses will not be suffered," Roosevelt pledged that "there will be no losses that possibly could be avoided." Furthermore, he wanted Americans to know the purpose of the Banking Relief Act was not just to momentarily rescue the banks but also to build a sound and stable financial system. Roosevelt closed by adding, "It is your problem no less than it is mine. Together we cannot fail."

Roosevelt's broadcast convinced Americans that he understood the precarious economic situation confronting the nation and that he genuinely cared for the citizens and their struggles. Long term, the speech marked the start of a process whereby Roosevelt personalized the presidency for the American people, nurturing the persona of a father-like figure in the White House. Over the next eleven years this paternal image became ensconced with the twenty-nine fireside chats that the president gave. Short term, the speech reduced public concerns and convinced people that the Emergency Banking Act was sound. The very next day after Roosevelt's fireside chat, when banks began to reopen, deposits exceeded withdrawals. Over the next several weeks, stability returned to the banking system. By mid-April over $1 billion had returned to the banks. Though structural problems within banking remained, Roosevelt could claim success with his first New Deal measure. The Banking Act momentarily halted a potentially dangerous financial crisis and restored confidence in the banking system. With that out of the way, Roosevelt had to discover a solution that guaranteed the solvency of America's banks over the long term.

Roosevelt followed up the Emergency Banking Act with the Economy Act. In keeping with his campaign pledge to balance the budget, this measure called for a $500 million reduction in the federal budget. To accomplish the task, Roosevelt proposed eliminating several federal offices, slashing government payrolls, and cutting pay for civilian and military personnel, including members of Congress. This time, the response was less favorable. Veterans stood to lose up to 50 percent of their benefits. With the Bonus Army in mind, many Congressmen, particularly Northern liberals, were leery about supporting the act. Introduced to Congress on March 10, it took ten days before the measure reached Roosevelt's desk, a far cry from the mere seven hours needed to steer through the Banking Act. Support came largely from conservative Southern Democrats, a group Roosevelt needed in his corner in order to pass future legislation. To help remove the sting of the Economy Act, two days later Roosevelt signed into law the Beer-Wine Revenue Act, which allowed for the manufacture and sale of beer and wine with an alcohol content of 3.2 percent or less. The act marked a step toward the repeal of prohibition, a move set in motion when Congress approved the Twenty-first Amendment just weeks before Roosevelt took office. It also demonstrated Roosevelt's political savvy. The Economy Act gave him necessary political cachet with Southern Democrats, a group lukewarm in their support of Roosevelt and whose backing he needed for other upcoming legislation. Meanwhile, by counterbalancing an unpopular piece of legislation like the Economy Act with a wildly popular one like ending Prohibition, he minimized public and political discontent.

Roosevelt closed out March by steering through Congress the Civilian Conservation Corps (CCC) bill. The measure, with its emphasis on conservation, was near and dear to Roosevelt's heart. He had initiated a similar program—though on a much smaller scale—while governor of New York. The CCC provided work relief to young, unemployed men. Under the program single men between the ages of eighteen to twenty-five would be placed on the federal payroll. They would be sent to work on the nation's parks and forests, building bridges, roads, and campgrounds. They taught rural farmers about soil erosion, fought forest fires, and planted trees, thereby earning the nickname "Roosevelt's Tree Army." In return for their labor, the men received room and board as well as $30 per month, of which $25 was automatically sent back home to their families.

The CCC demonstrated the ingenuity of Roosevelt's brain trust. It took young men, many of whom had been unemployed for a good portion of their adult lives, and gave them jobs. At its height in 1935, over 500,000 men worked in over 2,600 CCC camps spread across the United States. All told, over 2.5 million young men participated in the CCC, which ran until 1942. They learned a variety of skills and trades laboring on projects such as building the Great Smokey Mountains National Park or working on the reforestation of Manistee National Forest. They also learned valuable, marketable skills through training courses taught in the evening after work hours. Thus armed and occupied, young men were given hope for the future. But there was more to the program than just aiding unemployed young men. The success of the CCC lay in the wide array of people who benefited from the program. Parents received relief by having one less mouth to feed and assistance through the pay that the young men sent home. Finally, the nation benefited, as the CCC built a national park infrastructure that endured well beyond the 1930s and was enjoyed by generations of Americans to follow.

Roosevelt's CCC marked a major philosophical shift from the Hoover administration's response to the Great Depression. Whereas Hoover used government policy to jump-start the economy in the later years of his term, he remained fiercely opposed to programs that provided direct relief or assistance to the nation's poor. Like Hoover, Roosevelt was also leery of crafting legislation that might foster economic dependence and weaken people's work ethic. But unlike Hoover, the New York Democrat recognized the severity of the crisis and the need to raise the morale of citizens. Relief, like that provided by the CCC, thus became one of Roosevelt's key pillars in lifting America out of its economic doldrums.

Heading into April, Roosevelt's brain trust worked busily to give shape to the New Deal. A litany of legislation came from the White House in the weeks and months to follow. All told, the first hundred days of Roosevelt's administration produced an unprecedented number of proposals for political action from the Executive branch. The end result was a three-phased approach known as the "3 Rs": relief, recovery, and reform. The strategy aimed to provide temporary relief to the forgotten man, initiate a series of programs designed to jump-start economic recovery, and create necessary reforms to prevent a repeat of any future Great Depressions.

Whereas the CCC targeted a specific segment of the population, the Federal Emergency Relief Administration (FERA) was Roosevelt's broad-based attempt to help those hit hardest by the Depression. To administer the program, Roosevelt appointed Harry Hopkins, a former social worker who had taken the lead on several work-relief projects the president initiated while governor of New York. Rather than tasking the federal government with operating the program directly, Hopkins turned to state and local governments. Under his oversight, local governments could apply to FERA for grants to establish programs targeting the specific needs of the unemployed in their communities. Hopkins encouraged applicants to craft work-for-relief programs instead of handouts, which the administration preferred to avoid. Roosevelt established a budget of $500 million to fund FERA, drawing on monies available through the Reconstruction Finance Corporation.

To help stem the rising tide of farm and home foreclosures, Roosevelt put forward two pieces of legislation. The Emergency Farm Mortgage Act passed in May helped farmers stave off foreclosure by providing the means to refinance their mortgages. The program enabled farmers to extend their loan period at lower interest rates. Loans would be administered through a network of banks established by the Farm Credit Act and would be backed by the federal government. The Home Owners' Loan Act provided similar assistance to urban Americans. Like the Farm Mortgage Act, the program enabled cash-strapped homeowners to refinance their home loans. By lowering monthly payments and extending the length of the home loan, the administration expected to slow the rate of foreclosures across the nation.

Roosevelt's recovery programs for the general economy centered on two broadly based plans to bolster agriculture and industry. The agricultural legislation emerged in the first few days of his administration. Roosevelt's advisers believed that the key to agricultural recovery rested on bolstering prices and restoring purchasing power to farmers. To do so, they crafted a plan designed to restrict production and force prices upward. The Agricultural Adjustment Act (AAA) sought to inflate prices by paying farmers not to farm. Under the program, the administration targeted seven "basic crops"—wheat, cotton, corn, rice, peanuts, tobacco, and milk—and agreed to pay farmers who restricted production of these crops. In order to qualify, farmers had to agree to let their land lie fallow in "reduction contracts." In return, farmers received compensation equal to the value the land would yield if the crop had in fact been grown. By doing so, the AAA looked to scale back production, ending overproduction, and thereby inflate the prices of the crops. To fund the AAA Roosevelt established a tax on companies that processed farm products.

The National Industrial Recovery Act (NIRA) marked Roosevelt's efforts to stimulate industrial recovery. It consisted of two major components. The first established the Public Works Administration (PWA), a program that came at the behest of Secretary of Labor Frances Perkins. The PWA funded large-scale construction projects, earmarking $6 billion in its first two years, including $3.3 billion in year one. Unlike later programs, the PWA contracted directly with construction companies rather than put unemployed workers on the government payroll. The goal was to increase purchasing power by funding large scale construction projects that strengthened America's infrastructure. Among the more notable projects of the PWA were the Triborough Bridge and Lincoln Tunnel in New York, the Overseas Highway from Miami to Key West, and the Grand Coulee Dam in Washington state. The PWA also built schools, courthouses, hospitals, airports, and public housing.

The second component of Roosevelt's industrial recovery program established the National Recovery Administration (NRA). Rather than impose government control over the economy, Roosevelt viewed the NRA as the means for helping business and industry find their own path to recovery. The program took a page from Woodrow Wilson's War Industries Board during the Great War and another from the Trade Association movement initiated by Herbert Hoover and the Republican Party during the 1920s. The plan proposed to bring together businesses along their respective sectors. Business officials would then work jointly to craft fair practice codes for their particular industry, creating agreements that established prices, set wages, and determined production output. The NRA essentially permitted businesses the opportunity to plan and organize the economy according to their specific needs and interests. For his part, Roosevelt agreed to allow anti-trust prosecution to fall by the wayside, believing the NRA possessed the means to end cutthroat competition, stabilize prices, and stimulate economic activity.

The NRA gave business and industry tremendous economic latitude by easing government regulations. Roosevelt staffers understood the plan opened the door to potential manipulation and abuse. For example, concerns were expressed that businesses might conspire to drive down workers' wages or inhibit unionization. To minimize such threats and prevent wholesale collusion, Roosevelt insisted that a provision be included in the legislation to protect the workers' rights to organize. The administration also worked to ensure that labor be permitted to participate in the code hearings, believing that a strong worker voice would most effectively protect worker rights and mute criticism. Such provisions generated a great deal of criticism from business and industry leaders. Business officials were also upset that the NRA stipulated that they could not raise prices once their economic sector began to improve. Since involvement in the NRA was not mandatory, concerns arose that business and industry would not sign on in support of the measure. Roosevelt hoped that they would see enough of the positive potential in the NRA to support the program. However, he also looked to coerce participation. In a twist on Hoover's volunteerism, the NRA issued a "Blue Eagle" to businesses that supported the codes for their sector. The logo boasted the slogan "We Do Our Part." Compliant businesses could freely use the Blue Eagle in all advertising informing the general public that they were onboard with Roosevelt's programs for economic recovery. The hope was that the benefit of receiving a Blue Eagle, or threat of *not* receiving it, would be sufficient to encourage participation.

The reform component of Roosevelt's New Deal sought to tackle the systemic, structural economic problems exposed by the Great Depression. Roosevelt staffers believed that by establishing prudent fiscal policies and judicious government regulation, they could both curb the current economic catastrophe and establish long-term mechanisms to prevent future depressions. The Emergency Banking Act marked Roosevelt's first step in this direction, but it was by no means the last. The widespread collapse of America's lending institutions exposed the prevalence of reckless banking practices. Passed in June, the Banking Act further boosted American confidence in the banking system by protecting depositors' investments and deterring irresponsible lending practices. The main provision of the new law separated investment and commercial banking activities. The logic behind the legislation stemmed from the widespread belief that commercial banks had contributed greatly to the economic collapse by carelessly investing depositor monies in the stock market. Banks would be given a period of one year to decide their designation, whether commercial or investment. To curb speculative practices, commercial banks were restricted as to how much they could invest in the securities market. To further protect investors, the measure called for the creation of the Federal Deposit Insurance Corporation (FDIC), which guaranteed personal bank accounts up to $5,000. The creation of the FDIC may be the most enduring of Roosevelt's New Deal legacies.

To help control the rampant speculation that had grossly overinflated the stock market and precipitated the crash, Roosevelt's brain trust pushed forward two specific measures. Prior to the Depression most states had some form of legislation designed to prevent fraudulent practices and stock manipulation on their books. However, the local "Blue Sky Laws," as they came to be known, proved largely ineffective with businesses ignoring the measures. Passed in May, the Federal Securities Act placed trading practices under federal regulation and required full disclosure of all information regarding new stocks and bonds. The intent was to eliminate the insider trading practices that encouraged stock manipulation while guaranteeing investors complete and accurate information regarding stocks before making purchases. In order to curtail the practices that had led to the enormous stock bubble in the 1920s, the law also allowed for federal regulation of margin requirements.

Enforcement of the Federal Securities Act initially came under the purview of the Federal Trade Commission, the government agency created by Woodrow Wilson in 1915 to restrict monopolistic business practices. However, recognizing the need for a separate agency, in June 1934 Roosevelt signed into law a measure establishing the Securities Exchange Commission (SEC). The SEC was charged with supervising the new law and guaranteeing compliance. The agency was given authority to license stock exchanges, brokerage houses that bought and sold stocks, as well as individuals who traded stocks. The law also permitted SEC authority to bring civil and criminal charges against those who violated the Securities Act. By doing so, Roosevelt once again intended to restore public confidence in the stock market while preventing a repeat of similar problems.

Fifteen pieces of major legislation flowed through the halls of Congress during the first one hundred days of Roosevelt's presidency, with many more to follow in the months ahead. Though innovative, the programs created under Roosevelt's New Deal can by no means be classified as revolutionary. The possible lone exception was perhaps the Tennessee Valley Authority (TVA), a bold initiative that provided flood and erosion control, reforestation, and economic development to the Tennessee Valley region, while offering poor, rural areas long ignored by private utility companies with affordable electrical power. Instead, most legislation crafted in the first two years of Roosevelt's presidency built on Progressive Era traditions carved out by the likes of Teddy Roosevelt, Woodrow Wilson, and even Herbert Hoover. The Federal Farm Loan Act, established by the Wilson administration in 1917 to provide farmers with long-term credit to develop and expand farms, served as a pattern for Roosevelt's Emergency Farm Mortgage and the Farm Credit Acts. The NRA was grounded in the experiences of Wilson's War Industries Board and Hoover's Trade Associations. Federal regulation of the stock exchanges established with the SEC merely supplanted local, state regulatory policies or Blue Sky Laws that pre-dated the twentieth century in several cases. Similarly, several states experimented with bank insurance programs like the FDIC well before 1933, including Roosevelt's home state of New York in 1929. Indeed, calls for a federally guaranteed insurance program for bank deposits appeared in Congress as early as 1886. Even Roosevelt's CCC was patterned after a program he first created as governor of New York in 1931 and was built on the conservation principles of Teddy Roosevelt.

Rather than revolutionary, Franklin Roosevelt's distinction comes from the overall depth of the programs he promoted. Roosevelt brought forward more federally funded programs and initiated more government regulation than any previous sitting president in such a short period of time. The Great Depression necessitated strong, decisive action and Roosevelt delivered. Still, while Roosevelt greatly expanded the role of government in economic and social life, there were limits. In 1933, for example, Roosevelt initiated the Civil Works Administration (CWA), a federally funded public works project designed to aid the unemployed. The CWA was one of the few New Deal programs that put unemployed workers directly on the federal payroll. Until this point Roosevelt had been hesitant to engage such policies, fearing like many conservatives that it might create a sense of entitlement and sap the work ethic of the unemployed. However, after learning of the suffering Americans experienced the previous winter and recognizing the shortcomings of the state-sponsored relief programs created under FERA, Roosevelt relented. Beginning in November, unemployed workers were enlisted to work on CWA-sponsored work projects. Over the next four months more than four million people were put to work on a variety of CWA works projects building roads, schools, airports, playgrounds, and more. Costs for the programs exceeded over $1 billion. By April, alarmed over the growing cost of the program and renewed concerns about dependency, Roosevelt hastily dissolved the program, sending the workers back to the unemployment lines. As much as Roosevelt embraced the concept of change and encouraged the brain trust to be bold and experimental in combating the Great Depression, the president remained captive to his past, favoring judicious action over the reckless expansion of government policies and haphazard intervention. However, as the Depression lingered into the end of his first term, Roosevelt would be forced to reexamine his position, eventually turning toward policies he once refused.

Suggested Readings

A good starting point to the many studies of Franklin Roosevelt and the New Deal remains William Leuchtenburg's *Franklin D. Roosevelt and the New Deal, 1932–1940* (New York: Harper & Row, 1963), which provides a detailed overview of Roosevelt's presidency. For a look at Franklin and Eleanor Roosevelt's relationship, readers should consult *No Ordinary Time: Franklin and Eleanor Roosevelt* (New York: Simon & Shuster, 1995), by Doris Kearns Goodwin. Jonathan Alter's *The Defining*

Moment: FDR's First Hundred Days and the Triumph of Hope (New York: Simon & Shuster, 2007) provides an in-depth exploration of Roosevelt's rise to the presidency and the early formation of the New Deal. Amity Shales's *The Forgotten Man: A New History of the Great Depression* (New York: Harper Perennial, 2008) offers a critical look at the Roosevelt presidency and the politics of the New Deal.

3

The Environment and Science

"This Land Is Our Land"
—Woody Guthrie, 1940

WITNESSES DESCRIBED a sudden darkening of the sky and day turning to night, followed by the roar of a freight train before biting grit cut into exposed flesh. Large-scale industrial agriculture ripped soil from the Great Plains and made the wind heavy and dangerous with powdery dust. From 1931 to 1939, the band of states from the Dakotas to Texas—nearly a third of the nation—was plagued by dust storms that smothered livestock and buried houses whole. Storms descended on communities with relentless fury, sickening and killing people in their path. Oklahoma, Texas, Nebraska, and New Mexico were hardest hit, but the most severe damage occurred around the southwestern corner of Kansas and the Oklahoma and Texas panhandles. For nearly ten years, drought pulverized soil exposed by destructive farming practices and excessive grazing, resulting in dust storms that ripped the exposed topsoil away by the foot, withered crops, and forced many homesteaders to migrate. Some 3.5 million Americans would abandon their farms by the end of this environmental catastrophe. Most resettled in nearby states, but more than 350,000 Oklahomans moved as far away as California.

Social, political, and economic forces came together to create the conditions to drive a natural cycle of drought into the Dust Bowl, the worst ecological crisis in the history of the United States. It was exacerbated by the last wave of westward expansion that had begun in the nineteenth century and surged again in the early twentieth century when speculative farming became a popular venture. Migrants from the east who succeeded in midwestern and plains states embodied the best of the frontier spirit that had encouraged pioneers generations before. They were independent, self-reliant, highly motivated rugged individualists who worked hard and embraced sacrifice. They were also overconfident, underinformed, and ill equipped for the harsh side of the region's climate. Embracing the spirit of the industrial age, farmers adopted advances in agricultural technologies that made it possible to convert grass prairies to fields of grain—at least for a time. They used enormous gas-powered tractors to tear through the sod, creating efficient rows harvested by combines that quickened erosion. As a result, large-scale single crop or monoculture farming increased dramatically by the 1920s. Motivated by grain shortages following World War I, midwestern and plains farmers sought to reap profits from wheat production for export rather than to provide for the needs of regional communities as had the small, diversified, sustainable farms of the past. During the same period, ranchers and dairy farmers of Colorado, Wyoming, Minnesota, Wisconsin, and the Dakotas capitalized on the desires of an increasingly urban population for milk, cheese, and beef by increasing herds. Even though a few families prospered, more succumbed to failure when topsoil erosion and overgrazing added to the conditions that caused the ecological disaster known as the Dust Bowl.

The Dust Bowl began ignobly with drought in 1931 followed by fourteen dust storms in 1932. People in affected areas were alarmed, but stoic, sweeping or shoveling piles of dust out of their houses, digging out machinery, and accepting crop and livestock losses. Like the politicians who represented them, residents believed the bad weather would blow over. But in 1933 the number of dust storms grew to thirty-eight. "Black blizzards," as they would come to be known, could last for hours or days. They devastated the landscape and decimated the morale of farmers whose pride was inherently linked to their success on the land. Hoping to ward off the pneumonia-like symptoms caused by inhaling pernicious dust, residents donned surgical masks and treated children with homemade concoctions comprised of everything from whisky to turpentine.

By 1934, the storms were coming with alarming frequency. Government-mandated livestock kills, which were supposed to reduce overgrazing, further demoralized Great Plains communities and outraged a nation already worn down by the Great Depression. In 1935, after weeks of dust storms that destroyed 5 million acres of wheat, the worst storm of the era killed livestock and dumped tons of topsoil and red clay throughout Kansas, Oklahoma, and Colorado. With winds in excess of 70 miles per hour, the storm that lasted twenty-seven days and nights would be remembered for the day it began: Black Sunday. Black Sunday marked a major turning point in the crisis by convincing many residents to leave and stirring politicians and scientists into action. In addition, the label "Dust Bowl" emerged after Black Sunday when the Associated Press reporter Robert Geiger first used the term in his coverage of the storm.

Americans outside of the Midwest learned about the environmental crisis from coverage by reporters such as Geiger and especially travel dispatches written by the legendary journalist Ernie Pyle. Most often remembered as a Pulitzer prizewinning war correspondent from World War II, Pyle traveled throughout the United States for seven years beginning in 1935 with his wife, Geraldine "Jerry" Siebolds, who was known to readers as "that girl who rides with me." Sometimes working collaboratively with his wife and often relying on her editorial skills, Pyle produced as many as six seven-hundred-word columns each week that were published in hundreds of papers across the country. Twice he traveled through the Dust Bowl and "droughty" regions documenting his observations of the wind-ravaged, grasshopper-plagued landscape and the people who struggled to inhabit it. Whether writing about the decade-long drama in the Great Plains, or later from battlefronts in Europe and North Africa, Pyle's folksy style appealed to readers with an easygoing, unflappable perspective that both valued independence and promoted social responsibility. He reached millions of readers and was a favorite of the socially conscious First Lady Eleanor Roosevelt, who promoted Pyle's writing in her own daily column. Regardless of the topic, Pyle captured stories of ordinary people doing their best to overcome extraordinary obstacles.

Pyle had an everyman appeal that made him a representative voice for his generation. He is remembered as much for his hard work, dedication, and talent as he is for being a champion for the common man, whether an infantryman or a Dust Bowl refugee. Moreover, Pyle's life story offers an important parallel to the popular image of the Roaring Twenties, revealing the growing restlessness of a generation without the means to achieve an American dream that was increasingly visible, desirable, and out of reach. Born to tenant farmers in rural Indiana in 1900, Pyle attended high school before serving briefly in the United States Navy Reserve during World War I. He attended Indiana University, but moved to Washington, DC, during his senior year to write for a daily paper. Of medium height and slender build, Pyle worked as a writer and editor for a number of newspapers during the 1920s, earning an audience for his reports on feats of aviation by record-breaking aviators such as Charles Lindbergh and Amelia Earhart. Spectacular subjects notwithstanding, readers responded to Pyle's spare, compelling details and insightful observations. In a tragic final chapter, Pyle would become an important hero for the generation he comforted during the worst of hard times. In 1945, after reluctantly agreeing to cover the Pacific Theater, Pyle's life was cut short by machine-gun fire on a remote island near Okinawa, Japan, thereby solidifying his place in American history.

An inexhaustible reporter who lived his adult life from deadline to deadline, Pyle's writing demonstrates narrative prowess requiring both talent and skill. Leaning more toward realism and eschewing the detached tone of many of his contemporaries who favored modernism, Pyle wrote profiles of people and places during the 1930s with an earnest and unassuming midwestern voice. Collected and republished in *Ernie's America: The Best of Ernie Pyle's 1930s Travel Dispatches* in 1989, Pyle introduced characters such as young Mr. Roy Meehan, "of the South Dakota Meehans," who was handsome, tan, and as "fine a fellow" as a person could meet. When they met up in Miles City, Montana, Meehan was heading west to Fort Peck in search of a job on a government dam project, leaving a mother and two younger brothers behind to manage without him. Using understatements to powerful effect, Pyle reported the events that brought Meehan to his decision to hit the road: "He never knew anything about farming. His father died, and left three-quarters of a section for Roy and his mother to handle. They, with the help of the elements and things we can't understand, handed it into the hands of Rural Credit. They don't have a farm anymore." Pyle's tone is terse but sympathetic as he describes Meehan's desperate situation. Similarly, compassion is not erased by a sense of irony in Pyle's report of another man's ill-fated move from La Porte, Indiana, to South Dakota. Mr. Denien and his family packed everything into their old Cadillac and drove out to the land of opportunity to share a farm with a widowed uncle. Described as more bewildered and disheartened than anyone he'd ever met, Pyle predicted that "one of these days, when Mr. Denien gets his courage, and enough money to buy a license," the Cadillac would carry them away again.

Perhaps the most powerful and haunting images appear in Pyle's profiles of the land itself. He describes the ruined and despoiled countryside and calls wind storms "horizontal waterfalls." For Pyle, driving into a dust storm was like an airplane flying into black fog, and driving out was like bursting "into fresh air on the windward side of a forest fire." With unsettling precision, Pyle reported the horrific desolation that had formerly been lush and verdant western Kansas. It is clear from his dispatches that farmers and readers alike were aware that unsuitable farming practices and pasture overuse had played key roles in damaging the plains and prolonging the Dust Bowl; however, Pyle is careful not to assign blame. Metaphors subtly reinforce the central role of humans in ruining the land. He refers to sickening "pillars of sand—giant columns, miles away, rising from the horizon clear up to the sky, like smoke from a burning town." Pyle mentions the scientists and government officials responding to the crisis, alluding to the tension between progress, farmers, and the exploitation of the land. When reflecting on the painful question of what might happen to the Great Plains region, he acknowledges that the "experts are working on it. They are giving advice, but advice is mighty hard to follow when you're broke." Pyle helped Depression Era readers across the nation strengthen their own resolve with such accounts of life in the Dust Bowl.

Photographers, filmmakers, and other visual artists joined journalists in covering the Dust Bowl. Dorothea Lange made a name for herself documenting life during the Dust Bowl as a photographer with the Farm Security Administration. Driven, hardworking, and talented, Lange traveled with migrants and the images she captured portray the utter destitution of dispirited families. Photographs like Lange's iconic "Migrant Mother" brought the face of suffering to a sympathetic American public. Federal monies funded the filmmaker Pare Lorentz's significant documentary *The Plow That Broke the Plains*. Like Lange, Lorentz was driven and talented. He was also idealistic and motivated by a powerful conviction that film could provide more than distraction for audiences. He wanted to make substantial films of merit that might inspire answers to the problems faced by Americans during the Great Depression. By avoiding the relevant issues of the day, Lorentz believed that Hollywood filmmakers were guilty of self-censorship and he publically criticized studios for their escapist fare. This perspective would have serious consequences for him later, when Hollywood insiders prohibited access to stock footage he needed to complete *The Plow That Broke the Plains*, and worse, restricted the nationwide distribution of his films.

Having worked for years as a professional writer and popular, candid film critic, Lorentz believed film was a potent medium to educate, inform, and energize audiences. Until then its role in shaping public discourse had been sorely lacking. At the relatively young age of thirty and with no prior filmmaking experience, this ambitious West Virginia native convinced the Department of Agriculture official James La Cron that a new kind of documentary blending artistry and commentary on the Dust Bowl conditions would be an excellent opportunity to advance New Deal agricultural programs. Although the government had produced or funded documentaries prior to Lorentz's, films were typically narrow in scope and didactic in purpose. Lorentz proposed a completely new approach to content and production that included aesthetic appeal and experimental techniques. Working under the New Dealer Rexford G. Tugwell for the recently established Resettlement Administration, Lorentz produced, wrote, and directed the 25-minute film for a total of $19,500. Although the final cost was more than the modest $6,000 he was originally allotted, *The Plow That Broke the Plains* was significantly less expensive to make than even the lowest-budget Hollywood features.

Lorentz was familiar enough with the filmmaking industry to hire the best camera technicians and crew members he could find. He broke ranks with both Hollywood and government documentary traditions by choosing to film entirely on location and using local people rather than professional actors. He developed the highly elegiac script over time, resulting in nine chapters organized in seven major sequences including the history of the region, early causes and warnings, economic booms and busts, drought and dust storms, and finally, failure and exodus. Lorentz was deeply sensitive to the emotional currency of music and therefore dedicated a lot of attention to the score for *The Plow That Broke the Plains.* He found a kindred spirit in the composer Virgil Thompson, who agreed to collaborate with Lorentz on creating a soundtrack to match the stunning visual images and poetic narration of the film. Recorded by musicians from the New York Philharmonic, Thompson's score incorporated plains folk melodies, traditional hymns, and even songs sung by dirt farmers. The result was a film that remains evocative, stirring, and immensely compelling. Roosevelt brandished praise after its premiere in the White House. Critics lauded it in the press for its powerful portrayal of wind-ravaged landscapes and devastated farmers—even though the film condemned the ideologies and practices that created the Dust Bowl.

Another visual artist moved by his conscience to act in response to the crisis in the Great Plains was the painter Alexandre Hogue. Hailed by *Life* magazine in 1937 as the "artist of the US Dust Bowl," Hogue was a popular artist from the burgeoning Dallas art scene whose work had shown in prominent galleries across the nation in the 1920s and 1930s. Informed by a lifelong study of land use and geology, Hogue's Erosion series depicts water and wind erosion in the Great Plains as well as images of the Dust Bowl. According to his biographer Susie Kalil, these paintings memorialize the grim ambitions and extreme avarice that propelled twentieth-century ideas of progress, while maintaining an awe-inspiring reverence for Great Plains landscapes and a veneration of traditional cultures. Born the sixth child and only son of an erudite Presbyterian minister father and an independent, progressive-minded, artistically inclined mother in Memphis, Missouri, in 1898, Hogue grew up and spent much of his adult life in Texas. He developed a love for the landscapes of the Southwest, especially Texas, New Mexico, and Oklahoma, and he fostered an interest in geology that would add scientific credibility to his work as an artist. So keen was his understanding of soil and rock formations that the Department of Agriculture featured paintings from the Erosion series in a two-page spread in the March 1937 issue of *Soil Conservation: The Official Organ of the Soil Conservation Service.*

Hogue's landscapes offer a profound sense of place that is at once rooted in a specific location and moment and yet transcends space and time. His work exposes prominent beliefs and sensibilities that were part of a larger, collective, national experience. Palpable heat and wind emanate through

Hogue's canvases, mingling awe and dread. He lived through the Dust Bowl in Texas, working from a ranch in the panhandle owned by his sister and her husband; there, he determined to record his impressions in colors, lines, and shapes. To do so, Hogue developed a new technique involving the careful organization of symbols that appealed to the intellect as well as the senses. His style rejected modernist obsessions with the subconscious and reimagined realism as a technique. The first in the Erosion series, "Red Earth Canyon" (1932), shows the mutability of stone canyons etched by water erosion and traversed by power lines. A road diminishes in the distance where a farm appears, dwarfed and insignificant on the horizon. Clouds hang in a chartreuse sky above a wall of yellow rock and red earth, juxtaposing lines and curves in an uneasy alliance that has nonetheless withstood time. In "Dust Bowl" (1933), a broken and half-buried barbed wire fence is illuminated under a white sun and darkening sky. Tire tracks through a break in the fence offer evidence of failed human industry, while a lone set of footprints represents the retreat of "exodusters" from the region, and a low farm lies in shadow below the skyline. These paintings convey despair and foreboding, yet there is a lingering sense of hope and a promise of transcendence that emerges upon reflection.

Hogue was an early advocate for conservationism and his work promotes an astonishingly contemporary environmental perspective. His Erosion paintings highlight the violence and destruction that result from industrial agriculture. In characteristically small, controlled, repetitive brushstrokes, Hogue used vibrant color and dramatic swathes of light and shadow to distill complex feelings out of simple lines and shapes. This technique results in compositions that are at once harmonious and discordant, bewildering and enlightening, beautiful and terrifying. Over his lifetime, Hogue had witnessed the dwindling numbers of family farms and was critical of highly technical, commercial farming. He gained an appreciation for sustainable land use while studying the traditional folkways of Native Americans in Taos, New Mexico. These ideas reinforced an environmental ethic that had been instilled by his mother during his childhood when they gardened together. The painting that best represents these myriad influences and most accurately reveals Hogue's environmental consciousness in response to the Dust Bowl is "Erosion No. 2—Mother Earth Laid Bare" (1936).

At 44 by 56 inches, "Mother Earth Laid Bare" is one of the larger canvases in the series; the size reinforces the disorienting effect of a scene in which the torso and head of a woman emerges from a field eroded by water and agriculture. Although the enormous body is highlighted in a sickly yellow and framed by a stormy cerulean sky above and blue-streaked water flowing downhill below, many people who see the painting for the first time miss her form. Instead, viewers are taken by disparate impressions of proximity and distance, movement and stillness, desire and decay. The woman's face is obscured (or eroded) and turns toward an abandoned farm, while a forgotten plow remains embedded in the soil below her disintegrating thigh. Hogue chose a plow, instead a tractor, to represent the symbolic rape of the land. It is an eerie, brooding, yet incendiary image that intermingles intimacy and violation. While the painting was greeted with critical praise and national attention, not everyone appreciated Hogue's candor. The *Dallas Morning News* called Hogue a "terrifying prophet" who raised emotional dust storms among regional farmers who saw themselves as victims, not perpetrators.

Along with visual artists working in a variety of mediums, writers and musicians found ample material in the Dust Bowl. One of the great writers of the twentieth century, John Steinbeck, is remembered for his portrayals of the grim experience of working men as well as the plight of Dust Bowl refugees. He would earn a Nobel Prize in literature for his depiction of Oklahoma tenant farmers migrating to California in *The Grapes of Wrath* (1939). The novel was completed with support from the Federal Writers' Project and demonstrates Steinbeck's preference for realism. Detailed descriptions of the land and its people are conveyed by a detached narrative voice that resists both editorializing and sentimentality. At the other end of the spectrum, Meridel Le Sueur, one of the most prominent women writers of the decade, offered seething commentary in her reportage writing. In "Cows and Horses Are Hungry," published in the 1934 edition of *The American Mercury*, Le Sueur describes the conditions in the drought-plagued Midwest, including Minnesota, Montana, Wisconsin, Iowa, Nebraska, and the Dakotas, with powerful prose that is spare and stinging.

Essentially, "Cows and Horses Are Hungry" offers a sardonic look at starvation on American farms. Le Sueur confronts readers directly by naming specific towns and using the second person throughout. It is "you" driving through the droughty country, "you" trying not to look at bony livestock, and "you" who begins to suspect that the farmer and his family are emaciated underneath their ragged clothing. Her relentless assault on readers continues with the repetition of descriptive elements, such as protruding ribs and references to funerals. Cynical criticism of banks and the failure of relief programs slips through when she explains to readers that following government buyout of livestock for use by the Federal Emergency Relief Administration (FERA), "you'll be getting some starved meat for your own starved bones" in the breadlines. Leaving no doubt about her political convictions, Le Sueur encourages solidarity among rural and urban workers when she returns to this image again in the end of the piece.

For audiophiles, the folk singer Woody Guthrie traveled with migrant workers and recorded their experiences in a collection of songs known as *The Dust Bowl Ballads.* A popular radio personality and prolific writer, Woodrow Wilson "Woody" Guthrie was committed to representing the voice of the people, some of whom actually were his people. Born in 1912 to musically gifted parents in Okemah, Oklahoma, Guthrie developed a deep appreciation for rural life and experienced great personal loss growing up—trajectories that would chart the course of his adult life. His father was a cowboy and land speculator and the family weathered the volatility of economic booms and busts. As a result of these early experiences, Guthrie developed a wry outlook on life, great sympathy for working people, and an enduring love of the Great Plains landscape. In 1931, he moved to the Texas panhandle where he married and began a family. Like many men during the Great Depression, he left his family in search of work. During much of the decade, he eked out a rambling, marginal existence on the road. This lifestyle would cost him his marriage, but it would also launch a career and create an American legend. Eventually making his way to California and onto the KFVD radio station in Los Angeles, Guthrie gained an audience singing old time country music and providing folksy commentaries on social justice and the failure of capitalism.

Guthrie's enduring legacy comes neither from his prowess as a musician nor the quality of his voice, but from the heartfelt, dynamic expressions in his lyrics. Written and revised from 1935 until its recording in 1940, *The Dust Bowl Ballads* offer simple refrains and upbeat melodies, inspiring toe tapping and knee slapping in listeners. He wrote about the Dust Bowl from a variety of perspectives—as a farmer, migrant, and observer. In "Dust Storm Disaster," he conveys the concerns of residents of the decimated regions who huddle around radios listening to alarming reports and share fears of apocalyptic judgment. "Talking Dust Bowl Blues" begins with the image of a successful farm in 1927, before prices fell, rains stopped, and winds rose. Situations too painful to deal with directly are embedded within entertaining and sometimes fanciful verses. For example, migrating on poor roads in an unreliable jalopy wears down a desperate father who decides to push the limits. From "way up yonder in the piney wood," he pushes his stalled Ford back onto the road. It coasts, picks up speed, and careens down the hillside before coming upon a hairpin turn. The effect is both exhilarating and terrifying, resulting in "wives and childrens" being scattered all over the mountainside. Guthrie's delivery moves between rapid syncopation in the first lines and drawn out pauses and utterances in the last. Like Le Sueur, Guthrie rarely shied away from offering political criticism on behalf of the poor and downtrodden. The song closes after the hungry speaker panhandles for potatoes for "tater stew" thin enough to read through—though not thin enough to get the attention of politicians.

Guthrie is uncharacteristically grim in "Dust Can't Kill Me," which conveys a portentous, driving monologue at a feverish pace. The lyrics move through sadness and loss, grief and bitterness as Guthrie recounts familiar tragedies—dust storms killing family members, destroying farms and property, and driving people off the land. As in Le Sueur's writing, repetition is a thematic and structural component reinforcing the emotional force of the words. The song has a cadence that beats like a pounding windstorm. Guthrie repeats specific words (the "boys" he's talking to, and "Lord"), he repeats ideas and concepts (baby, family, relatives in one series, and house, furniture, barn, tractor in another), and most obviously, he repeats the driving refrain. With only infrequent, minor variations, the thirteen verses are structured like the first. The first verse is also the last, completing the final level of repetition. Returning to the beginning suggests both the inevitability of natural cycles and the dogged persistence required to weather them. References to predatory landlords and pawn shops provide the social commentary Guthrie's audience expected from him.

While artists successfully communicated their impressions and responses to the ecological tragedy playing out in the middle third of the country, they offered few solutions. Answers would have to come from the development of new approaches to land use. In 1935, the same year as Black Sunday, Congress passed Public Law 74-46 establishing the Soil Conservation Service (SCS) as a permanent agency under the US Department of Agriculture (USDA). The SCS was charged with protecting the welfare of the nation by reducing damage to farmland, pasture, and forests. Although its name would change to the Natural Resources Conservation Service in 1994, it has promoted the conservation of the nation's soil and water resources since its inception.

The Progressive Era conservationist and visionary Hugh Hammond Bennett was tasked to lead SCS and oversee a team of surveyors as they drew maps and analyzed aerial photographs of every county affected by dust storms. Recognized as the father of soil conservation and known to his colleagues and friends as "Chief" or "Big Hugh," Bennett had warned farmers for decades that their agricultural practices caused incalculable damage to the landscape. Raised on a 1,200-acre plantation in Anson County, North Carolina, Bennett learned to value hard work and sustainable land use. His father plowed along contour lines and built terraces to slow rainwater runoff and increase absorption of water into the soil—techniques Bennett shared with Dust Bowl farmers a generation later.

For Bennett and his contemporaries, soil conservation was understood as a scientific endeavor wherein highly trained specialists used the most advanced technology to catalogue soil types and erosion, analyze the damage, and propose viable solutions. As the head of SCS, Bennett utilized Civilian Conservation Corps (CCC) participants in repairing ruined areas, building erosion-control structures, and planting cover crops and trees. In addition to introducing the farming techniques that had preserved his father's land, Bennett proposed farmers plant soil-conserving grasses and legumes in place of wheat. Farmers were reluctant to change and the federal government initially offered few incentives. However, small changes were rewarded by less erosion and improved soil fertility. By 1937, the federal government was paying farmers to adopt practices that had been proven by scientists, thus beginning a system of federal entitlements for farmers that persist until the present day. Nevertheless, the strategy worked and by 1938 farmers and the SCS achieved a 65 percent reduction in soil loss. The drought finally ended in 1939 when rains returned and brought closure to the Dust Bowl.

Science played a major role in the SCS, USDA, and many New Deal agencies and programs, including those that responded to the Dust Bowl. Much of the infrastructure that was made possible by President Roosevelt's Public Works Administration, including the construction of bridges, dams, train stations, and airports, would not have been possible without great numbers of scientists, engineers, and technicians. Scientific work introduced radical changes in all aspects of American life, in the home, the workplace, and shared public spaces. By the end of the decade, the majority of American households were wired for electricity thanks to the Tennessee Valley Authority (TVA) project and Rural Electrification Act (REA), both New Deal initiatives. Highway systems extended through every region in the United States, connecting major cities and providing access to resources from the countryside. High-rise skyscrapers (with more than twelve floors) transformed urban skylines, worker safety and productivity improved, and the proliferation of media technologies that Americans continue to enjoy today emerged from the work of scientists of this period.

At home, inventions and new technologies facilitated housework, caregiving, and the cultivation of personal style. Leftovers were wrapped in moisture-proof cellophane, patented in 1933, and preserved in refrigerators cooled by Freon, invented in 1930. While the TVA and REA brought electricity to the majority of Americans, homes were illuminated by General Electric brand florescent light bulbs that were on the market by 1938. The powerful antibacterial tyrothricin was discovered in a routine study of microorganisms in soil in 1939. Polarized lenses to protect vision were developed in 1937. Nylon resulted from research into polymer chemistry by Wallace Carothers in 1930, and was the first synthetic fiber developed by the E. I. Du Pont laboratories five years later. It was used to make bristles for toothbrushes before replacing silk as a popular alternative to stockings in 1938. Later, it would prove useful in everything from parachutes to sutures during World War II. Teflon, invented by a Du Pont chemist during the 1930s, was another advance that benefited the war effort. Although it would not find its way into American kitchens until the early 1960s, Teflon's slippery, insulating properties rendered the components required to make the atomic bomb resistant to corrosion.

From the invention of the ballpoint pen by Hungarian brothers in 1938 to the fluorescent tube showcased at the 1939 World's Fair in New York City, office work improved in ways that continue to be essential today. The physicist Chester F. Carlson transformed business forever with the invention of xerography in 1938, which used electrostatic charges to attract dry powder ink to a reflection of the desired image and then seal it with heat. Arguably the greatest advance in business technologies is the personal computer, and its origins can be traced to the 1930s when a wide variety of electromechanical machines were developed. The Massachusetts Institute of Technology engineer Vannevar Bush invented a device called a differential analyzer or integraph in 1930. A full-scale working model followed in 1935. The integraph weighed more than 100 tons, consisted of 150 motors, hundreds of miles of wire connecting diodes, and a complex constellation of electrical relays. Bush's integraph was a mathematical problem-solving device that laid the groundwork for the development of smaller, more efficient analog computers, and eventually the digital computers we use today.

Like Bush's integraph, many of the technologies that impacted Americans in the 1930s resulted from advancements made to existing technologies. For example, the caterpillar track used in construction equipment and tanks in the 1930s emerged from Benjamin Holt's 1904 design for a commercial vehicle using a self-laying track system. Modifications to the original Crookes cathode ray from the 1880s led to a prototype television screen in the early 1930s. By the end of the decade, Roosevelt would broadcast the first presidential speech ever to be televised—even though it was available to a very limited audience. The best example of an existing invention that was improved significantly in the 1930s is the automobile. Technology streamlined the production of automobiles, increased their reliability, and improved their performance. In addition, the automobile became more accessible to average Americans and a powerful symbol of American identity, a trend begun in the 1920s. Automobile culture changed the commercial landscape while transforming the natural landscape when a proliferation of new car-friendly businesses like supermarkets, gas and service stations, motels, diners, fruit stands, and drive-in theaters appeared on roadsides coast to coast.

While the results of scientific work during the 1930s seem laudable today, there were many public accusations that scientists played a part in bringing about the Depression by creating technology that eliminated the need for human labor. Anxieties about the role of science in society had been festering in the years preceding the decade. People around the world responded with horror to the warfare showcased during World War I involving chemical weapons and munitions capable of devastating carnage. Citizens in the 1920s channeled their anger toward the scientists who had developed such weaponry. In the 1930s, following Albert Einstein's revolutionary revelations about the atom, they could imagine weapons even more terrifying than those used in the First World War. Americans' anxiety intensified with media coverage of spectacular developments in weaponry and "weapons platforms." Concerns grew with the discovery of the neutron, which marks the beginning of the atomic age in the mid-1930s.

Making matters worse for scientists, the public believed they had been slow to respond to the needs of a suffering nation during the Depression. Government scientists were deployed to help farmers in the Dust Bowl regions, but were unable to produce perceptible relief until the drought was nearly over. Under fire for enabling the terrifying weaponry during World War I, scientists withdrew from public life and remained outside of politics from the mid-1920s until the mid-1930s. They migrated away from universities and government agencies to private industrial and commercial settings where they were shielded from public scrutiny. Consequently, there was a significant decline in the number of scientists working for the public good. Funds for independent research dried up as more and more businesses directed the research of salaried scientists. As a sign of their diminished presence in public life, scientists were only marginally represented in Roosevelt's first New Deal. The president's Science Advisory Board included prominent scientists representing different disciplines, but their purview was slim and their resources limited.

In spite of the challenges for scientists between the wars, the impact of the shifts within science could not be contained. Scientific research of the 1920s and 1930s penetrated the atom and extended to the outermost reaches of space; however, new theories increasingly disproved what had formerly been understood as fact. Since the Enlightenment, science competed with religion as a way to understand the natural world. By the twentieth century, scientists, doctors, and their ideas informed all aspects of human life, from theories of evolution to rules for childrearing. Following the work of Einstein and his contemporaries, scientists in all fields had to account for uncertainty in their research because if motion, time, and matter were not constant, what was? Reverberations of these groundbreaking discoveries were felt throughout American society and around the world.

The message transmitted by science was unsettling. Embracing relativity and acknowledging uncertainty resulted in resistance to formerly absolute worldviews. Upsetting ideas and values that were unassailable to previous generations opened the door to more esoteric—though no less important—questions about personal responsibility, the efficacy of standards, and the intractability of class distinctions. People began to question conventional wisdom and religious institutions, and to challenge rigidly defined race and gender differences. Many people renewed their faith by turning to increasingly popular evangelical ministries. Others attempted to impose stability through the political activism and radical movements that flourished during the 1930s—more so than at any other time during the century.

A circle of intellectuals at Vanderbilt University in Nashville, Tennessee, organized the Southern Agrarian movement in response to the anxieties of modern life. They admonished the scientifically supported industrialization of agriculture, condemned the urbanization of America, and demanded a return to small-scale agrarianism. The group was comprised of students and faculty that included Robert Penn Warren, Donald Davidson, John Crowe Ransom, Frank Lawrence Owsley, Andrew Lytle, and Allen Tate, among others. They were ardent regionalists who believed it imperative to challenge the ideology of progress made possible by science. These genteel revolutionary poets, writers, historians, and administrators adopted the name "the Twelve Southerners" and together produced the manifesto "I'll Take My Stand" in 1930. In it, they condemned capitalism as threatening Southern identity and advocated a return to traditional Southern cultural values and practices, exempting slavery. In a style characteristic of the time, the Twelve Southerners spoke collectively in "I'll Take My Stand," while at the same time maintaining the individual voices and promoting the unique perspectives of each writer regarding the problems facing the nation. Written using concrete, formal language meant to contrast what they saw as the hollow, experimental abstractions of modernism, the Twelve Southerners offered biting criticism of modern life and the science that made it possible.

Whereas the Twelve Southerners speak with solidarity, the statement of principles that opens "I'll Take My Stand" represents a distinct multiplicity of voices. The writers align themselves with "many other minority communities opposed to industrialism, and wanting a much simpler economy to live by." They understood industrialization in terms of capitalism, whereby the results of production were more important than the means of production—including labor (the workers) and work practices (technologies and regulations). Chief among their reservations was the role of the applied sciences in propelling industrial capitalism. Offering an agrarian variation of labor theory and value, the Twelve Southerners prized hard physical labor that tempered the body and brought contentment to the spirit. People spent most of their adult lives working, they reasoned; therefore, finding satisfaction—even pleasure—in work was a valid goal for science and industry. Although scientists could have been developing technologies and practices that ensured safety and security for workers, they instead focused their energies on improving efficiency and reducing labor, both of which serve the interest of industry at the expense of skilled and unskilled workers.

The writers' indictment of science offers telling insights into the attitudes of this era. Delivered with thoughtful zeal, they enumerate the failures of modern life, industrial capitalism, and the applied sciences, and describe a "cult of science" that has attained sanctities beyond all reason. The capitalization of the applied sciences, they charge, "has now become extravagant and uncritical; it has enslaved our human energies to a degree now clearly felt to be burdensome." Eschewing the techniques of modernism, the Twelve Southerners nevertheless share some of its tenets, as illustrated in the following: "The constitution of the natural man probably does not permit him to shorten his labor-time and enlarge his consuming-time indefinitely. He has to pay the penalty in satiety and aimlessness. The modern man has lost his sense of vocation." In addition to diminishing the individual human spirit, industrial capitalism and the applied sciences weakened society by discouraging the conditions in which human culture flourishes. Modern life undermined religious beliefs and institutions, reduced creativity in and enjoyment of the arts, and discouraged civility. Perhaps most alarming, the "progress" permitted by industrial capitalism divided the population into classes: worker, manager, owner, or consumer. Rejecting progress and returning to the values instilled by working the land, they argued, would remedy these abuses.

Even as scientific certainty dissolved and scientists drifted away from public work during the 1920s, the actual number of science workers in the United States increased. Thanks to a renaissance of humanism among scientists in the latter half of the 1930s, the authority and influence of scientists in American culture would be reconstituted by the time the United States entered World War II. Scientists returned to public debates as ethical leaders and political activists by the mid-1930s and played an important role in establishing new standards regarding the quality of life at home, work, and in society. Their reemergence included a degree of self-reflection. Max Schoen, professor and head of the Department of Psychology at the Carnegie Institute of Technology, admitted two major failures of scientists in the 1937 article "Can We Be Socially Intelligent?" published in *The Scientific Monthly.* He believed scientists had failed the public "by misusing the fruits of the physical sciences and thereby bringing numerous social ills down upon ourselves," and because of their reluctance "to apply to social ills . . . as much scientific knowledge about social life as we possess."

Scientists like the zoologist and parasitologist Maurice C. Hall, who served as chief of the Zoological Division of the Department of Agriculture from 1925 to 1937, and then chief of the Zoological Division of the National Institute of Health until his death, began staking a claim for the moral authority of scientists. With strident urgency, he argued that "sooner or later, the business world must accept the idea that when scientific research points out conditions menacing to public health, business must cooperate in carrying out its share of control measures and permit others to carry out theirs." Continuing with patriotic idealism, he noted that the United States guarantees free speech and a free press in its Constitution, and so "the idea that science must be supervised by business, and that business must 'put the heat' on the scientists when his findings are not the liking of business, [was] peculiarly unwholesome."

For a brief period during the late thirties, there was a radical transformation in the beliefs, attitudes, and assumptions of scientists that redefined their identity as well as their role in society. In his presidential address to the American Association for the Advancement of Science in 1939, Wesley C. Mitchell noted the dwindling public esteem for scientists and the "widespread disposition to hold science responsible for the ills men are bringing upon themselves—for technological unemployment, for the rise of autocracies, for the suppression of freedom, for the heightened horror of war." He recognized that a formerly "glowing picture of science as benefactor of mankind" must be set against "a dark picture of science putting more power into the hands of certain individuals, classes, nations, generations, giving them a differential advantage over others which they exploited." When scientists finally began to mobilize, they moved into public discourse with a vigorous social and political consciousness bolstered by an increasingly international perspective. They addressed issues in industry, public health, personal well-being, and the environment, while conducting a difficult but necessary self-assessment of their role in society.

Never before and not since have scientists been called on to provide leadership in addressing more social, economic, and environmental problems than they were in the 1930s. In addition to distinguishing the interests of science from the interests of business and industry, scientists reached even further to establish themselves as moral authorities in American culture. A manifesto signed by 1,284 science workers including 64 members of the National Academy of Sciences, and by 85 college presidents, deans, and directors of industrial labs, established the Association of Scientific Workers and charged them with three goals: to bring science workers together to promote science-based understandings of social problems, to present their findings to the public, and to promote action based on their conclusions. The world-renowned anthropologist Franz Boas made the first concerted effort to galvanize the scientific community behind a number of progressive causes. He even organized a conference on the science of race in the United States and challenged race-based theories espoused by Nazis.

Whether in biology, geology, chemistry, physics, sociology, psychology, or medicine, science offered tools to increase production, improve safety and access for people, and what seemed at the time the continual improvement of natural systems. Significantly, two of the most important environmental thinkers of the twentieth century, Rachel Carson and Aldo Leopold, would forge their environmental ethics among scientists during the 1930s. Though their approaches and perspectives were distinctly different, Carson and Leopold shared significant commonalities. Both enjoyed a lifelong love of the natural world that had been nurtured by Progressive Era mentors in early childhood. Trained by scientists in academia, both later applied their knowledge and experience in government service. In their professional careers, both were exposed to cutting-edge scientific research that would inform their unique environmental philosophies and both would link human success with scientific achievement.

The pioneering ecologist Rachel Carson was a scientist, naturalist, philosopher, and educator, as well as an accomplished writer. Representing the best qualities of 1930s scientific humanism, Carson believed scientists had a moral responsibility to benefit society. She advocated the translation of complex scientific information to citizens and championed the rights of individuals to be protected from environmental degradation resulting from business and industry. Born on a farm near Pittsburgh in Springdale, Pennsylvania, on May 27, 1907, Carson was the youngest of three children. Her mother taught her to love and respect nature from an early age, spending hours with her children identifying plants and animals on the rural hillside surrounding their homestead and orchard. The family had a lot of land but little money, and like many Americans left out of the prosperity of the 1920s, they struggled to get by. From the Carson homestead, the family could watch the transformation of the region by industry. Even though they were located high above the Allegheny, the Carsons suffered from periodic waves of a sickening stench emanating from the Pennsylvania Glue factory below that was comparable to the noxious odors produced by tanneries and paper mills.

Wastewater produced during the glue manufacturing process fouled the water but did not significantly impact residents until the construction of a federally funded dam prior to Carson's birth. The dam permitted discharges from the glue factory to grow stagnant in shallow basins that quickly became both a nuisance and menace to public health. Although the company submitted detailed plans to remedy the problem as early as 1906, the pollution and damage to the river was apparent. When the glue factory and other manufacturing enterprises waned, they were replaced by two large power plants and a coal and coke company that continued to sustain the regional economy at the expense of the environment. By the time Carson left Springdale in 1929 for graduate school at Johns Hopkins, the river looked dirty and smelled awful, especially in summer months. Many of Carson's biographers have claimed that the environmental consciousness that would direct her life's work began with her awareness of the ruin that industrial pollution wrought on her family's homestead.

Carson's love of the environment was in equal measure to her devotion to science. She was among the last generation of women to be swept into the sciences by Progressive Era currents. Affluent women had been attending colleges in increasing numbers from the turn of the century through the 1920s, when university education became more available to middle-class women. In contrast to the retreat of scientists during the decade, the number of women working in science actually increased. That changed quickly after the stock market crash in 1929. Shortly before the crash, she began graduate school at Johns Hopkins University, concentrating on marine zoology. Upon completion of her master's degree in 1932, Carson began work on her doctorate, but was forced to quit in 1934 in order to assume financial responsibility for her family. Following the death of her father in 1935, Carson took a part-time job with the US Bureau of Fisheries (now the US Fish and Wildlife Service), where she wrote radio scripts on marine life. Carson understood the language of science, but she did not write like a scientist. Her work was based on the most recent research available, yet easy to understand and beautiful to behold.

In 1936, Carson accepted a full-time position as junior aquatic biologist at the Bureau. Only the second woman hired in a professional position at the agency, she was fortunate to be employed by the fair-minded Elmer Higgins, who recognized and nurtured her multiple talents. He encouraged her to find a larger audience for writing he called "too good for government work." Carson valued his praise and looked forward to fulfilling her lifelong dream to be a writer of significance. However, she was also motivated by a pressing need to support her family, which included an aging mother and a divorced sister and two nieces, as well as the intermittent support of her brother and his wife during the Great Depression. Published in *Atlantic Monthly* in 1937, "Undersea" demonstrated the coherent ecological consciousness that Carson would convey throughout her career as a nature writer and provided a foundation for her first book, *Under the Sea-Wind* (1941). She would publish two more books about the sea that would make her a household name and build a readership for her most famous book, *Silent Spring* (1964).

Carson's favorite subject was the sea as the source and symbol of life. "Undersea" is a brief yet comprehensive overview of ocean ecosystems, from the coastal shorelines to the continental shelf, from teeming pastures of plankton and kelp gardens to the hidden, lightless realms of the deep abyss. With a characteristic and appealing sense of wonder, Carson shared information that would have been completely new to readers. At the same time, she leveled the difference between expert and novice without sacrificing her own ethical authority. With imagination and the relevant scientific details, anyone could "see" habitats that would otherwise remain hidden. Carson offered readers a new way to relate to the natural world that was substantial and meaningful, yet void of personification and anthropomorphism.

In the introduction to the reprint of "Undersea" in *Lost Woods: The Discovered Writing of Rachel Carson*, the editor and environmental historian Linda Lear explains that the piece contains two of Carson's signature themes: "the ancient and enduring ecology that dominates ocean life, and the material immortality that encompasses even the smallest organism." With heartening confidence supported by the best scientific research available, Carson explains again and again that all things that exist and all things that die are returned to the earth only to be reconstituted and used again by future generations. She resists reinforcing the tension between predator and prey by reminding readers that the predator of one species becomes the prey of another. All living things share an elemental world that can be nurturing and sustaining in the best case and indifferent and severe in the worst. In this way, she constructs the tension between the ephemeral and the eternal rather than between "us" and "them." Carson's message about the power of interdependence and the promise of continuity offered reassuring comfort to readers worn down by the economic hardships, social upheaval, and diminishing environments of the thirties.

Like Carson, Aldo Leopold's work was shaped by Progressive Era ideas and reflects the best of what 1930s science had to offer. Considered by many to be father of wildlife management and the United States' wilderness system, Leopold was a conservationist, forester, philosopher, educator, writer, and outdoor enthusiast. Born in 1887 and raised in an affluent family in Burlington, Iowa, Leopold developed an interest in the natural world at an early age. He spent hours outdoors hiking, hunting, and recording his observations in journals and sketchbooks—activities he would continue until his death. He also witnessed the accelerating rate of industrial progress as it transformed the Mississippi River and environs near his home. He graduated in the first class of the Yale Forest School in 1909 and pursued a career with the newly established US Forest Service in Arizona and New Mexico. During this time, Leopold experienced two life-altering events: the first was an encounter with a dying wolf that initiated a significant change in his attitude toward land use, the second was his marriage to María Alvira Estella Bergere.

In 1922, Leopold was instrumental in developing the proposal to manage the Gila National Forest as a wilderness area, which became the first such official designation in 1924. Also in 1924, Leopold was transferred to the US Forest Products Lab in Madison, Wisconsin, where he began to publish his work. Eventually, he migrated to the University of Wisconsin in 1933, where he chaired a new game management program for the Department of Agricultural Economics and continued to refine his philosophy on conservation. In 1935 Leopold, along with Estella and their five children, began reclaiming an exhausted farmstead in Sand County, Wisconsin. Between his research at the university and his personal rehabilitation activities, Leopold forged his convictions into a coherent philosophy during the 1930s and delivered a major paper to a joint meeting of the Society of American Foresters and the Ecological Society of America in 1939.

In "A Biotic View of Land," Leopold set forth his proposal for an ecological foundation for land management grounded by science. He insisted that a comprehensive understanding of "functioning" land was critical, not just to guide the work of scientists but also for proper maintenance of the land to ensure productivity and recreation (primarily hunting). Later that year, Leopold published a version of his paper in the *Journal of Forestry*. A decade later, another revision appeared in *The Sand County Almanac*, one of the most respected books about the environment ever published, where it supplied the scientific foundation for Leopold's now-famous essay "The Land Ethic." In the original version, Leopold was critical of human systems that disrupted natural systems—whether outdated agricultural practices or unrestrained industrial progress. When referring to the Dust Bowl, Leopold blamed overtilling as much as the new emphasis on monoculture farming for accelerating erosion.

Whereas Carson's tone conveyed gentle authority, Leopold's was brusque, buoyant, and self-assured. He valorized the role of science by advocating a land ethic based on scientific principles rather than religious or sentimental ones. Although he claimed that farming was the most important use of land, he criticized farmers for failing to keep up with current scientific discoveries. He cautioned against industry's adverse impact on natural systems through pollution and refers to dense human populations as a form of violence. Leopold's conviction that scientists were well prepared to provide redress for social and environmental problems was consistent with the perspective of many Americans by 1939. Scientists could respond appropriately to a variety of social and environmental problems and could even reconcile rifts among farmers, sportsmen, and recreational tourists. He even suggested that public and private land use might be regulated—with the oversight of scientists—to promote better land conservation.

Leopold was fully aware of public concerns about science and conceded that scientists could be guilty of overspecialization and social isolation. He even criticized scientists who remained isolated in their discrete disciplines. He acknowledged that some scientific work caused confusion and that some inventions resulted in devastating consequences. Finally, Leopold opposed land use based on the narrow definition of utility rooted in industrial progress. Instead, he asserted that ecology could be strengthened by the collective effort of scientists from many fields and advocated for scientist-activists. Scientists in the 1930s were in closer contact with international colleagues than perhaps any other sector of society and Leopold's essay shows a broad awareness of global issues and trends. He offered lessons learned by West German foresters and compares the American Great Plains to semi-arid Asian regions. He cautioned against the planting of non-native species and proposed the development of national as well as international food networks.

Both Leopold and Carson are more famous now than they were in the 1930s; however, both came of age as environmental thinkers and writers in the ferment of Depression Era America. The most visible reflection of that influence is that both used the language of economics as well as science in discussions of natural systems. For example, Leopold referred to biota (natural resources) as capital and his biotic pyramid is literally a model of consumption. In addition, Leopold frequently described a necessary balance between competition and cooperation—between scientists and farmers, farmers and hunters, scientific organizations and government agencies, and finally, between humans and the natural world. He explained that "each species, including ourselves, is a link in many food chains" and the biotic pyramid "is a tangle of chains so complex as to seem disorderly, but when carefully examined the tangle is seen to be a highly organized structure. Its functioning depends on the cooperation and competition of all its diverse links." Carson also used the language of economics in "Undersea"; however, she set the terms "producer" and "consumer" off in quotation marks—as she does the "monster" of an imagined abyss—in order to highlight the intentional analogy.

The 1930s was a period of tremendous scientific and technological innovation that stands in contrast to grim assessments of the Great Depression. When the economy plummeted in the United States, the quality of life for most Americans diminished. Although plenty of Americans suffered in a worsening economic crisis, everyone enjoyed some of the benefits produced by science and technology. Both at home and in the workplace, labor was reduced and in many cases rendered less hazardous. Media technologies educated and inspired a population in need of distraction. Advances in mass media helped unify a collective national identity. Trains, planes, automobiles, and ocean-liners reinforced popular themes of movement and interconnection. In so many ways, science provided the conveniences to accommodate a struggling but significant middle class by offering new options for the "good life."

At the same time, Americans confronted the devastating effects of unregulated and ill-informed scientific work. Evidence in written accounts of the Dust Bowl conveys immeasurable suffering along with the awareness of human complicity in the crisis. Artistic representations of dust storms reveal changing ideas about the relationship between humans and the natural world. Scientists responded to these conditions and publically committed to work to better society and improvement land use. Although these commitments proved more idealistic than practical, the dynamic intersection between science and social thought that occurred during the 1930s fostered an environmental consciousness that precipitated the modern environmental movement today.

Suggested Readings

Three of the very best sources for students to learn more about the Dust Bowl are Timothy Egan's *The Worst Hard Time: The Untold Story of Those Who Survived the Great American Dust Bowl* (Boston: Houghton Mifflin, 2006); Donald Worster's *Dust Bowl: The Southern Plains in the 1930s* (New York: Oxford University Press, 1979); and Ken Burns's stunning two-part documentary *The Dust Bowl* (Florentine Films, 2012). Each of these important works approaches the topic from a different perspective. R. Louis Baumhardt's article "Dust Bowl Era," produced by the USDA and appearing in the *Encyclopedia of Water Science* (2003), provides a brief but comprehensive analysis of the Dust Bowl. The environmental ethic that began to emerge in the 1930s is addressed in Benjamin Kline's *First along the River: A Brief History of the U.S. Environmental Movement* (Lanham, MD: Acada Books, 2000). The reemergence of scientific humanism and the increasing authority of science as an institution is examined in Peter J. Kuznick's impressive book *Beyond the Laboratory: Scientists and Political Activists in 1930s America* (Chicago: University of Chicago Press, 1987), and in Joel Genuth's article "Groping towards Science Policy in the United States in the 1930s," published in *Minerva: A Review of Science, Learning and Policy* (1987). Both authors examine changes that occurred as a consequence of science and the changing role of science and scientists in public life.

4

African Americans

"(What Did I Do to Be So) Black and Blue"
—Fats Waller, Harry Brooks,
and Andy Razaf, 1929

IN THE SUMMER OF 1936, nearly four thousand athletes representing forty-nine nations gathered in Berlin, Germany, to compete in the XI Olympiad. By all accounts it was a lavish affair. Germany poured millions into the venture, including the construction of a state-of-the-art track-and-field stadium that could seat one hundred thousand people. For Adolph Hitler and the Nazi Party, which had just come into power three years earlier, the Olympics represented far more than a series of sporting events. They saw the international affair as their coming-out party, an occasion to showcase to the world Germany's economic and spiritual resurgence under their rule. Convinced that German athletes would dominate the contests, Hitler also saw the events as a proving ground to demonstrate the superiority of the Aryan race and affirm his racist ideology.

Three days into the Olympics on August 3, Jesse Owens, an African American sprinter from the United States, stepped into the starting blocks for the final heat of the 100-meter dash. The stadium seats were filled with tens of thousands of people looking on in eager anticipation. One can only imagine the thoughts racing through the mind of the twenty-two-year-old runner. Racism was nothing new to Owens. The son of Alabama sharecroppers, Owens had endured discrimination growing up in Cleveland and again while competing in track and field for The Ohio State University, where he and other black athletes were required to live off campus. Yet the openly racist ideology of the Nazis was far beyond anything he had encountered previously. Compounding the situation was a growing public debate that emerged in the United States over America's participation in the games. The controversy centered on the Nazi's strict policy prohibiting non-Aryans from competing on state-sanctioned athletic teams. Hitler brazenly attempted to compel other nations to adhere to the policy, while the Nazi newspaper *Völkischer Beobachter* called for the exclusion of black and Jewish athletes. Only the threat of a boycott from several nations led German officials to back away from its demand. The incident sparked a heated discussion in the United States. Some critics feared that by participating in the games, the United States would add fuel to the Nazi propaganda machine. Others loathed even the appearance that the United States was sanctioning such overt discriminatory practices. Owens, a quiet and unassuming sprinter, simply looked to avoid the controversy and refused to comment. Instead, he focused on running.

On August 3, Owens was ready to go. When the starter's pistol went off that afternoon, he shot out of his running block and covered the 100 meters in 10.3 seconds, faster than any other runner, and won the gold medal. Following the event, a humiliated Hitler refused to meet Owens, just as he avoided the African American high jumper Cornelius Johnson, who had won a gold medal for the United States a day earlier. Over the next three days, Owens went on to capture three more gold medals, winning the 200-meter dash, the long jump, and the 4 x 100-meter relay. His physical prowess marked one of the greatest athletic displays of the twentieth century and publicly shattered Hitler's myths of Aryan supremacy.

Owens's achievements at the Berlin Summer Olympics captured the hearts of the American people, catapulting him into the public limelight. The "Buckeye Bullet," as he came to be known, returned to a hero's welcome that included a ticker-tape parade on Fifth Avenue in New York City. Yet the nation's reverence for its star athlete could not erase the flagrant racism he endured at home. Invited to a dinner in his honor at the Waldorf Astoria on the very day of the parade, Owens was barred from using the hotel's main lobby and forced to ride a freight elevator to the room. Hitler had snubbed the sprinter, so too did President Franklin Roosevelt, who did not send so much as a congratulatory note to the Olympic champion. In the weeks and months to follow, Owens suffered additional indignities in spite of his earned celebrity. Unlike many white athletes, Owens received no financial endorsements and very few financial opportunities following his stellar performance. To support himself, Owens reverted to the public spectacle of racing against dogs and horses for gawking onlookers willing to pay money to catch a glimpse of the Olympian.

Owens's experiences reflected the conditions facing most African Americans during the Great Depression. By the 1930s visible signs of progress demonstrated the important strides African Americans had made since the Reconstruction Era. Furthermore, a cohesive African American identity began to emerge in the face of changing internal demographics and the economic crisis of the Great Depression. Like many marginal ethnic groups in America, this historically underrepresented group was drawn together by a common experience. Together African Americans worked to overcome their hardships and laid the groundwork for even greater progress in the post-Depression Era. Still, for all the advances, vivid problems continued to plague the African American community, attesting to the racial chasm engulfing America. Gains achieved in the 1930s were circumscribed by blatant racial discrimination and pronounced economic hardships, far beyond what white America encountered. Even though much had changed, much remained the same for African Americans, who continued to live as second-class citizens.

On the eve of the 1930s the African American community was restless. During World War I, tens of thousands of Africans Americans had begun to flee the South. As sharecroppers mired in a system that provided little hope for economic advancement, frustrated by the failed promises of emancipation, and bitter about the lack of justice, African Americans began abandoning life below the Mason-Dixon Line. Individuals, families, and even whole neighborhoods boarded trains heading north, looking to capitalize on the growing economic opportunities offered by America's expanding wartime industries. What followed was a massive internal exodus. The Great Migration, as it became known, lasted well after the ink was dry on the Treaty of Versailles and continued through the twenties before tapering off during the Great Depression. All told, between 1910 and 1930, over 1.6 million African Americans left the South to settle in northern urban centers such as Chicago, Detroit, Pittsburgh, New York, Boston, Buffalo, and Cleveland. For migrants, the move offered hope for a better life. The North symbolized an almost mystical "promised land" where migrants could finally enjoy the fruits of their labor and the rights of full citizenship, the potential fulfillment of a dream long denied them after the Civil War.

Though conditions in the North offered the possibility for improved lives, it was not guaranteed. Too often migrants learned that their new homeland presented its own set of challenges, often on a par with those of the South. Upon arrival in the North, African Americans typically found themselves relegated to dilapidated slums and ghettos. White real-estate agents were unwilling or unable to lease apartments to African American outside delegated "black neighborhoods." With communities unable to expand, overcrowding soon became a problem that added to already deteriorating conditions. For migrants who went north hoping for better opportunities for their children, they too grew disenchanted. Although northern schools were superior to their southern counterparts—no difficult feat given the state of education below the Mason-Dixon Line—the northern black educational experience was often appreciably inferior to that of whites. Many school boards engaged in de facto segregation by redistricting to minimize interaction between the races. Programs in black neighborhoods were underfunded and undersupplied. Curricula provided blacks with only a basic, remedial education to prepare them for unskilled jobs. Schools failed to hire qualified instructors to teach black students. The result was a poorer educational experience that differed appreciably from that of northern whites. Finally, adding insult to injury, the economic opportunities that lured many out of the South quickly dried up and migrants struggled with the effects of unemployment in the wake of the postwar recession. When the economy eventually rebounded, blacks found the employment doors once opened to them now closed. What work remained was typically low-wage service industry jobs that made it next to impossible for African Americans to lift themselves out of poverty. The North, as African Americans soon discovered, was far from the "promise land." And the so-called Era of Prosperity was an era that rarely touched the lives of African Americans in the 1920s.

The changing racial demographics in northern cities also brought with it a backlash. Northern communities became transformed by the influx of black migrants. Chicago saw its African American population expand from 44,103 in 1910 to over 234,000 by 1930. Detroit's black population skyrocketed from 5,741 to 120,066. Pittsburgh, Buffalo, New York, Cleveland, and Boston experienced similar growth in their black populations. Whites, threatened by the growing presence of blacks, lashed out as tensions turned to conflict. In the summer of 1919 race riots engulfed the American landscape. Between June and December, twenty-five major race riots exploded across the United States. The most serious took place in Chicago, one of the major destinations of the Great Migration. Violence and lawlessness reigned in the Windy City for thirteen days, even though the Illinois militia was mobilized four days into the riot. When it finally ended, thirty-eight people lay dead, over five hundred were injured, and more than a thousand families were left homeless.

The 1919 race riots highlighted the hardships and discrimination that followed African Americans to the North. But the conflicts also showed something else. Embracing the spirit of independence and determination that led them north, African Americans showed a readiness to fight and die for their own defense. The resolve evident during the race riots was emblematic of a greater sense of cultural awareness emerging among African Americans. Heading into the 1920s and 1930s, bonds formed in the wake of the Great Migration, unifying the African American community unlike never before. The Harlem Renaissance, as it came to be known, was a by-product of the migration. Northern cities became not only an end destination but also a cultural hub that flourished with black culture. Writers, painters, poets, sculptors, and musicians embraced their African heritage, articulating an identity that celebrated the African American experience. The Harlem Renaissance helped raise racial consciousness among African Americans through the expression of their collective experiences revealed in an explosion in the arts. Increasingly over a period of twenty-five years beginning after 1910, African American musicians recorded spirituals, blues, and jazz. Artists created visual images using a broad range of traditional, realist, and cutting-edge modernist techniques. Writers produced an impressive collection of poetry, fiction, drama, and essays. An optimistic and affirming movement, the Harlem Renaissance echoed Progressive Era confidence in social reform and the belief that culture was the ideal vehicle for change. The change sought by artists emphasized African American perspectives and celebrated the creative and intellectual ability of black Americans. Much of their endeavors caught the attention of mainstream white America.

Harlem, once an ethnic neighborhood home to mostly Russian Jews, became the center of the New Negro Art Movement. The official beginning of the Harlem Renaissance is still debated. For some scholars, it was launched in 1914 by a show of the Philadelphia artist Meta Warrick Fuller's bronze statue *Ethiopia Awakening*. At 67 inches tall, it is a life-size depiction of a black woman in an ancient Egyptian headdress. Her hand is on her heart, her face is raised and tilted regally, her gaze is focused mournfully toward the ground. With a blend of African motifs and modern appeal, the statue became a symbol of the spirit of the Harlem Renaissance. More recently, scholars have cited the 1923 publication of Jean Toomer's *Cane*, an experimental novel that integrated poetry, prose, and drama in three complex and layered vignettes of African American lives, as the official beginning of the Harlem Renaissance. Others mark the beginning not in the arts, but in social unrest. In 1917, following a series of lynchings in Waco, Texas, and Memphis, Tennessee, and a massacre of forty African Americans in East St. Louis, Missouri, the National Association for the Advancement of Colored People (NAACP) organized a silent protest in New York. Eight thousand African Americans, formal, solemn, and of all ages, marched silently down New York's Fifth Avenue carrying picket signs and banners while thousands looked on. Still others point to 1919, seeing the arts movement as an outgrowth of the postwar disillusionment African Americans endured after loyally serving their country only to see their optimism and hope dashed amid continued segregation, declining economic opportunities, and rising racial violence.

In truth, the Harlem Renaissance resulted from a convergence of factors that had been percolating for some time. By the 1920s, it emerged as a vibrant, thriving movement epitomized by significant literary publications, beginning with two serials produced by the NAACP. The first was the official monthly of the organization, *The Crisis: A Record of the Darker Races*, that began in 1910 with W. E. B. DuBois as editor. Costing 15 cents a copy, by 1920 the magazine claimed a monthly readership of one hundred thousand. The magazine gained a reputation for its opposition to racial discrimination and violence, and later sponsored a literary contest that promoted some of the greatest voices of the Harlem Renaissance, including Countee Cullen, Claude McKay, and Langston Hughes. *The Brownies Book*, likewise under the direction of DuBois with literary editor Jessie Redmond Fauset, was the first magazine designed specifically for African American children. First issued as a monthly in 1921, the cost was 15 cents, and inside readers found short stories, poetry, and articles of interest to African American families. Many of the writers who contributed to *The Crisis* and *The Brownies Book* would move on to publishing in mainstream publications like *The Mercury Reader* and *The New Yorker*, among others.

DuBois's influence in shaping the emerging arts movement extended beyond his promotion of black writers. The noted civil rights activist and scholar also introduced one of the dominant themes of the Harlem Renaissance, that of divided identity, or "twoness," as he called it in this often quoted passage: "One ever feels his two-ness—an American, a Negro; two souls, two thoughts, two unreconciled stirrings: two warring ideals in one dark body, whose dogged strength alone keeps it from being torn asunder." This theme resonated powerfully among African American artists and intellectuals in the 1930s. Aaron Douglas's 1936 painting "Aspiration" portrays divided identities by linking African and African American cultures in an allegorical representation of the journeys from slavery to freedom and from Southern sharecropper to Northern industrial laborer. The image is both haunting and alluring. In translucent layers of muted colors characteristic of Douglas, broad-shouldered figures with faces turned toward an urban landscape on a distant mountain rise above the shackled arms of slaves. Standing figures have their backs to their past as well as the viewer, while the shining city looms out of reach. The vitality and yearning emanating from their open postures and outstretched arms is as appealing as it is futile. In this one, complex, layered image, Douglas captured the unreconciled and conflicting feelings DuBois described in words.

The Great Migration introduced a new image of African Americans in American culture, one that was urban, sophisticated, and accomplished. Harlem writers and intellectuals sought to break down racial stereotypes by emphasizing the dignity of black experience and participating in public discourse through the arts, the academy, and politics. In the early part of the twentieth century, that often meant cultivating the preoccupations and pursuing the interests popular among affluent whites. Portraits and group photographs of Claude McKay, Arna Bontemps, Jean Toomer, and Countee Cullen show men in smart suits with ties and polished shoes looking as handsome and self-possessed as their white contemporaries. Although fewer in number, prominent women of the Harlem Renaissance such as Gwendolyn Bennett, Nella Larson, Angelina Welde Grimke, and Jessie Redmond Fauset were as modern and self-assured as the images of young women in popular magazines of the time.

The new image of African Americans competed with entrenched stereotypes making their way into the mainstream culture of the 1930s. In the 1930s, African American actors and actresses carved out a visible niche on the silver screen playing a host of racially charged caricatures. Bill Robinson, Herb Jeffries, and Louise Beavers were some of the many performers who became household names to audiences during the decade. One of the most recognizable performers in the film industry during the Depression Era was Lincoln Theodore Monroe Andrew Perry, or "Stepin Fetchit," as his fans popularly knew him. Perry broke into the entertainment industry working the vaudeville circuit as part of a two-man comedy team. In the midtwenties, Perry made the move to films and performed in thirteen films by the end of the decade, appearing mostly as a secondary character. Perry's film career took off in the 1930s when he appeared in twenty-nine films. By 1934, after playing opposite Will Rogers in two comedies, *David Harum* and *Judge Priest*, Perry was a recognizable figure to American audiences. Cast as Rogers's comical sidekick, Perry's characters were known for their exaggerated physical features, slow mannerisms, and baggy clothes. The "laziest man with soul," as one film critic later dubbed the characters, Perry struck a chord with moviegoers. Soon he began receiving feature billing. Many directors allowed Perry a great deal of latitude with scripts, permitting him to improvise his scenes as they filmed. The one-time vaudeville comedian found himself propelled into the upper echelon of Hollywood society, earning him the distinction of being the first African American actor to become a millionaire. Perry became equally famous for his lavish lifestyle. At the height of his career he maintained six houses with numerous servants and owned at least a dozen automobiles, including a champagne Cadillac with his name emblazoned on the side in neon.

Of equal celebrity in the 1930s film industry was Hattie McDaniel. Born in Wichita, Kansas, in 1895, McDaniel was the daughter of former slaves. The youngest of thirteen children, she made her way into the entertainment industry after dropping out of high school her sophomore year. She started performing in an older brother's traveling minstrel show, where she sang and acted. In the 1920s, McDaniel landed a part on the *Melody Hounds*, a touring black musical ensemble. With the start of the Great Depression, McDaniel was unable to find regular work, so she moved to Los Angeles and joined a brother and two sisters who were already out West. In 1932, she began appearing in films in minor background roles, mostly singing in choruses, for which she received 5 dollars per movie. McDaniel's first feature-length film appearance came in *The Golden West*, when she landed a small role as a maid. She continued to find work in uncredited roles as a maid and house servant, including an appearance in Mae West's *I'm No Angel* in 1933.

McDaniel's big break came the following year, when she appeared in John Ford's *Judge Priest*, a romantic comedy about a confederate veteran working as a judge in a small Kentucky town. Cast as Aunt Dilsey, a washerwoman working for the main character, the film generated a great deal of attention for McDaniel's musical talents. She sang several songs, including a duet with the film's lead actor, Will Rogers. Afterward, Fox Films put McDaniel under contract, giving her steady work. Gradually, she began receiving more prominent roles, appearing in films alongside the biggest stars of the era: Shirley Temple, Lionel Barrymore, Jean Harlow, Clark Gable, Ginger Rogers, and Jimmy Stewart. Though McDaniel continued to be typecast as a maid or servant, her characters became noted for their sassiness and strong demeanor. Far from acting the docile servant, she gave her characters a forcefulness and boldness typically not seen in such roles. By the end of the 1930s, McDaniel had appeared in nearly sixty films, including David O. Selznick's memorable adaptation of Margaret Mitchell's best-selling novel *Gone with the Wind*. In *Gone with the Wind*, McDaniel played "Mammy," the strong, moral matron who protects the virtue of the whimsical Scarlett O'Hara. The performance garnered McDaniel an Academy Award for Best Supporting Actress; she was the first African American to win an Oscar.

The racial stereotypes played by Perry and McDaniel appealed to white audiences. Black responses were more complicated, however. On the one hand, black audiences applauded the success of Perry, McDaniel, and others. On the other hand, they disliked the demeaning and derogatory stereotypes in which the actors were cast. Many blacks expressed frustration over the tired racial caricatures that failed to accurately represent the living conditions they faced in their day-to-day lives. These frustrations illustrated America's lack of racial progress and helped fuel the cause of civil rights throughout the 1930s. The results, while modest, laid an important foundation for the civil rights struggle in succeeding decades. One of the organizations that stood at the forefront in the battle against racial discrimination was the NAACP. Formed in 1908, the NAACP fought to secure for African Americans all rights guaranteed under the Constitution of the United States. Early on, the organization broadly defined its aims, focusing its energies on eliminating all elements of racial segregation and improving the social, political, economic, and educational opportunities afforded black Americans. NAACP officials pursued its agenda by trying to craft an economic program designed to widen the opportunities afforded African Americans while simultaneously eliminating racial inequality through political action. The emphasis they placed on improving economic conditions for African Americans marked a "tip of the hat" to Booker T. Washington, one of the leading African American figures at the time and a strong advocate of industrial education. The NAACP's economic program, however, failed to materialize as leaders struggled to define a coherent plan. Instead the organization's energy centered principally on challenging the institutional racial inequality that pervaded America, particularly as it pertained to the South in the post–Reconstruction Era.

The NAACP developed a two-pronged strategy. First, it lobbied government agencies to voluntarily pass laws or establish policies to end discrimination. For example, NAACP officials pushed for the creation of a federal anti-lynching law and legislation eliminating poll taxes and literacy tests that obstructed black voting. It also worked to overturn federal discrimination, an issue that took on growing importance after Woodrow Wilson's administration ushered in a series of measures establishing greater segregation at federal facilities and restricted government employment opportunities for African Americans. The second strategy employed by the NAACP sought to overturn segregation and discriminatory practices by challenging the legality of such measures in the courts. Officials presumed this approach held the potential for tremendous success, believing they could find a degree of impartiality in the courts that did not exist in the other branches of government. They were right. The organization's legal offices won several significant cases in the latter part of the Progressive Era, toppling restrictive housing policies in Louisville, Kentucky, and eliminating the use of grandfather clauses that allowed literacy tests to determine voting rights.

In the 1930s, the NAACP's efforts to secure the full rights of citizenship through the court system picked up steam. The push came from Charles Houston, who was appointed the NAACP's special counsel in 1934. Houston was among the most committed and formidable civil rights activists in the twentieth century. Born in Washington, DC, in 1895, Houston came from a modestly comfortable middle-class family. An exceptionally bright student, Houston excelled academically, graduating from Amherst College with honors, despite being only nineteen years old. Following graduation, he taught English for a short time at Howard University, an all-black institution in the nation's capital. When America entered World War I in 1917, Houston enlisted in the armed forces, earning a commission as a first lieutenant in the US Infantry. His stay in the military proved to be life altering. Assigned to a segregated unit, Houston experienced firsthand the degradation, humiliation, and frustrations of racism. Houston came away from the experience determined to use his career for the furtherance of social justice.

After returning from France, Houston enrolled in Harvard University Law School, convinced that the law offered the best means to combat racism. At the Ivy League school, Houston once again distinguished himself by becoming the first black to serve as editor for the revered *Harvard Law Review* before graduating with a PhD in jurisprudence in 1923. Returning to Washington, Houston briefly worked at his father's law office, where he started taking on civil rights cases. In 1929, Houston's private practice took a backseat when the young litigator accepted a position as vice dean at Howard University Law School. From the start, Houston vigorously plunged into the challenges of his new career, working tirelessly to improve the institution's academic standards. By recruiting qualified faculty, revising curricula, and raising student expectations, Houston steered Howard's law school to a position on a par with leading white institutions across the nation. Soon he began recruiting the brightest legal minds in the black community, including future Supreme Court Justice Thurgood Marshall. For Houston, attaining national prominence for the law school was a means to an end, as he viewed the school as a training ground for future lawyers interested in "litigation against racism."

In 1934, Houston accepted the post of special counsel for the NAACP. The civil rights organization was starting to lay the groundwork for an attack on the infamous 1896 *Plessy v. Ferguson* Supreme Court ruling that sanctioned segregation in the South. It was the challenge Houston had been working toward since embarking on a legal career. He surrounded himself with the most gifted black lawyers to make their way through Howard University Law School, including the likes of James Nabrit, Oliver Hill, and of course his young protégé, Thurgood Marshall. Houston was convinced that the best way to undo the South's Jim Crow laws was through the educational system. The idea stemmed from an internal report produced by an NAACP investigation in 1930. The Margold Report detailed the woefully inadequate educational facilities available to black children across the region. Southern black schools may have been separate, but they certainly were not equal, a fact that raised the question of whether communities stood in violation of the *Plessy* ruling.

Shortly after accepting the position with the NAACP, Houston and several of his aides conducted an exhaustive investigation of the educational facilities in the South. Houston came away from the trip convinced that there was sufficient evidence to sustain a court challenge, as suggested in the Margold Report. If the courts accepted Houston's argument that Southern schools were in effect unequal, providing fewer educational resources and opportunities to black students, communities faced the costly prospect of radically improving the inadequate and underfunded education facilities. Given the potential financial costs, Houston believed the more viable option for cash-strapped Southern communities would be to integrate their schools rather than try to make up the funding gap that existed in the segregated educational system. If they succeeded in ending school desegregation, Houston was convinced it would open the door for wider integration throughout the South. However, Houston disagreed with the Margold Report as to where the NAACP should focus its initial energies. Whereas the report suggested targeting the South's elementary schools, Houston instead decided to focus the initial assault on the region's higher educational facilities. The approach would have a limited effect, at least initially, as it would impact a small segment of Southern society. However, Houston believed that by doing so the NAACP would be less likely to arouse a hostile reaction from white Southerners who had grown accustomed to segregation. The cautious approach also would establish important precedent, increasing the NAACP's chance for success when the organization pursued integration for younger students. By establishing a foothold in higher education, Houston was convinced it would be more difficult for the courts to maintain the *Plessy* decision elsewhere.

In 1936, Houston's strategy began to pay dividends when the NAACP filed suit against the University of Maryland on behalf of Donald Murray. Murray had applied to the university's law school, only to be rejected since the school did not admit African American students. Instead, the university offered to aid Murray in finding an adequate alternative. Since Maryland did not have a black law school, Murray would be forced to go out of state. Before the Maryland Appeals Court, Houston and Marshall argued that because no separate black law school existed in the state, Maryland was in violation of the law. In effect, by providing no other alternative to Murray than the opportunity to attend law school outside the state, Maryland was preventing Murray from being adequately trained to practice law in his home state. As Marshall argued, the University of Maryland had a "moral commitment" to admit Murray into its law school. The court agreed, and in 1936 Murray successfully enrolled in the University of Maryland Law School.

Even though the case marked an important victory, its scope was limited. Since the Murray case was resolved in the Maryland State Appeals Court and never made its way to the Supreme Court, it lacked binding effect on the national level. Nevertheless, Houston and the NAACP had clearly exposed an exploitable weakness in the South's segregation practices. Next, Houston took his argument to the US Supreme Court in 1938. This case centered on Lloyd Gaines, a twenty-five-year-old college graduate from Lincoln University, an all-black school in his native Missouri. An extraordinary student, Gaines graduated from Lincoln with honors, earning a degree in history. He was also the senior class president and a member of the Alpha Phi Alpha fraternity. At the urging of the Lincoln history professor and noted civil rights activist Lorenzo Greene, Gaines applied for admission into the University of Missouri Law School. As in Maryland, Missouri lacked a separate all-black law school and offered to provide Gaines with aid to attend a law school outside the state. Denied admission into Missouri and unwilling to attend an out-of-state school, Gaines filed suit against the university and its registrar, Sy Woodson Canada. In *Gaines v. Canada*, the Supreme Court ruled that Missouri had to either admit Gaines into the university's law school or it had to create a separate and equal facility.

The *Gaines* case laid the first bricks in the legal foundation to dismantle *Plessy v. Ferguson* and destroy the South's system of institutionalized segregation. The case also earned Houston the reputation of "the man who killed Jim Crow" for the significant precedent it set. But for all the success, the *Gaines* ruling also highlighted the limitations and failings of the civil rights struggle in the 1930s. Far from striking down the *Plessy* ruling, the court simply required the University of Missouri to admit Lloyd Gaines if a separate facility was not available. Not surprisingly, Missouri leaders chose the latter option, hastily transforming an old cosmetology school in St. Louis into the Lincoln University School of Law, an all-black institution where Gaines and other African Americans could study law. Other states responded in similar fashion, finding ways to circumvent the *Gaines* ruling. Faced with a similar lawsuit in South Carolina, state leaders funded the creation of a separate all-black law school. Virginia increased the amount of financial assistance available to black residents who attended school out of state, hoping they would be less inclined to push the issue. Though the *Gaines* case established an important precedent, it would be twelve years until segregation was struck down in the nation's postgraduate educational system. As for Gaines, he never attended the law school created for him. Instead, in March 1939, just a few short months after the ruling, he mysteriously disappeared. Rumors as to Gaines's whereabouts circulated for years: some speculated that he quietly decided to walk away from his sudden notoriety, others suggested a more sinister demise.

Without a doubt, African Americans made important strides during the 1930s, but many bitter reminders of the obstacles still facing black Americans and the nation's continued reluctance to combat racism remained. Even a study of success stories reveals the grim consequences of racial discrimination. Although Lincoln Perry and Hattie McDaniel set new heights for African Americans in Hollywood, they did so playing subservient and menial roles that accentuated degrading racial stereotypes. McDaniel understood the industry's limitations, famously quipping, "I'd rather play a maid than be one." But for many performers, the humiliation was too difficult to endure. Bill "Bojangles" Robinson experienced a meteoric rise in his career when cast as the loyal sidekick to Shirley Temple in the 1935 film *The Little Colonel.* An accomplished dancer, Robinson went on to appear in four films with the Depression Era star, the last of which was *Rebecca of Sunnybrook Farm* in 1938. In all these films Robinson played an "Uncle Tom" caricature. Forever the docile, obedient servant who placed the interests of Temple's character above his own, the stereotype represented white American's idealization of race relations. Unable to break out of the stereotype, Robinson chose his dignity over his career in Hollywood and returned to the theater.

Many of the best and brightest in the Harlem Renaissance suffered from a similar untenable double standard. By the early years of the 1930s, the literary and intellectual lights of the Harlem Renaissance began to wane. Some, including Countee Cullen, Arna Bontemps, and James Weldon Johnson, built sufficient momentum in the twenties to carry them into the next decade. Cullen, for example, had been writing poetry since early childhood before beginning a distinguished career writing for the NAACP and other literary magazines in New York during the 1920s. Like Cullen, Bontemps was a talented, lifelong poet who gained fame during the height of the Harlem Renaissance. They collaborated on a novel, *God Sends Sunday* (1931), which would be adapted as a play and then a musical titled *St. Louis Woman. God Sends Sunday* has been called the last novel of the Harlem Renaissance, but Cullen would complete his first solo novel, *One Way to Heaven,* in 1932 and Bontemps would publish his novel *Black Thunder: Gabriel's Revolt: Virginia, 1800* in 1936. Although Cullen and Bontemps produced important work during the 1930s, they were among the last to popularize the early Harlem Renaissance vision of black consciousness.

Johnson was another of the waning lights of the Harlem Renaissance. Poet, novelist, journalist, songwriter, educator, civil rights activist, and statesman, Johnson had worked tirelessly for the NAACP during the 1920s, but grew weary when his efforts failed to produce the legislative and social reform he desired. During the 1930s, he traveled and lectured widely on racial advancement and civil rights. Johnson also continued to write, penning a history of black life in New York, *Black Manhattan* (1930); an autobiography, *Along This Way: The Autobiography of James Weldon Johnson* (1933); a book arguing for racial integration and cooperation, *Negro Americans, What Now?* (1934); and his last major collection of poetry, *Saint Peter Relates an Incident: Selected Poems* (1934). Johnson's body of work produced in the 1930s reflects the depth and integrity of ideas and attitudes he developed over a lifetime of civil rights activism and public service. Yet, like Cullen and Bontemps, he ignored the impact of the economic crises and rising class differences that emerged in the African American community in 1930s.

Not all writers and intellectuals ignored the suffering brought to African American communities by the Great Depression. Others, such as E. Franklin Frazier, Langston Hughes, and Zora Neale Hurston, addressed economic and class issues that resonated powerfully for both black and white readers. They responded to the additional challenges faced by African Americans during the Great Depression by fostering new insights and techniques that helped them maintain both relevance and readers. Frazier was new on the scene, but both Hughes and Hurston had been major players in the Harlem Renaissance during the 1920s, and all three were successful during the thirties because they pursued interests beyond the increasingly narrow providence of the early Harlem Renaissance. A sociologist and Howard University professor, Frazier earned his doctorate from the University of Chicago with his dissertation *The Negro in Chicago*, published in 1932. In 1939 he published *The Negro in the United States*, a detailed study that offered significant insights into the complex and interrelated factors of race, economics, and society confronting African Americans.

Known as the poet laureate of Harlem, Hughes produced a large volume of work in the 1930s that addressed the most dominant themes and issues of the times. He was a prolific writer who published extensively until his death in 1967. After the stock market crash, Hughes became politically active and published with other Proletariat writers. He continued to experiment with the poetic themes and techniques popular among Harlem Renaissance and modernist writers of the 1920s, but with a lens focused clearly on present conditions and current events. His poetry continued to reflect New York life and culture and celebrate the genesis of a unique black consciousness, although now it included an examination of class differences from a variety of perspectives. For example, Hughes addressed economic oppression as a means to control workers, both black and white, in his poem "White Man." Energetic and confrontational, Hughes proposed that in spite of the additional burden of racism faced by blacks, workers share a common cause against the wealthy. Pessimism and grim experience temper the optimistic idealism that characterized his earlier work, although much of his Depression Era poetry, like "Tired," "Christ in Alabama," and "Let America Be America Again," returns to the theme of dual identities.

Hughes enjoyed the company of intellects, artists, and many other elite urbanites of all races, and his work in the 1930s reflects this elegant mélange. Unlike many of the notable black poets of the period, he refused to differentiate between his personal experience and the common experience of black America. He wanted to tell the stories of his people in ways that reflected their actual culture, including both their suffering and their love of music, laughter, and language itself. Like Hughes, Hurston persevered during the 1930s by channeling her unique artistic energy to more accurately reflect the times from the perspective of African Americans, including the often neglected experience of women. One of the few African American women to gain a nationwide, interracial readership prior to the civil rights movement, Hurston had combustible relationships with a number of prominent members of the Harlem Renaissance, including a long-term, public feud with Richard Wright. She and Hughes had a brief alliance working together to produce the play *Mule Bone* (1931), but the collaboration ended their friendship.

Hurston's writing began to appear in the 1920s, but her most significant work was published between 1931 and 1943. While attending Howard University, she attracted attention for her vibrant, affirming, and unembellished stories of African American communities in the South. Even though she enjoyed Harlem and all it had to offer, she was convinced that the South was the only place to find authentic black culture. After studying under the anthropologist Franz Boaz and with the support of a white patron, Hurston traveled extensively through Florida and the Caribbean to collect folklore. With keen powers of observation and a vivacious personality, many of Hurston's stories were based on her personal experiences growing up in the first incorporated, all-black town of Eatonville, Florida. Preserving the dialect, traditions, and dignity of the cultures she observed, Hurston's 1933 short story "The Gilded Six-bits," which is counted among her best, describes how newlyweds Joe and Missy May Banks overcome infidelity in a community where personal business is a matter for public deliberation. Hurston's fresh voice was filled with spunk and humanity, and Depression Era readers of all races enjoyed the ending when love and forgiveness overcame adversity and betrayal.

The efforts of people like Cullen, Bontemps, Johnson, Frazier, Hughes, and Hurston secured them a place in American history and culture; however, it was not enough to sustain the Harlem Renaissance as a movement. Over time, African Americans withdrew their support from artists who seemed out of touch with the experiences of those they aspired to represent and intellectuals whose proximity to wealthy whites made their optimism appear disingenuous. The presence of African Americans in mass media would continue to grow steadily from the thirties on, but it would be increasingly mediated or simply appropriated by white artists, producers, distributors, and ultimately, audiences.

Symbolic of the decline of the Harlem Renaissance and the racial dichotomy that existed across America was the deterioration of Harlem itself. Prohibition did little to restrain the party atmosphere of the area, and starting in the midtwenties many upscale whites looking for thrills, legal and illegal, made their way uptown from Manhattan to Harlem's jazz clubs. Known popularly as "slumming," the songwriter Irving Berlin immortalized the good times enjoyed by both black and white patrons on "Lennox Avenue"—a main street through Harlem—in his 1929 song "Puttin' on the Ritz." In 1932, the fashionable men's magazine *Esquire* published a detailed map of Harlem nightspots, complete with advice and commentary. Places such as the "Club Hot-Cha," "Radium Club," "Cotton Club," "Small's Paradise," "Connie's Inn," and "Savoy Ballroom" were on the map, along with descriptions like "Nothing happens before 2 a.m." and "Ask for Clarence." These insider notes only added to the borough's mystique and helped build up Harlem's appeal.

At its height, Harlem's allure had much to do with the impression that it had transcended the racial chasm dividing America. To the casual observer, Harlem seemed to defy the strict racial segregation code—both formal and informal—that existed in most communities. Places like Small's Paradise became known as a "black and tan club" where races intermingled openly. Drawn to the clubs by great jazz from artists such as Count Basie and his orchestra and "Fats" Waller, mixed audiences also enjoyed top-notch white jazz musicians. Dancers could head to the Savoy Ballroom, another racially integrated club in Harlem that opened its doors in 1926. By the 1930s, the club was ground zero for the swing-dance movement captivating the nation's attention. Black and white dancers performed acrobatic dances like "The Lindy Hop" and "the Hucklebuck." The Savoy hosted popular "battle of the bands" or "cutting contests," which pitted swing orchestras against one another. Audiences decided which band swung harder and won the night. In 1937, the most famous cutting contest occurred between Chick Webb and Benny Goodman. Five thousand people reportedly filled every inch of the ten-thousand-square-foot ballroom, while another five thousand people stood outside to hear the noted African American bandleader and reigning King of the Savoy rival one of the most popular white musicians of the era. The two bands musically mixed it up on stage before Webb's band won with a sound that could fell even the mightiest orchestra. Such mixed-race revelry helped to carve out a quixotic image of Harlem as a "racial Eden," an idyllic place where blacks and whites enjoyed a thriving culture together. But, beyond the glamour and pizazz of the region's 120 nightclubs, life in the "real Harlem" was a different story.

Harlem served as a microcosm of the problems confronting African Americans during the 1930s. With the Great Migration, the African American population in New York City soared, growing over 150 percent in the 1920s. Nowhere were the effects of the migration more palpable than in Harlem, a neighborhood of less than 4 square miles located in the city's upper borough of Manhattan. By 1930, Harlem's black population reached nearly 165,000 residents—accounting for about 72 percent of Manhattan's entire African American population. This massive population explosion produced immediate logistical problems that were intensified by systemic racism. Rents skyrocketed as Harlem's population swelled. Unable to move into white neighborhoods outside Harlem, African Americans found themselves at the mercy of unscrupulous landlords who charged black residents in Harlem significantly higher rates than the rates in New York's white, working-class neighborhoods. To make ends meet, black tenants shared apartments or took in boarders, leading to rampant overcrowding and rapidly deteriorating conditions. Attesting to the deplorable and unhealthy environment in Harlem, the infant mortality rate for blacks in Harlem was 111 per 1,000 births, nearly double the rate of whites living in New York City. Poverty became an epidemic among Harlem's African American population, with most of the region's inhabitants mired in unskilled, low-wage occupations—working as general laborers, domestics, chauffeurs, waiters, elevator operators, and in other menial jobs. Vice thrived, further adding to the Harlem's appeal among white visitors who came to the upper Manhattan neighborhood lusting for such illegal activities as gambling, drugs, and prostitution. By the 1930s, Harlem was far from a thriving community, and instead an emerging slum.

In many respects, Harlem's famed nightclubs symbolized the push and pull of racial disparity and economic hardship that plagued the neighborhood's African American community. Although blacks could find work in clubs as entertainers, cooks, or servers, they rarely rose above low-status jobs. When blacks achieved higher positions, their tenure was either provisional or short lived. Ownership typically fell to white businessmen or even white mobsters, like Owen "Owney" Madden. Through intimidation, Madden gained control of the Cotton Club from Jack Johnson, the first black heavyweight boxing champion. Operating the nightclub while serving a prison term, Madden redesigned the club as a Southern plantation open exclusively to whites. The experience was complete with racially charged imagery and an elaborate floor show featuring a scantily clad, light-skinned black chorus described in advertisements as "tall, tan, and wonderful." Early in his career Duke Ellington, America's great musician and composer, provided music for the ornate shows at the Cotton Club. A radio broadcast described Ellington's jazz sound as "jungle music," though his sophisticated compositions had little to do with tribal sounds. From 1923 to 1940, the Cotton Club provided upper-class whites an exotic but safe experience at the expense of ordinary African Americans in Harlem. In 1932, Madden loosened up his "whites only" policy by admitting light-skinned black patrons and dark-skinned celebrities, but the Cotton Club remained off-limits to mixed parties.

The Cotton Club, as well as the many other clubs owned by white businessmen, highlighted the lack of upward economic mobility plaguing the Harlem community. Even though African Americans made up the vast majority of the neighborhood's residents, financial and material resources benefited whites living outside the community. In fact, African Americans owned less than 20 percent of Harlem businesses. With dead-end jobs, little prospect for economic advancement, and deteriorating living conditions, Harlem was a community filled with internal turmoil. In March 1935, tensions erupted when a black Hispanic teenager was killed while in police custody after his apprehension for shoplifting at the Kress Five and Ten Store across from the Apollo Theater. A two-day riot ensued, resulting in the death of three people and more than $2 million in damages. Afterward, the riot generated a profound sense of fear among outsiders. Between the riot and the continued financial struggles caused by the Great Depression, slowly Harlem lost its luster as cash-strapped pleasure seekers scaled back their leisurely activities. Harlem's reign as a cultural hot spot all but ended after 1935.

The institutional problems plaguing Harlem and other African American communities were further compounded by the economic calamities of the 1930s. When New York City Mayor Fiorello LaGuardia convened a biracial commission to investigate the Harlem riot, they concluded that it was a by-product of "injustices of discrimination in employment, the aggressions of the police, and . . . racial segregation." Stated more broadly, the Great Depression worsened an already precarious existence for America's black population. African American communities suffered disproportionally from rising unemployment, poverty, and homelessness. Already living on the economic margins, black sharecroppers throughout the South found themselves displaced as cotton prices plummeted. In Southern cities such as

New Orleans and Atlanta, Depression Era frustrations led whites to organize protests against the hiring of black workers and in favor of hiring whites. By 1931, 40 percent of black men in Chicago were unemployed, compared with 20 percent of white men. Similarly, unemployment among black women skyrocketed when employers opted to hire unemployed white women or cut menial service jobs altogether. By 1931, the unemployment rate for Chicago's black women was 55 percent, as compared with only 13 percent for white women. Estimates place the overall unemployment rate for African Americans at over 50 percent in the 1930s, far above the 30 percent estimate for white Americans.

As African Americans struggled with unemployment, they also found themselves subject to an uneven and racially biased relief system that placed them at a disadvantage. For example, by early 1933, the daily relief allotment for black households in Norfolk, Virginia, was $1.25 per family, compared with the daily rate of $2.00 for whites. Officials in Houston, Texas, simply rejected relief applications from African Americans. The Roosevelt administration tried to eliminate relief inequities with its New Deal; however, disparities persisted. Wage differences became the norm in employment codes established by the National Recovery Administration. Government relief programs—though officially open to blacks—often prohibited access to benefits. As a case in point, the Civilian Conservation Corps informally gave preference to young white workers. When black men were accepted by the CCC, they were housed in segregated camps and struggled to ascend to leadership positions. Far from a New Deal, many of Roosevelt's programs remained entrenched in the old story of racial discrimination.

No event symbolized the disparity and injustice facing black Americans in the 1930s better than the Scottsboro trials. In March 1931, a group of nine black youths ranging in age from thirteen to twenty-one were arrested in Paint Rock, Alabama. They had been "hoboing" to Memphis on the Southern Railway line when they got into a fight with several white youths. Local authorities stopped the train and arrested the young black men. As they were taken off the train, authorities discovered Ruby Bates and Victoria Price, two young white girls, hiding in the back. It would later be revealed that the young women had been selling sexual favors in the freight car, but at the time, they accused the nine black riders of rape.

Despite flimsy evidence and the fact that one of the young women withdrew her allegation, an all-white jury declared the accused guilty in a series of hastily convened trials. As thousands of cheering whites gathered outside the Scottsboro, Alabama, courthouse where the trials were held, eight of the young defendants were sentenced to death. For the ninth defendant, Roy Wright, a mistrial was declared as the jury came back hung, unable to agree on his sentence. In Wright's case, prosecutors requested a life sentence, citing the fact that he was only thirteen years old. Although jurors agreed on Wright's guilt, they disagreed on his sentence; seven jurors held out for the death sentence for the youngster. After the trial, appeals and retrials followed in one of the most widely publicized cases of the time. On two occasions, the Supreme Court took up arguments relating to the "Scottsboro boys." Eventually charges were dropped against four of the defendants. The remaining defendants were ultimately pardoned, but not before the fiasco of the Scottsboro trial showcased the precarious and sometimes life-threatening circumstances afflicting African Americans in the 1930s.

The Scottsboro case spoke to the lengths African Americans had yet to go to attain their full rights of citizenship. Although the 1930s saw important strides in civil rights for African Americans, it would take World War II and a new generation of civil rights activists before the country finally fulfilled the promises made after the Civil War. Nevertheless, the 1930s is an important period for African Americans. The continuation of the Great Migration brought a visible African American presence north of the Mason-Dixon Line, and communities created in America's northern urban centers became important conduits of changes—political, social, and cultural. Despite the constant economic hardships of the era—which continued from the 1920s—the decade saw progress for African Americans.

Suggested Readings

Several studies offer a detailed examination of African Americans and civil rights during the 1930s. Harvard Sitkoff's *A New Deal for Blacks: The Emergence of Civil Rights as a National Issue* (New York: Oxford University Press, 1978) provides a comprehensive overview of the political struggle over the civil rights struggle during the thirties. In *Black Culture and the New Deal: The Quest for Civil Rights in the Roosevelt Era* (Chapel Hill: The University of North Carolina Press, 2009), Lauren

Rebecca Sklaroff looks at the civil rights issue through African American participation in the Federal Arts Project. Cheryl Greenberg's *"Or Does It Explode?": Black Harlem in the Great Depression* (New York: Oxford University Press, 1997) offers a detailed case study of Harlem during the 1930s. For a look at African American artists and performers during the decade, readers should consult Mel Watkins's *Stepin Fetchit: The Life and Times of Lincoln Perry* (New York: Vintage, 2006) and Jonathan Scott Holloway's *Confronting the Veil: Abram Harris, Jr., E. Franklin Frazier, and Ralph Bunchie, 1919–1941* (Chapel Hill: The University of North Carolina Press, 2002). Stacy I. Morgan's *Rethinking Social Realism: African American Art and Literature, 1930–1953* (Athens: University of Georgia Press, 2004) reconsiders the influence of African American artists on mainstream American culture. Finally, James W. Loewen's *Sundown Towns: A Hidden Dimension of American Racism* (New York: Simon & Schuster, 2006) offers a chilling reminder of institutionalized racism and the challenges of persistent discrimination.

5

The Second New Deal, 1933–1940

"The Clouds Will Soon Roll By"
—George Brown and Harry Woods, 1932

IN SEPTEMBER 1936, *Literary Digest* mailed out ten million postcards to people across the nation for the straw poll the magazine was conducting on the upcoming presidential election. The questionnaire simply asked respondents for whom they intended to vote in the November contest. Participants were chosen from every phonebook across the nation, automobile registration records, and the membership rolls of a variety of local community clubs. The poll's outcome was much anticipated. Over the years *Literary Digest* had touted itself as one of the foremost prognosticators of presidential contests, having correctly forecasted the winners in the past four elections. In fact, the weekly news magazine had been "amazingly right," predicting not just the victor but also near-exact percentage points by which the candidates won their respective races.

On October 31, *Literary Digest* finally unveiled the results of the poll. Based on the responses of over 2.2 million people, the magazine concluded that the Republican candidate Alf Landon would decisively win the election, easily defeating the incumbent Franklin Roosevelt by a margin of 57 to 43 percent. Three days later Americans officially cast their votes. The outcome was very different. When the polls closed, Roosevelt emerged victorious, receiving nearly 61 percent of the vote to Landon's 36.5 percent—nearly a nineteen-point swing for FDR, compared with *Literary Digest's* prediction. Accentuating the decisiveness of the 1936 contest, Roosevelt took every state in the nation except two, Maine and Vermont. Not since the 1820 presidential election, when James Madison ran unopposed, had a president won by such a landslide. *Literary Digest*, which had been "uncannily accurate" in its previous polls, proved to be uncannily wrong in 1936. With its reputation forever tarnished, less than two years later the newsmagazine closed its doors.

Literary Digest's failed straw poll represented one of the colossal blunders in election polling history, on a par with the *Chicago Tribune's* ill-fated "Dewey Defeats Truman" headline in the 1948 presidential race. One reason for the fiasco stems from poor and inaccurate polling techniques that skewed the results. But there is also more to it. A closer examination of the poll results tells the story of a significant voter shift beginning to occur among the electorate in the later years of Roosevelt's first term in office. When *Literary Digest* sent out the questionnaire, it did so to people who owned phones and cars, groups that were typically better off than the majority of Americans after the stock market crash. There were also people who were more apt to vote for the Republican Landon. Conversely, voters who cast their ballots for Roosevelt were the downtrodden of the Great Depression: farmers, workers, minorities, the elderly, and other groups who identified themselves economically with the policies of Franklin Roosevelt and the Democratic Party. These otherwise disparate groups were united by shared economic insecurity, and looked to Roosevelt to lead them out of the Depression. This shift marked the start of a political realignment that gave rise to Roosevelt's New Deal Coalition. And though it speaks to the universal adulation Americans came to hold for the president, this political realignment was also the product of a significant transformation occurring within Roosevelt's New Deal. By 1935, facing the continued onslaught of the Depression and growing public criticism, Roosevelt's New Deal took a dramatic political turn to the left. The "second New Deal," as it was termed, called for greater government intervention in the economy and looked to level the playing field in society by empowering the downtrodden. In effect, it brought a redistribution of power within American society. And though it failed to end the Great Depression, it brought lasting changes to America and the political landscape. Groups once marginalized found a voice in a democracy that became more responsive to its people on a federal level.

The ambitious New Deal programs unfurled by Franklin Roosevelt and his brain trust over the first one hundred days of his presidency began showing signs of success by 1934. The Emergency Bank Relief Act and the Banking Act restored public confidence in the banking system and stopped in its tracks a growing financial crisis that threatened to topple America's lending institutions. Already by June 1933, bank deposits had increased by $2 billion. The Federal Emergency Relief Administration (FERA), the Civilian Conservation Corps (CCC), and Public Works Administration (PWA) provided relief that helped ease the suffering of millions of Americans struggling under the weight of the Depression and its crushing unemployment. Such programs also built up America's infrastructure and contributed to the nation's long-term development by creating roads, bridges, airports, schools, and parks. The industrial sector also began to show signs of life as Roosevelt's National Industrial Recovery Act (NIRA) appeared to produce its desired effect, increasing industrial production by nearly 22 percent by May 1935. Meanwhile Roosevelt's Agricultural Adjustment Act (AAA) showed signs of improving the farm economy. Crop prices rose steadily with the AAA's crop reduction program, leading farm incomes to climb to an estimated 50 percent by 1936.

Still, for all the New Deal's apparent success, it was equally clear by 1935 that Roosevelt's program was sputtering along rather than unleashing the wholesale economic recovery the president had promised. With FERA, Roosevelt wanted local and state officials to implement and oversee relief programs rather than creating a federal network to do so. Urgency fueled the initiative, as Roosevelt wanted to provide aid to those in need as quickly as possible. The problem was that local and state agencies were equally unprepared for the task, often lacking the same administrative experience that led Roosevelt to refrain from establishing federal oversight of the works projects. Waste and delays characterized the early years of many FERA grants. Equally troubling was the unevenness of the application of the program. With local administration came local prejudices. Many FERA relief projects excluded women. Others, particularly in the South, neglected to provide assistance to

African Americans. As one African American explained in a letter to President Roosevelt, "hard as it is to believe, the relief officials here are using up almost everything that you send for themselves and their friends. They . . . give us black folks . . . nothing but a few cans of pickle meat and to the white folks they give blankets, bolts of cloth, and things like that." Going against Roosevelt's intent, it became clear that a number of the FERA programs were not meeting the needs of many of the most vulnerable in society, who continued to suffer from the effects of the Depression.

Equally troubling were the failings of Roosevelt's recovery programs. Despite signs of success, there existed significant problems in both the AAA and the NIRA. The AAA was particularly important to Roosevelt, who believed that the New Deal would stand or fall based on its success or failure. The program got off to a rough start. By the time it was passed in 1933, farmers had already planted many of their crops for the season. Henry Wallace, Roosevelt's secretary of agriculture and the man in charge of the AAA, reluctantly agreed to have farmers destroy their crops in order to comply with the program's call for crop reduction. Cotton farmers plowed under their crops in Arkansas, Mississippi, and elsewhere throughout the South. The same held true for corn and wheat farms across the Midwest. Meanwhile, hog farmers slaughtered over six million piglets to help prevent a glut in the pork market. Similar cattle kills occurred out West. The destruction of crops and slaughter of livestock horrified a nation in which millions lived in poverty and hunger. For Roosevelt and Wallace, the decision was an unmitigated public-relations disaster. Adding to the AAA's woes, the program suffered from the same local administration problems that plagued FERA. Policies favored agribusinesses and large farmers and denied benefits to small farmers. Furthermore, as landowners accepted the federal farm subsidies, they took out of circulation the land they leased to tenant farmers and sharecroppers instead of the land they farmed. Thus, the program's crop reduction policies led to the displacement of countless numbers of tenant farmers and sharecroppers. For a program Roosevelt placed so much hope in, by late 1934 it was clear that serious problems plagued the AAA.

The NIRA suffered similar difficulties. Roosevelt chose Hugh Johnson, the hard-drinking, obstinate, former United States Army General to head the National Recovery Administration (NRA), the agency tasked with overseeing implementation of the NIRA. Johnson and the NRA struggled to find footing almost from the start. The guiding premise behind the NIRA was to establish a rationally planned industrial economy that would eliminate overproduction, restore employment, and usher in prosperity. Businesses, joined by labor, and overseen by Johnson's office, would organize code hearings to establish production practices, determine production output, and set labor standards across their respective industries. To work, the plan required business leaders to buy in completely. Drawing on his experience working with the War Industries Board during World War I, Johnson relied on volunteerism to coax business support rather than impose government control. Unfortunately, Johnson's strategy permitted larger businesses to dominate the code hearings, leading to price fixing, which was not the intent of the NIRA. Compounding the problem, business leaders continually evaded the wage standards Johnson sought to attain under the NIRA. When the former general pushed for a maximum forty-hour workweek and a 30-cent-per-hour minimum wage, businesses ceded to the request, only to raise prices even more in order to offset the added costs and maintain profit margins. Thus, any wage gains garnered under the NIRA code hearings were lost as workers' wages failed to keep pace with rising prices, thereby hindering the administration's efforts to stimulate purchasing power. Adding to the NIRA's failure, industrial leaders evaded the collective bargaining provisions guaranteed under the program. Without effective labor representation at the code hearings, workers failed to realize significant change under the NIRA. As a result, resentment grew over the program from labor unions, the working class, and the public in general. Business leaders also joined the list of the NIRA's critics. Despite the economic gains businesses attained under the program, executives bristled over what they saw as needless government intrusion into the economy. By 1934, many manufacturers agreed with the assessment of newspaper magnate William Randolph Hearst that the NRA stood for "No Recovery Allowed."

As Roosevelt's programs struggled, criticism of the president mounted. Not surprisingly, a vocal element came from the Right, as conservatives and business leaders assailed Roosevelt's so-called socialistic tendencies. Leading the charge was the American Liberty League, an organization formed by conservative Southern Democrats opposed to Roosevelt's liberal policies. By late 1934, the group included industrialists, chief among whom was John Jacob Raskob, former chair of the Democratic National Committee and board member for DuPont Corporation, one of the nation's leading chemical companies. The League's ranks later swelled to include Alfred Sloan of General Motors, Ernest Weir of Weirton Steel, Sewell Avery of Montgomery Ward, James Pew of Sun Oil, the movie producer Hal Roach, and the Roosevelt nemesis and one-time presidential candidate Al Smith. Formed in August 1934, the America Liberty League's mandate was to uphold the ideals of the US Constitution and "to teach the necessity of respect for the rights of persons and property as fundamental to every form of government." Although the Liberty League denied that it was anti-Roosevelt, the president's New Deal programs were the main targets of its attacks. The NIRA was condemned for its "unwarranted excesses of attempted regulation," while the AAA was denounced as little more than a fascist attempt to control agriculture. By 1936, the American Liberty League claimed to enjoy a national membership of over 125,000 people.

Criticism of Roosevelt and the New Deal was not limited to conservatives. Joining the chorus of critics was a group of well-known liberal detractors who charged Roosevelt with selling out to business interests and callously ignoring the suffering of millions. Among the most vocal of Roosevelt's left-leaning critics was Francis Townsend, a retired California physician. After a failed career in farming, Townsend turned to medicine and at the age of thirty-one graduated from the Omaha Medical College in 1907. Afterward, he alternated between medicine and a variety of other jobs. In 1930, Townsend landed a position as public health officer for the city of Long Beach, California. Three years later, he was forced to retire when city officials eliminated the position. One morning in 1933, the unemployed sixty-six-year-old Townsend walked out to his back alley and stumbled on three elderly women rummaging through the garbage. The scene horrified him. What Townsend soon discovered was what many elderly already knew—that the Depression had fallen particularly hard on the nation's senior citizens. Many had lost their life savings in the wave of bank crashes. Making matters worse, seniors faced discrimination on the job market as many employers preferred to hire from the plethora of younger workers flooding the nation's unemployment lines. Too old to work and too young to die, the elderly found themselves thrust to the margins of society. Some were forced to turn to their children or extended family members to provide care, while others took up residence in the many Hoovervilles sprouting up on the outskirts of towns.

Townsend soon became a forceful advocate for the elderly. Joined by the former real estate agent Earl Clements, Townsend crafted his Old Age Revolving Pension Plan. The plan called for the federal government to provide senior citizens with a guaranteed monthly income of $200. The program was to be funded by a 2 percent national sales tax. Everyone over the age of sixty would be eligible for the program, provided they were retired and not "habitual criminals." Recipients were required to spend the monthly stipend in its entirety, thereby distributing $200 each back into the local economy. No portion of the monthly pension could be placed into savings. Townsend believed the plan would not only aid seniors but would also help solve the nation's economic crisis. As seniors purchased food, paid rent, and bought consumer goods, he argued, they would stimulate demand, create jobs, and bring an end to the Great Depression. However, critics were quick to dismiss his reasoning. The noted journalist Walter Lippmann characterized Townsend's ruminations as overly simplistic and economically naïve. Yet it was soon apparent that the retired physician had struck a chord with the American people, and Townsend Clubs began to pop up across the country. By 1935, his plan had over five million supporters. A few months later, the physician-turned-activist handed Roosevelt a petition signed by twenty million Americans calling for the creation of a pension program for the elderly.

Townsend's criticism of the New Deal was tame compared with that of other liberal critics. Among the more outspoken detractors on the left was the Catholic priest and national radio personality Father Charles Coughlin. Born in Hamilton, Ontario, to Irish parents, Coughlin was ordained a Catholic priest in 1916 at the age of twenty-four. After teaching at a college in Canada for several years, Coughlin was assigned to oversee the National Shrine of the Little Flower, a newly established parish in Royal Oak, Michigan, in 1923. The church served as Coughlin's home base for the next forty-three years. In 1926, Coughlin gave his first radio address on WJR, a small station operating out of nearby Detroit. His early shows did little more than offer catechism instruction to young listeners, but his popularity in the region was a harbinger of things to come. Coughlin came to recognize the powerful potential of broadcasting on the nation's airwaves. His message soon moved to broader religious themes and drew a larger audience of adults. By the early thirties, Coughlin's focus shifted again when he began to incorporate commentary on national political issues of significance to his listeners.

Initially, Coughlin supported Franklin Roosevelt and the New Deal enthusiastically. The priest saw in Roosevelt a leader who possessed the strength and determination to pull America out of the economic mire of the Great Depression. Coughlin also believed that the president was strong enough to beat back the threat of communism, which the Michigan priest believed was among the greatest threat to the American way of life. In 1932, Coughlin called on listeners to turn out and support Roosevelt's election bid. Following the election, Coughlin continued to champion the president and his economic programs, telling listeners it was "Roosevelt or ruin." In one show he declared that "the New Deal is Christ's deal." Later, he testified before Congress that Roosevelt was doing "God's work." By 1934, however, Coughlin's relationship with Roosevelt began to sour.

Roosevelt was never an enthusiastic supporter of Coughlin. Though the president appreciated Coughlin's public endorsement, he remained wary of Coughlin, uncertain of his motives and distrustful of his overtures. Roosevelt's misgivings soon proved correct. In 1934, Coughlin turned on Roosevelt with a vengeance and became one of the president's most formidable critics. Proclaiming a commitment to social justice, Coughlin began to attack Roosevelt's New Deal measures as unconstitutional. He took new exception to the president's economic policies, deriding Roosevelt for giving in to the dictates of Wall Street and selling out to the "money changers." Eventually, Father Coughlin's anti-Roosevelt assault disintegrated into an anti-Semitic harangue about Jewish plans for world domination, a perspective that ultimately contributed to the cancellation of his radio show in 1940. But between 1934 and 1935, there was no denying that Coughlin was a potent force. With an estimated weekly audience of thirty million listeners, he possessed the potential to sway public opinion and shape politics. And during that time, the radio priest had Roosevelt in his crosshairs.

Then there was Huey Long, the flamboyant senator and political demagogue from Louisiana. Of Roosevelt's liberal critics, Long was without question the most controversial and perhaps the most dangerous. Born in 1893, Long came from a small, impoverished farm community in north-central Louisiana. Although his family was modestly well off, Long grew up keenly aware of the poverty afflicting his neighbors in Winn Parish, among the poorest counties in the Bayou State. From an early age, Long distinguished himself as offbeat, outspoken, and fiercely independent. When he was in the eleventh grade, the local school added a twelfth-year requirement for graduation. In response, Long circulated a petition to have the decision repealed, a move that provoked the ire of school officials and led to his expulsion. Despite the setback, Long won a debating scholarship to Louisiana State University, an early testament to his strong oratory skills. However, the future politician was forced to pass up the opportunity because he could not afford the cost of textbooks.

Unsuited for and uninterested in farm work, Long bounced around working as a traveling salesman, selling books, canned goods, and patent medicines. After his marriage in 1913, Long tried to return to school, first attending Oklahoma Baptist University to become a preacher and then the University of Oklahoma Law School to study law. Both of these stints in school were brief. Long was unfit for the classroom and soon realized that he had little interest in becoming a preacher or a lawyer. At the urging of an older brother, Long eventually returned to law school in 1915, this time enrolling at Tulane University in New Orleans. After a year, Long petitioned the Law Board for permission to take the state bar exam before completing his degree. Despite possessing only one year of formal legal training, Long passed and was admitted to the Louisiana Bar. Although he never received a diploma of any kind, Long opened a small office in his hometown of Winnfield in 1915 and began practicing law.

Long's political career began when he was elected to the Louisiana Railroad Commission in 1918. He won public support largely by attacking the excesses of Standard Oil, a corporate giant whose presence was felt across the state. The contest was an early example of the folksy, populist campaign style that would characterize Long's political career. This style had strong local appeal, as Winn Parish had always been a hotbed for radical politics. The impoverished residents had embraced the Populist insurrection of the 1890s. Then in the early 1900s they supported the Socialist candidate

Eugene Debs. In fact, in the 1912 presidential contest, nearly 36 percent of Winn Parish residents turned out to support Debs, favoring the third-party candidate over progressive reformers Teddy Roosevelt and Woodrow Wilson. Long's anti–Standard Oil campaign in 1918 was consistent with the insurgent political climate of his youth and reflected his deep commitment to Winn's impoverished residents. Drawn more to old charismatic populist candidates like William Jennings Bryan than to stodgy contemporary progressives like the party standard-bearer Woodrow Wilson, Long cultivated an image of a down-to-earth country bumpkin out to defend the weak and defenseless against rampant lawlessness and corruption. Furthermore, he offered a powerful message that transcended the South's racial barrier. Unlike traditional Southern Democrats, Long refused to engage in race baiting. Instead, he crafted a class-based approach that had universal appeal to all of Louisiana's poor, regardless of race. Long essentially cast himself as the consummate outsider, building a strong following as the politician out to rescue the "little guy."

In 1928, Long's political strength grew when he succeeded in winning election to the governor's seat. He quickly consolidated power and liberally dispensed patronage to political allies, all the while isolating opponents. Long further ingratiated himself with Louisiana's poor by launching an ambitious works program that built roads, bridges, schools, hospitals, and a host of other public services, many of which were located in the most neglected areas of the state. He established free textbook programs that enabled poor children to attend school. He sanctioned the creation of adult literacy classes designed to improve Louisiana's ranking as the state with the lowest literacy rates in the nation. The program helped many, and it also showed Long's political savvy by preparing residents to pass the literacy tests that had barred them from voting in state elections. Gradually, the colorful and bombastic Long emerged as a folk hero among Louisianans, particularly for the rural poor. Yet the great irony of Long's political career is that while portraying himself as a champion of the poor who rallied against corruption, "the Kingfish," as he later became known, built one of the most corrupt political regimes in Louisiana history.

People who won appointment to political office under Long's reign were expected to kickback portions of their salary to aid his reelection campaign, helping Long build and maintain a sizeable war chest. He utilized bribery, extortion, intimidation, and blackmail as weapons to maintain a firm grasp on the state's political apparatus. In 1929, Long's opponents tried to impeach him. He fired back by taking his case to the people and portraying the efforts of his political adversaries as little more than a thinly veiled effort by corrupt corporations to remove him from office. After successfully deflecting the attack, Long embarked on a scorched-earth policy, decimating his opponents systematically and without mercy. Whenever possible he removed from office those who supported the impeachment effort, as well as their extended family members. If Long could not take them out of office, he threw his considerable weight behind candidates who could defeat the so-called traitors at the polls. When state newspapers came out in support of his impeachment, Long created his own newspaper, the *Louisiana Progress*, to laud his exploits and attack his critics. As he explained unabashedly, "I used to try to get things done by saying 'please.' Now . . . I dynamite 'em out of my path." Testifying to Long's growing political aggrandizement, after winning election to the US Senate in 1930, the cantankerous politician refused to vacate his position as governor before the end of his term because he did not want the office to pass to his lieutenant governor, Paul Cyr, who happened to be one of Long's staunchest opponents. Instead, from March 1931 through January 1932, Long let the Senate seat sit vacant. When Cyr tried to take the governor's seat, Long mobilized the Louisiana National Guard and ordered troops to surround the capitol building to fend off the lieutenant governor's "coup d'état."

In Washington, Long continued to extol his fiery brand of populism. Colorful, outgoing, and charismatic, the Louisiana senator steadily gained national attention with his outspoken and often outlandish assaults on banks and big business. He attacked the Washington establishment, including leaders of his own party, for their lethargic efforts in combating the Depression and "cozying up" to Hoover. When Roosevelt entered the political fray, the loquacious Long initially lined up to be among his more vocal supporters. Long threw his support behind the New Yorker's nomination and campaigned for Roosevelt across the Midwest. The alliance was short lived. Long broke with Roosevelt soon after he took the White House. In part, the break came over policy. Ever suspicious of America's powerful national banking system and the Federal Reserve in particular, Long staged a three-week filibuster over proposed legislation for Roosevelt's Banking Act. He ended it only when provisions were included to guarantee the creation of a depositors' insurance plan. Long was also highly critical of Roosevelt's NIRA, believing that the president kowtowed too much to big business. For Long, the only way to successfully overcome the Depression was through programs that radically redistributed wealth in America, an approach Roosevelt refused to entertain. As the Louisiana senator saw it, the New Deal simply failed to address the root problem plaguing the nation.

Long's divorce from Roosevelt and the New Deal was also partly personal. Neither man had ever fully embraced the union, and for good reason. Roosevelt saw Long as a dangerous political demagogue and looked to limit his power and influence as much as possible. When it came time to dispense federal patronage in Louisiana, Roosevelt passed the appointments to Long's political adversaries rather than to Long. Long saw Roosevelt as an impediment to his own presidential ambitions. Indeed, Long planned to challenge Roosevelt for the presidency in 1936. In an ambitious plan that spoke to Long's political maneuvering, the Louisiana senator hatched a scheme to contest Roosevelt for the Democratic nomination. Long understood Roosevelt's appeal and political strength and held no illusion of becoming the Democratic nominee or even winning the presidency in 1936. Instead, Long hoped to use his candidacy to spur the creation of a third party buttressed by his ideas. Although it would not deliver Long the presidency, it held the appeal of possibly derailing Roosevelt's efforts to win reelection by splitting the Democratic Party and giving the election victory to the Republican Party in 1936. With Roosevelt out of the way, Long then planned to swoop in and rescue the Democratic Party by winning the presidency in 1940.

In February 1934, Long set his plan in motion. On a national radio broadcast, he unveiled the "Share Our Wealth" plan, his solution to the nation's economic woes. Long's vision for redistributing wealth in the country was radical. He proposed that every American was to receive a minimum yearly income of $2,500 from the federal government. Families were to receive an additional $5,000 cash grant per year. In addition, the plan called for reduced work hours, paid college education for qualified students, and pensions for the elderly. To pay for the expenditures, Long proposed capping yearly incomes at $1 million and limiting personal wealth to $50 million dollars. Proceeds earned above these amounts would be forfeited to the government to support Long's initiatives. When critics called the proposal socialistic, Long discounted the claim, stating that the inspiration behind Share Our Wealth came from the Bible and the Declaration of Independence. When opponents claimed the economics of it would not work, Long dismissed the criticisms outright. As he told a group of Iowa farmers, "Just shut your damn eyes and believe it. That's all." While the wealth redistribution legislation Long proposed in the Senate gained little traction, it struck a chord among Americans mired under the weight of the Great Depression. By early 1935, Long claimed to have amassed a following of over 7.5 million people.

With the New Deal struggling and political criticism growing, Roosevelt's situation became even more precarious when the Supreme Court began questioning the legality of his programs. The court Roosevelt inherited leaned to the right of the political spectrum, controlled by a group the press dubbed the "Four Horsemen." The four justices—Pierce Butler, James McReynolds, George Sutherland, and Willis Van Devanter—formed a solid conservative block. With three of the five remaining jurists aligning with liberal commitments, court rulings typically turned on the decisions of the two remaining judges, Charles Evans Hughes and Owen Roberts. Roberts regularly joined the Four Horsemen, giving them a majority. In spite of this, Roosevelt's administration was mildly optimistic early on when, in 1934, Roberts aligned himself with the liberal jurists in two cases upholding state legislation dealing with government regulation of the economy. In one case, Roberts delivered the majority opinion acknowledging the "inherent" power of government to promote the "general welfare" of the people, a major tenant of Roosevelt's line of thinking. So, while the court had yet to rule on a case involving New Deal legislation directly, Roberts and the jurists appeared receptive to Roosevelt's tactics during his first two years in office.

The administration's optimism for an accommodating court was dashed in early 1935, when the court began whittling away at Roosevelt's New Deal. A January ruling raised questions over the NIRA's ability to set production quotas as a means to control overproduction in the oil industry. In the *Hot Oil* case, the Supreme Court found that Congress had given the president too much authority to regulate the interstate and foreign trade of oil. Though the court's ruling did not directly invalidate the NIRA and Roosevelt's right to regulate intrastate commerce, it raised questions about his methods. In a second case four weeks later, the court allowed Roosevelt's legislation to stand, but took the administration to task for what it deemed to be a growing usurpation of power. The *Gold Clause* cases revolved around several policies Roosevelt initiated shortly after talking office to try to restrict gold circulation. Through executive order, Roosevelt required citizens to surrender all but the smallest amounts of gold coins, gold bullion, and gold certificates owed them by the Federal Reserve for just over $20 per ounce. He also signed a Congressional measure that canceled all gold clauses in public contracts, whereby creditors could be paid in gold or a gold equivalent. The policies, Roosevelt argued, were designed to prevent gold hoarding, which he and his advisers believed threatened to undermine the federal monetary system. Though the court acknowledged the government's right to initiate such policies, Chief Justice Hughes issued a scathing rebuke in the majority opinion declaring the tactic legal but "immoral." Justice McReynolds in writing the dissenting opinion went one further, declaring the gold policies an example of "Nero at his worst." In a third case just weeks later, the Four Horseman, joined once again by Roberts, issued a majority ruling invalidating the Railroad Pension Act established by the Roosevelt administration in 1934. The majority found the legislation, which created a retirement plan for railroad workers, an arbitrary imposition on railway carriers and questioned whether the creation of such a plan was a function of intrastate transportation and thus open to federal regulation.

The rulings were by no means a death sentence for the New Deal, but the court's decisions troubled Roosevelt and his staff. New Deal advisers argued that the Great Depression produced exigent circumstances, an emergency more calamitous than war, and therefore necessitated a broad expansion of federal power. The Supreme Court took exception to that line of thinking. In May 1935, the final blow fell when the court declared unconstitutional the whole of the NIRA. The case centered on Joseph, Alex, Aaron, and Martin Schechter, four orthodox Russian Jewish butchers in Brooklyn, New York. The Schechter brothers were far from one of the many small butchers servicing immigrant communities. Together they operated the largest kosher poultry supply shop in Brooklyn, earning yearly profits in excess of $1 million. In July 1934, just weeks after passage of the NIRA production code for the poultry industry, the brothers were charged with sixty violations. Although they were not the first or only business to disobey the NIRA, they were among the most egregious. One charge leveled against the brothers was that they recklessly undercut their competitors' prices. Another was that they violated the wage and work hour provisions of the code, which set wages at $.50 per hour and established a forty-eight-hour workweek for employees. Instead, the brothers paid workers $.30 per hour and worked them seventy-three hours per week. They were also accused of selling chickens allegedly "unfit" for public consumption.

A Federal District Court initially found the Schechter brothers guilty of violating the NIRA. The ruling imposed a fine of $7,425 and sentenced them to prison for one to three months. In April 1935, the Supreme Court took up the brothers' appeal in *Schechter Poultry v. US*, or "the case of the sick chicken." The justices determined that Congress conceded too much power to the president when it created the NIRA and overturned the convictions in a unanimous 9–0 verdict. They also declared that even though the Schechter brothers purchased their poultry outside of New York State, since they sold their products solely within it, the Roosevelt administration and the National Recovery Administration had no authority whatsoever to regulate their trade. The NIRA violated the basic tenants of the intrastate commerce provisions of the Constitution, according to the ruling. The unanimous verdict shocked the White House. Roosevelt was particularly perturbed by the court's narrow interpretation of the Intrastate Commerce clause, declaring it antiquated and reminiscent of the "horse-and-buggy days" of intrastate trade. The ruling proved to be the final nail in the coffin for the president's first New Deal.

Roosevelt, in the months leading up to the court case, came to understand the limitations and failures of his New Deal programs. Ever the advocate for experimentation, Roosevelt realized the need to find new approaches to combat the economic crisis. As a seasoned politician Roosevelt also recognized the changing political climate emanating across America. The panaceas and criticisms from the likes of Long, Coughlin, and Townsend found a growing audience among discouraged Americans seeking solutions to their suffering. Frustration steadily pushed Americans more and more to the left politically, producing a growing class divide. Roosevelt recognized the cleavage. During the first two years of his presidency he sought to maintain a degree of balance. The increasing attacks leveled by business leaders befuddled the president. Far from being a "socialist" or "communist," as critics labeled him, Roosevelt saw himself as the savior of capitalism. The New Deal was, as Roosevelt put it, an attempt to save business leaders from committing suicide. But by 1935, as the intensity of conservative attacks continued, Roosevelt recognized the growing class divide and the ire of the public toward business. It led him to push the New Deal to the left politically.

The second New Deal, or Roosevelt's second one hundred days, began in 1935. In April, Roosevelt signed into law the Emergency Relief Appropriation Act. The legislation allocated $4.8 billion for works projects that employed the unemployed. Oversight of the program fell under the control of a new agency, the Works Progress Administration (WPA), the largest and most expansive New Deal agency. Whereas local oversight created problems in the implementation of FERA, the WPA placed the unemployed directly on the federal government's payrolls. To head the agency, Roosevelt tapped Harry Hopkins, the gregarious, outgoing social worker who had directed FERA and who was one of the president's closest advisers by 1935. Like Roosevelt, Hopkins believed that the program needed to center on job creation rather than cash handouts. Avoiding "the dole" by offering a job to those in need was psychologically important because it allowed the destitute to maintain their dignity. It also reinforced the merits of a strong work ethic, which Roosevelt and Hopkins feared would be lost if cash payments were simply handed out. Guided by this principle, Hopkins turned the WPA into the largest employer in the country. Over 8.5 million people worked on WPA projects. Workers built over 650,000 miles of roads and highways, 1,000 airports, and over 2,500 hospitals. Bridges, post offices, schools, parks, and countless other public buildings were erected during the WPA's seven-year run before it ended in 1943.

The WPA was more than just a building-trades works project. Hopkins understood that not everyone unemployed was a construction worker or laborer. The key was to develop projects that utilized the diverse skills and talents of the unemployed. Many artists supported the New Deal's spirit of social and political change and happily responded to Hopkins's call. Artists working in all mediums created positive images of America and increased public appreciation of art while they earned a living wage. Illustrators designed posters for WPA projects and public information campaigns, while photographers documented the dignity of ordinary Americans at work. Some artists even taught art in schools. WPA funded the Federal Theater Project that organized theater shows and other live performances, while employing out of work actors, writers, and directors. Thornton Wilder's play *Our Town*, about idyllic life in small-town New England, was funded by the WPA and completed in 1938. The future film star and acclaimed director Orson Welles directed Shakespeare's *Macbeth* for the New York Negro Theater Unit under the WPA.

The Federal Writers' Project (FWP), another WPA initiative, put writers, historians, and anthropologists to work compiling local histories, recording oral accounts, and writing children's books. The FWP's *American Guide Series* provided detailed travel guides and histories of all forty-eight states. The noted author Richard Wright wrote a New York City guidebook in 1938. Although writers were not meant to create literature while on the government payroll, field research influenced much of the fiction they produced. Sam Ross's novel *Windy City* describes the Chicago music scene he saw while interviewing jazz musicians for the FWP. Mari Thomasi based her novel *Like Lesser Gods* on the life stories of Vermont granite carvers she documented for the FWP. Encouraged to record authentic idioms and vernacular, Ralph Ellison began including the speech patterns of black Americans in his creative work as a result of his time as an FWP writer. James Agee and the photographer Walker Evans teamed up to produce *Let Us Now Praise Famous Men* (1941), a book that was said to be on the coffee table of every progressive household for the next decade. The future Pulitzer prize winner Saul Bellow's first job was working for the Federal Writers' Project. Other luminaries who worked on WPA projects included Studs Terkel, Zora Neale Hurston, and John Cheever. At its peak, the Writers' Project employed approximately 6,500 men and women around the country, paying them a modest but livable wage of $20 a week. Between 1935 and 1942 the writers assembled a collection of work that included field research and reports, drafts of essays, speeches, scripts, plays, oral histories, folklore material, newspaper clippings, transcripts, inventories, correspondence and other administrative records, drawings, maps, graphs, instructions, and surveys. FWP workers documented the life stories of more than ten thousand men and women from a variety of regions, occupations, and ethnic groups. One of the most important and fascinating collections archived are slave narratives from the last remaining generation of people born into slavery in the United States. Recorded between 1936 and 1938, the collection contains seventeen volumes of more than 2,300 first-person accounts of slavery, as well as 500 black-and-white photographs of former slaves. Of invaluable historical importance, the vast store of unpublished material that was accumulated by the FWP is housed in the Library of Congress.

Another significant piece of legislation established during the second New Deal was the National Labor Relations Act (NLRA). In July 1935, Roosevelt signed into law the NLRA, or the Wagner Act, as it was popularly called in honor of New York Senator Robert Wagner, who had authored the legislation. The Wagner Act clearly established the right of workers to organize into labor unions and engage in collective bargaining. For the first time in the nation's history, it became illegal for companies to deny workers this right. To oversee the legislation and ensure compliance, the Wagner Act also established the National Labor Relations Board (NLRB). The board was entrusted to administer elections for union representation and certify the results based on majority rule. The NLRB also heard complaints for violations of the Wagner Act and was granted the authority to issue cease and desist orders in cases where companies refused to adhere to the principles of the legislation. In effect, the NLRB served as a court, ensuring proper oversight of the Wagner Act.

Not surprisingly, the Wagner Act and the NLRB proved controversial. Led by the American Liberty League, critics assailed the act as socialistic and complained that it infringed on workers' individual freedoms. Roosevelt was forcing unionization on unwilling workers, they protested. The president vehemently disagreed. Never a strong supporter of unionization, Roosevelt simply believed that the rights of those who wanted to unionize should be protected. Still, the Wagner Act marked a shift in philosophy from the NIRA, which only affirmed the rights of workers. The change was partly pragmatic. When Wagner brought forward the legislation to the Senate it passed by a large margin, 63 to 12, even though Roosevelt did not publicly back the measure. Roosevelt saw the outcome of the vote as symbolic of the changing mood in America and quickly supported it afterward, declaring the Wagner Act part of his "must have" legislation in 1935. But Roosevelt's support was also based on his changing views on the nature of labor relations. By 1935, Roosevelt realized that only organized labor could meet organized capital on a level playing field. By protecting workers' rights to unionize, the president sought to empower workers and create an opportunity in which they could pursue the issues that were best for them. This way of thinking marked a significant shift in perspective for Roosevelt and his New Deal.

Even though Roosevelt acknowledged workers' right to organize, he recognized that not all workers wished to join a labor union. The key for the second New Deal was to provide a minimum safety net to protect workers who remained outside the labor movement. In 1938, this thinking became the impetus for the Fair Labor Standards Act (FLSA). First proposed in 1932 by then Senator Hugo Black, the goal was to establish a floor for wages and a ceiling on hours of work. Southern politicians initially resisted the measure, fearing it would raise the region's historically low wage scales and make the South less appealing to manufacturers. With the backing of Claude Pepper, a pro-New Deal senator from Florida, Roosevelt succeeded in bringing the legislation forward in 1938. The FLSA established a minimum wage of $.25 cents per hour, to be raised to $.40 in 1945. It also created a maximum workweek of forty-four hours, to be reduced to forty hours in three years. Finally, the FLSA outlawed child labor, fulfilling a goal progressive reformers had long advocated and effectively paving the way for the elimination of most child labor. From then on, all children under the age of sixteen were prohibited from working in industries that engaged in interstate commerce.

Perhaps no legislation symbolized the philosophical shift to the left for the New Deal more than the Social Security Act. Francis Townsend's call for an old-age pension program struck a chord with the public and exposed a glaring weakness with Roosevelt's New Deal. Townsend was not the first to come up with the idea. Progressive reformers had unsuccessfully advocated such legislation thirty years earlier. The conditions during the Great Depression highlighted the need for a pension program, and Roosevelt responded. In June 1934, Roosevelt established the Committee on Economic Security to develop a workable social insurance program for the elderly. To head up the committee, the president tapped Frances Perkins, a one-time social worker and current head of the Department of Labor. In January 1935, the results of the committee laid the groundwork for social insurance legislation. To shepherd the plan through Congress, Roosevelt turned to Senator Robert Wagner (D-NY) and Congressman David Lewis (D-MD). Both men felt a deep connection to the legislation. Wagner, the son of German immigrants, came of age in the tenements of New York City. Lewis, meanwhile, grew up toiling in Pennsylvania's coalmines. He studied law in his spare time and was eventually admitted to the bar in Maryland, paving the way for a political career. Both men intimately understood the potential impact of the pending legislation in aiding the most vulnerable of America's working class in their golden years.

As with most New Deal initiatives, critics lined up quickly to attack Roosevelt's pension bill. Conservatives saw the legislation as an assault on the traditional American value of self-help, fearful that a social insurance program would foster dependency. Southerners complained that Roosevelt's plan threatened the region's race relations by encouraging laziness among poor African Americans and bitterness among well-off whites called on to finance it. Yet, as politicians wrangled over Roosevelt's social-insurance plan, the possibility of even more sweeping legislation arose. John McGroarty, California's poet laureate and a Congressman from Los Angeles, brought to the floor a bill to establish the popular Townsend plan, complete with mandatory $200 monthly pensions. Weeks later, Congressman Ernest Lundeen, a member of the Minnesota Farm-Labor Party, reissued a call to establish an extensive social welfare plan operated by the federal government, including old-age pensions, unemployment benefits, and health insurance. Both McGroarty's and Lundeen's plan were voted down quickly. But the prospect of more "radical" measures allowed support to coalesce behind Roosevelt's plan. After passing the House in April, and the Senate in June, Roosevelt signed the Social Security Act into law on August 15, 1935.

The Social Security Act consisted of three primary provisions. First and foremost was the old-age pension plan, which called for a 1 percent payroll tax to be levied on all employees and employers. Workers could begin to collect benefits once they turned sixty-five. The initial rate varied from $10 to

$85 per month, depending on how much they contributed while working. To administer the fund the act called for the creation of a Social Security Board, with payments to commence in 1942. In 1939, Congress amended the legislation to include payment of survivor benefits to families in the event of a worker's premature death, and expanded the program to include benefits for spouses and minor children of retired workers. The change enlarged the program even further, making it a broader family-based program. It also accelerated the start date of the program to 1940. Finally, the other two provisions of the Social Security Act centered on unemployment and relief, two problems that became chronic in the wake of the Great Depression. Under Roosevelt's legislation, the act extended federal-state unemployment insurance to approximately twenty-eight million workers. The program was to be funded by a tax on employers. Benefits were to be paid to workers who had momentarily lost their jobs through no fault of their own. Roosevelt created a safety net to aid workers in between jobs as they searched for employment. Finally, the legislation also established federal aid for states to help provide relief programs targeting the elderly, dependent children, and the blind, and to establish public health services.

Roosevelt's Social Security Act is typically viewed as marking the "high tide" of the second New Deal. Roosevelt proclaimed the legislation as the foundation of his reconfigured New Deal. Nevertheless, problems existed with the legislation. For example, the regressive payroll tax hit lower-income workers harder than those in higher brackets who earned more than the maximum taxable limit. Economists also speculated that by taxing workers' income, Roosevelt's plan inadvertently hurt recovery efforts by removing money from the economy. However, the president insisted that the program be financed through a payroll tax in which workers and employers jointly contributed. Roosevelt's motives were a mix of his ideas of self-help and political pragmatism. First, he believed that by funding the programs through joint contributions it would guarantee the programs' financial viability, making them self-supporting. Roosevelt did not want the programs to be subsidized by the federal government. Instead, the government would simply administer the programs. Second, Roosevelt was convinced that by financing Social Security and unemployment insurance through payroll deductions, it would be impossible for later generations of politicians to overturn the legislation.

As Roosevelt later explained, "We put those payroll contributions there so as to give the contributors a legal, moral, and political right to collect their pensions and their unemployment benefits. With those taxes in there, no damn politician can ever scrap my Social Security program."

Roosevelt's second New Deal also re-addressed the problems confronting farmers. Overproduction, declining prices, and the ecological effects of the Dust Bowl had wreaked unrelenting havoc on the nation's farmers. In January 1936, the Supreme Court ruled the AAA unconstitutional. The decision was based on the program's funding, which came from a tax levied on companies that processed farm products. In a 6-to-3 decision, the court declared it a violation of the Tenth Amendment and illegal to tax one specific group or segment of the population to benefit another—in this case, farmers who received payments for restricting their crops from a tax on suppliers. The lone consolation the administration could take from the ruling was that justices did not find fault with the basic premise behind the program, namely, paying farmers to restrict crop production.

Roosevelt's staffers remained convinced that taking land out of circulation was the best way to deal with agricultural overproduction. Just weeks after the Supreme Court's ruling on the AAA in February 1936, Roosevelt's administration rolled out the Soil Conservation Act (SCA), which paid farmers to restrict land production in the name of soil conservation. The program targeted midwestern lands impacted by the Dust Bowl. Under the program, farmers received benefits or bounties for taking out of circulation the soil-depleting cash crops that ravaged the land and planting soil-conserving crops such as soybeans, legumes, and clover in their place. Two years later, in 1938, Roosevelt brought forward the second Agricultural Adjustment Act. Like the first, the second AAA tackled the problems of overproduction by paying farmers to restrict their output. Unlike the previous measure, the second one paid farmers out of proceeds from the general tax fund.

While the SCA and second AAA provided relief to many rural communities and helped eliminate overproduction, Roosevelt's brain trust recognized that it needed to do more to help the most impoverished farmers, particularly tenant famers and sharecroppers. Therefore, the administration steered through the Domestic Allotment Act alongside the SCA in February 1936. This legislation closed the loophole that, under the federal government's previous land restrictions programs, had squeezed out tenant farmers and sharecroppers. The measure required landowners to share any proceeds they received from the government with sharecroppers and tenant farmers if either group used the land taken out of circulation. Meanwhile, in a similar attempt to help impoverished agricultural workers, the administration threw its support behind the Farm Tenancy Act in 1937. Alabama Senator John Bankhead and Texas Congressman Marvin Jones, two of Roosevelt's strongest supporters south of the Mason-Dixon Line, brought the legislation forward. The Tenancy Act offered distressed farmers low-interest rehabilitation loans to improve their farms. The goal was to keep struggling farmers from falling into farm tenancy. The program also offered loans to farm tenants seeking to purchase their own land. Over $190 million in loans would be available under the legislation, helping thousands of struggling farmers, their families, and, by extension, their communities.

Ollie Burnett was typical of the countless number of tenant farmers helped by second New Deal programs. In 1935, the twenty-eight-year-old African American farmer grossed an income of $350, of which $170 was paid to merchants for seed and fertilizer. The situation led to a precarious existence for Burnett and his family, and they moved frequently in search of a better life. By 1937, Burnett listed an estimated net worth of $571 for the following possessions: an eighteen-year-old mule, a cow, two small pigs, seventeen chickens, a half ton of hay, and fifty bushels of grain. In 1938, Burnett applied to the Farm Settlement Administration (FSA) for a loan under the Tenancy Act in order to purchase the modest 132-acre farm he had been leasing. He received a loan for $3,200 from the FSA, which included an option to borrow an additional $2,300 for repairs, if needed. The forty-year loan was secured at a modest interest rate of 3 percent. With the help of FSA officials, Burnett steadily improved his farm and in just five years repaid his debt, gained title to his farm, and earned the distinction of becoming the first farmer to repay a loan under the Tenancy Act.

Unlike the legislation of Roosevelt's first hundred days, the second New Deal sought to directly improve conditions for groups vulnerable to the persistent poverty of the Great Depression, namely, workers, farmers, minorities, and the elderly. The strategy was a success and played brilliantly to the growing class divide emerging across the nation. By putting forward the Wagner Act, the Social Security Act, the Farm Tenant Act, and the WPA, Roosevelt built on his public persona as a champion for the "forgotten man," winning admirers at a time when criticism of his presidency and the New Deal mounted. In June 1935, Roosevelt solidified that image. Just as the Wagner and Social Security Acts were making their way through the halls of Congress, Roosevelt issued a call for sweeping tax reform. He attacked the growing economic imbalance plaguing America and asked for inheritance and gift taxes, significant increases to tax rates for those in the upper brackets, and the creation of graduated corporate tax rates. The measures were more "must have" legislation, Roosevelt declared, necessary expedients to redistribute the wealth and repair the growing gulf dividing rich and poor.

Roosevelt's tax plan was the most stringent to be proposed since the Progressive Era. Not surprisingly, it met with a firestorm of controversy. Critics declared the tax proposals as another cloaked attempt to "soak the rich." The media magnate William Randolph Hearst went so far as to instruct his newspapers to identify the tax as "soak the successful" and refer to the New Deal as the "Raw Deal." Others saw it as a heavy-handed political maneuver because, after pronouncing the tax package as imperative, Roosevelt seemed disinclined to push the matter. At one point he indicated a willingness to allow Congress to adjourn even though it had yet to vote on tax legislation. The Revenue Act of 1935 that eventually came through Congress bore little resemblance to Roosevelt's initial proposal. The estate tax was minimal. The graduated corporate tax structure remained, although it was significantly watered down. As to the income tax rates, the legislation raised tax rates on yearly incomes above $50,000, with progressive rates extending to 75 percent on incomes exceeding $5 million. Loopholes, though, significantly minimized the impact of the rate increases. In total, the Revenue Act generated approximately $250 million in taxes, a far cry from the reform proposed by the president.

Still, the legislation proved beneficial to Roosevelt. Although the Revenue Act came nowhere near redistributing the wealth as Roosevelt pledged, he secured what he needed out of the tax debate. The tax proposals infuriated business leaders and many among the wealthy. In their eyes, Roosevelt was already a villain. The proposed Revenue Act only confirmed their fears. At the same time, the tax proposal won over the disadvantaged and those struggling daily in the face of the Great Depression. For these Americans, Roosevelt's tax proposal stood as a form of retribution, holding accountable the people they believed had caused their suffering. Taxing the wealthy to this segment of society was more than justifiable. Thus with the tax proposal Roosevelt firmly cast his lot with the masses and against the rich. It became an image he played well, attacking the "unjust concentration of wealth and economic power."

Roosevelt's shift to the left with the second New Deal worked to his political advantage heading into the 1936 presidential election. The new programs allowed Roosevelt to solidify his political base around laborers, farmers, the elderly, minorities, and others counted among the disadvantaged. The programs also minimized the sting of Roosevelt's Left-leaning critics. The Social Security Act won over Francis Townsend's fans. The WPA and the unemployment insurance program drowned out the histrionics of Father Charles Coughlin. And the Revenue Act undermined the populist swagger of Huey Long. In September 1935, any remaining political challenge Long might have presented to Roosevelt vanished when the Louisiana senator fell victim to an assassin's bullet. With his critics quieted, Roosevelt remained the overwhelming choice to lead the party.

The Republican Party tried to counter Roosevelt's appeal by enlisting Kansas Governor Alf Landon as its standard bearer. Landon's candidacy held an attraction to the GOP. Recognizing the sway Roosevelt held over voters, Republican leaders did not want a candidate who could be identified with the "Hate Roosevelt" coalition within the party. Landon, an old Teddy Roosevelt progressive, appealed to that line of thinking. The Kansas governor, GOP strategists believed, was liberal enough to win over the president's supporters. He was seen as a friend to organized labor and had supported several New Deal measures. So rather than directly attack Roosevelt, Landon and the Republican Party's initial approach centered on exploiting the perception that the New Deal was hostile toward business and emphasizing the waste and inefficiency generated by the administration's programs. The strategy failed to generate any traction. Between Landon's lack of campaigning and a message that failed to resonate among voters, the GOP became desperate by fall 1936. Landon's campaign soon shifted its focus to directly assailing Roosevelt, a strategy that failed miserably. With the president's popularity riding high, Roosevelt thoroughly vanquished Landon, paving the way for a second term.

The 1936 election ushered in another four years for Franklin Roosevelt. It also brought a sweeping vindication for the Democratic Party and the President's New Deal supporters. Fall elections saw Democrats garner twelve additional seats in Congress, giving the party a commanding advantage over Republicans by a margin of 334 to 88. A similar advantage existed in the Senate, where Democrats picked up five more seats, giving them a 76-to-16 advantage in the upper chamber. With over three-fourths the majority in both Houses, the Democrats enjoyed the largest majority in Washington since the Reconstruction Era. Looking at the election as a referendum on Franklin Roosevelt and the New Deal, it is clear that the American people were buying what the president was selling. With such commanding majorities, Roosevelt was poised to push the New Deal even further in his second term. As he boldly told Americans at his second inaugural address, "I see one-third of a nation ill housed, ill clad, ill nourished. . . . The test of our progress is not whether we add more to the abundance of those who have much; it is whether we provide enough for those who have too little."

The Supreme Court remained Roosevelt's chief nemesis, in spite of his popular mandate. Following the fateful Schechter ruling in May 1935, the court steadily dismantled the first New Deal. By January 1936, the AAA was added to its list of Roosevelt programs deemed unconstitutional. The administration went on to lose two more cases in early spring, bringing the total number of cases in which the court ruled against the New Deal to seven. Equally disconcerting, in June 1936, the court struck down a New York State law establishing a minimum wage across the Empire State. The decisions distressed Roosevelt, who believed the court was creating a "no man's land" where state and federal government were unable to act. Equally troubling, the court had on its dockets cases pertaining to both the Wagner and Social Security Acts heading into 1937. Given their past actions, Roosevelt had every reason to fear that the justices might overturn both measures and rock the foundation of his second New Deal, as they had the first. Even worse, the court's antagonism to the New Deal stood as a roadblock to any future legislation. Essentially, the administration saw itself boxed into a corner by the Supreme Court, unable to act.

Roosevelt's advisers struggled to find a response to the seemingly hostile Supreme Court. Just over two years earlier, Attorney General Homer Cummings had broached the idea of expanding the court as a means of offsetting the conservative domination of the bench. Roosevelt could staff it with like-minded judges, advisers argued, and counteract the conservative influence of Roberts and the Four Horsemen. On the surface, the idea had merit. Congress, not the Constitution, determined the size of the Supreme Court, which had varied over the years from as few as six to as many as ten. Roosevelt, though, remained cool to the plan. Simply adding justices to the bench seemed heavy handed to the president. Nine justices had been the standard since 1869, and Roosevelt feared the political fallout from a proposal to expand the court. Instead, the president favored the passage of a constitutional amendment to reign in the court, either by limiting its powers or offsetting them by granting new powers to Congress to counteract the court. The problem was that securing passage of such an amendment required time, which the White House had very little of in late 1936. So, despite initial misgivings, Roosevelt switched gears and supported the idea of expanding the court's size.

On February 5, 1937, Roosevelt proposed the Judicial Procedures Reform Bill. The measure called for the president to appoint a new justice to the court for every justice who had more than ten years of service and who did not retire within six months after turning seventy. The origin of the plan could be found in the oddest of places. In 1913, Supreme Court Justice James McReynolds, then attorney general for Woodrow Wilson, had proposed a very similar plan. That Roosevelt resurrected the measure in 1937 undoubtedly rankled the conservative jurist, much to the enjoyment of the president and his advisers. McReynolds's connection to the plan brought added political benefits, as Roosevelt could argue that his proposal was not radical, heavy handed, or even new, since a sitting Supreme Court member had already supported such legislation. Also, by linking the legislation to a jurist's age, Roosevelt hoped to minimize public reaction, claiming he was simply trying to expedite the court and help the aged and overworked justices. The bill was about reforming the court to make it more effective, or so the president argued.

As it turned out, Roosevelt's court proposal faced strenuous opposition. Even though the judicial reform bill was fully constitutional, it was seen by most critics as little more than a pretense to manipulate the court. The press had a field day attacking Roosevelt's "court-packing plan," and his concerns about the inefficiency of elder justices were quickly refuted. Liberal supporters of the president were disquieted by the proposed legislation as well. Although Roosevelt claimed that judicial reform was necessary given the unique and extreme circumstances of the Depression, many opponents feared the precedent it would set, expressing concerns that future reactionary leaders might use similar tactics to subvert the court and the Constitution. The judicial reform bill alarmed even Democratic Party leaders and New Deal advisers, especially since they received no advance warning of Roosevelt's intention. In fact, other than Attorney General Cummings, none of Roosevelt's cabinet members received notice of the legislation before the president made it public. Left out in the cold and hung out to dry, few Democrats were willing to support the president's reform bill.

In late March 1937, as the Senate Judiciary Committee was roasting Roosevelt's court-packing plan, the controversy took an unexpected turn. In a strange sequence of events, the Supreme Court did an about-face with respect to Roosevelt's New Deal. The shift started when Justice Roberts broke with the Four Horsemen to support a ruling that sanctioned a state minimum-wage law in Washington, one that was strikingly similar to the New York statute the court had struck down just ten months earlier. In mid-April the switch looked complete when the court came out in favor of Roosevelt and upheld the Wagner Act in a 5-to-4 ruling. One month later, seventy-eight-year-old Willis Van Devanter, a stalwart opponent to the New Deal, announced his intention to step down from the bench. Van Devanter's impending retirement permitted Roosevelt to appoint his first justice, thereby altering the composition of the Supreme Court. Finally, in late May the court ruled in favor of the Social Security Act, sanctioning both the old-age pension and the unemployment insurance provisions of the legislation. Heading into summer 1937, Roosevelt relished the changing tide and looked forward to a more optimistic future with the Supreme Court.

Speculation quickly surfaced as to the possible cause for the Supreme Court's sudden reversal in attitude toward Roosevelt's New Deal. Some thought that the court simply caved in to Roosevelt's political pressure. Rather than allow Roosevelt to alter the court, so this line of thinking suggested, Roberts decided to switch gears and support the New Deal. As the popular saying went in 1937, Roberts's "switch in time saved nine." However, no evidence exists to support such allegations. Instead, it appears Roberts's support for the Washington minimum-wage law may have stemmed from the fact that he was never comfortable with the original ruling that overturned the New York State law. In fact, Roberts voted in favor of hearing the Washington state case, a vote that occurred before the 1936 presidential election. In December 1936, after arguments were heard, he voted to uphold the Washington statute. The vote occurred well before Roosevelt's court-packing proposal became public knowledge. As to the broader shift in the court's decision to sanction other New Deal programs, Chief Justice Hughes later attributed it to the recognition that the Supreme Court, and Roberts in particular, accepted the changing political tide in America as evidenced by the 1936 election. Whatever the cause for the court's changing views, the shift marked a dramatic victory for Roosevelt. It also brought an end to the judicial reform bill, which was unceremoniously dropped months after the turnaround. Though Congress passed the Judicial Procedures Reform Act in August 1937, the measure was watered down and bore no resemblance to Roosevelt's initial proposed piece of legislation. Rather, the new judicial act was little more than a piece of face-saving legislation crafted by Roosevelt's supporters to allow the president to claim victory in his battle over the court.

Roosevelt emerged victorious from his fight with the Supreme Court, but it came at a tremendous cost. His popularity took a hit among citizens who saw the Supreme Court as sacrosanct. More important, the affair provided an issue around which his opponents could rally. Prior to 1936, Roosevelt's many critics struggled to find common ground. In the court-packing plan, Roosevelt unwittingly handed his New Deal adversaries an issue on which to attack the administration. Republicans took the court episode as a symbol of Roosevelt's arrogance and used it to expose him as a ruthless power monger. The episode also aligned conservatives, drawing together

Republicans and Southern Democrats in their opposition to the New Deal. The unity that the Democratic Party had experienced during Roosevelt's first term in office started to unravel. It was not Roosevelt's finest hour, politically. Worse still, the opposition he faced in the courts shifted to Congress. After 1937, Congress began to contest forcefully the president's New Deal legislation. Republicans joined by conservative Southern Democrats succeeded in blocking Roosevelt's more liberal agenda, dealing significant blows to his plans for the second New Deal.

Nevertheless, Roosevelt continued to win victories during his second term in office. For example, he successfully pushed through Congress the Fair Labor Standards Act in 1938. It established a national minimum wage and put American workers on the path to an eight-hour workday and a forty-hour workweek. The following year the administration's New Deal supporters succeeded in amending the Social Security Act to include payment of survivor benefits to widows and dependent children. Yet Roosevelt's victories came with limitations. For example, the Fair Labor Standards Act passed only after a bitter and acrimonious battle. Considered by Roosevelt to be among the most important pieces of legislation passed by his administration, the political haggling over the bill saw over seventy separate amendments proposed to the original measure. In the end, the original proposed $.40 per hour minimum wage was dropped to $.25 cents per hour to placate Southerners who were determined to preserve the region's lower wage scale. Though Roosevelt's supporters secured a provision to raise the wage to $.40 per hour, as advocated by the president, it would not take effect until 1945, seven years after the legislation was signed into law. Even though over seven hundred thousand workers were covered by the new legislation, whole segments of the workforce were excluded from coverage, many of them among the lowest-paid wage earners in the nation, particularly women and minorities. Roosevelt's struggle over the Fair Labor Standards Act underscored the political fallout from the court battle. His critics became emboldened and opponents increasingly found common ground in their resistance to the New Deal. Thus, although Roosevelt may have won the battle with the court, he lost the war.

Political fallout over the court fiasco may have hindered Roosevelt's plans, but the second New Deal created a lasting imprint on America. In the short run, the programs from Roosevelt's administration helped Americans cope with the immediate effects of the Great Depression. Measures such as the Wagner Act, Works Progress Administration, Social Security Act, Agricultural Adjustment Act, and Farm Tenancy Act collectively eased the daily suffering of millions of Americans struggling to survive an unfathomable national financial crisis. Whether through employment on government works projects operated by the WPA or the impetus of self-help fostered under a measure like the Wagner Act, the programs of the second New Deal made a real difference. And though the programs of the second New Deal were a mixed bag of political triumphs and failures, Roosevelt's initiatives succeeded in bolstering public confidence in the federal government at a time when many Americans held grave doubts about the nation's political leadership and its ability to steer the country out of the depths of the Great Depression.

In the long run Roosevelt's New Deal exerted a lasting impact on American politics on a number of levels. Roosevelt's determined and forceful leadership in trying to navigate the nation out of the Great Depression redefined the role of the presidency. Never again would the presidency retreat to the weak, laissez-faire leadership style of Warren Harding and Calvin Coolidge. Instead, following the path blazed by Roosevelt, the executive office came to be seen by the American people as a strong, driving force for shaping society far beyond the Washington beltway. In directing the second New Deal toward the forgotten man, Roosevelt also permanently altered the focus of federal politics. In effect the second New Deal gave voice to groups historically ignored or marginalized on the federal level politically. By the end of the 1930s, an entire nation and especially farmers, workers, immigrants, women, minorities, and the elderly all came to have a very different outlook of the role of the federal government. Whereas these "special-interest" groups had previously looked to local and state political institutions to address their problems, by Roosevelt's second term they increasingly turned to the nation's capital to redress their grievances. Roosevelt's ability to answer their call, or at the very least to give the impression of his ability to do so, redefined the Democratic Party. The dispossessed of the 1930s would become the backbone of the Democratic Party, making Roosevelt's "New Deal Coalition" a political juggernaut up until the Reagan years. The approach also transformed federal politics, forcing Washington to become responsive to the interests of such varied groups. Empowered by their experiences of the Great Depression, workers, farmers, minorities, and women came to expect a federal government attentive to their interests as well as to those of business or industry. In effect, the outcome was to turn the nation into what one historian has called the "brokerage state." Although it is debatable whether the move to constituency-based bloc politics is good for the American political system, there is no denying that Roosevelt is responsible for transforming the federal government to become more responsive to the needs and interests of broader social, economic, and political groups.

As for Franklin Roosevelt and the Great Depression, the economic catastrophe lived on until his third term, ending only after America's entry into World War II in 1941. In fact, not until 1943 did the Depression finally end, finding its demise in the massive infusion of government spending created by America's Lend-Lease program and its military build-up. This was a formula Roosevelt turned to periodically during the second New Deal. For example, with the WPA the administration put forward an initial investment of $4.9 billion to fund works projects that utilized the unemployed—an amount that eventually climbed to over $13 billion by the time the program ended in 1943. Through the WPA and other federally funded programs the economy began showing signs of recovery by late 1936. In 1937, believing the economy had stabilized, Roosevelt suddenly scaled back federal spending. The reason for the cutbacks was that the president feared a rising federal deficit. He also expressed concerns that if the programs continued too long, they might foster dependency and negatively impact private initiative and personal work ethic. Better the program end too quickly than go on too long.

Roosevelt, however, overestimated the strength of the economy. As he slashed federal spending, the economy bottomed out yet again. The resulting Roosevelt Recession was an economic drop that rivaled the great crash of 1929. Over four million workers found themselves unemployed, while stock prices plummeted throughout the summer and into the fall in 1937. With the economic gains of the past two-plus years erased, Roosevelt once again in 1938 turned to federal spending as a means to try to jumpstart the economy. Over $3 billion suddenly flowed into various New Deal initiatives. However,

Roosevelt refused to go along with more aggressive spending measures advocated by several advisers, again fearing the social and economic implications of such policies. Ultimately, although Roosevelt possessed the solution for the Great Depression, he found himself unable to carry it through. Doing so violated major tenets of his political and social philosophy. And therein lies the complex, and at times contradictory, legacy of Roosevelt. Whereas on the one hand Franklin Roosevelt stood as a revolutionary leader who transformed American politics and society, on the other he was a stalwart conservative reluctant to fully embrace the very changes he at times advocated.

Suggested Readings

Two recent biographies that offer a comprehensive overview of Roosevelt and his presidency are Jean Edward Smith, *FDR* (New York: Random House, 2008), and H. W. Brands, *Traitor to His Class: The Privileged Life and Radical Presidency of Franklin Delano Roosevelt* (New York: Anchor, 2009). Alan Brinkley, *Voices of Protest: Huey Long, Father Coughlin, and the Great Depression* (New York: Vintage, 1983), provides insight into two of Roosevelt's leading critics. T. Harry Williams, *Huey Long* (New York: Vintage, 1981), offers the most detailed examination of the controversial Louisiana politician. Kirstin Downey, *The Woman behind the New Deal: The Life and Legacy of Frances Perkins—Social Security, Unemployment Insurance, and the Minimum Wage* (New York: Anchor, 2010), provides a thoughtful exploration of the key political battles of Roosevelt's presidency, particularly as it relates to the second New Deal. In *The End of Reform: New Deal Liberalism in Recession and War* (New York: Vintage, 1996), Alan Brinkley explores the political implications of Roosevelt's presidency and how it impacted America.

6

Workers and the Labor Movement

"Down on the Picket Line"

—Sarah Gunning, 1932

JOHN L. LEWIS was filled with anger when he arrived at the American Federation of Labor (AFL) National Convention in Atlantic City in 1935. At the AFL convention in San Francisco the previous year, the president of the United Mine Workers' of America (UMW) succeeded in extracting from the union's executive leadership an agreement to broaden its organizational horizons and explore the potential of organizing unskilled mass production workers. To purists in AFL circles, what the combative labor leader proposed was heresy. Historically the AFL's conservative hierarchy jealously guarded its craft union philosophy, often refusing to even entertain discussion of industrial organization. However, Lewis was no fundamentalist. Throughout 1933–1934 he saw a growing militancy emerging among America's working class. While radicals and other labor supporters were stepping forward and seizing the unprecedented opportunities presented by Franklin Roosevelt's pro-labor New Deal, the AFL sat quietly on the sidelines, seemingly content to do nothing. For Lewis this was too much to bear.

During the previous two years, the bushy-browed labor leader rebuilt the UMW, resurrecting the decaying miners' union into one of the most powerful labor unions in the nation. Now he wanted the AFL to do the same. In 1934, Lewis believed that he succeeded in convincing the AFL leadership to turn the page on its craft structure and expand the scope of its activities, reaching out to unskilled workers in the mass production industries. Now, one year later, he realized the futility and hollowness of that pledge. Frustrated by the Old Guard's refusal to act on the agreement and initiate massive organizing drives, Lewis gave a scathing rebuke of the leadership's passivity before the Atlantic City conventioneers. Lewis told onlookers, "At San Francisco they seduced me with fair words. Now, of course, having learned that I was seduced, I am enraged and ready to rend my seducers limb from limb." He went on to declare, "if we let this opportunity slip, the enemies of labor will be encouraged and a high wassail will prevail at the banquet tables of the mighty."

Despite Lewis's impassioned plea for action, the AFL leadership shot down the request in short order, steadfastly refusing to branch out of its narrow provincialism, insisting that it include only craft workers within its union structure. The Old Guard won. The fiery and combative Lewis was not finished. As he walked past Bill Hutcheson, head of the United Brotherhood of Carpenters and Joiners of America, the two exchanged words. Though Lewis considered Hutchinson a friend, the head of the Carpenters' union also symbolized the AFL's conservative leadership. There were, in fact, few in the AFL leadership ranks as conservative as Hutcheson. "Big Bill," as he came to be known by friend and foe alike, was among the staunchest critics of Roosevelt and his New Deal, at one point publicly declaring the president a "dictator." Hutchinson also vigorously supported the AFL's craft orthodoxy, strenuously opposing any effort to organize unskilled workers in the mass production industries. As the discussion between the two became heated, Hutchinson lashed out a Lewis, calling him a "bastard." In a fit of rage Lewis leapt past onlookers and delivered a blow across Hutcheson's jaw, bloodying the Carpenters' president. Soon the two were rolling on the ground of the convention floor.

Lewis's battle with Hutcheson symbolized the intellectual divide separating the AFL leadership over the question of the union's organizational structure. Namely, should the AFL continue to pursue a narrowly defined craft union philosophy that excluded significant segments of the industrial workforce from joining its ranks, or should it embrace the opportunities afforded by the Roosevelt's New Deal and move to a more inclusive industrial union philosophy that organized workers of all skills, genders, and races? Lewis's punch also represented a significant break in the AFL. The next day Lewis and the heads of seven other AFL unions met on Atlantic City's famed boardwalk. There, they mapped out plans for the creation of the Committee for Industrial Organizations (CIO). With the Old Guard incapable and unwilling to organize the mass production industries, union leaders behind the CIO looked to pick up the task. The decision by Lewis and the other union leaders to forge a new labor organization had deep and far-reaching consequences for the American working class.

In looking at the 1930s, there are two significant developments to come out of the era. The first was the growing realization on the part of the federal government that it had an obligation to preserve and promote the well-being of its citizenry. The second development was the rise of industrial unionism. With the emergence of the CIO, tens of thousands of workers gained the benefits of unionization. As the CIO found success organizing labor's new millions, the AFL's Old Guard had little choice but to reach out and join the fray, finally and reluctantly abandoning its narrow craft provincialism. The activities by first the CIO and then the AFL revitalized a once dormant labor movement. By 1941 over 8.4 million workers belonged to labor unions, accounting for over 23 percent of America's industrial workforce. More important, the industrial unionism that took root in the 1930s improved the economic well-being of workers, offered workplace protection, and ultimately laid the ground work for the entry of the working class into the middle class following 1945.

Coming out of World War I, American workers and the labor movement enjoyed a sense of hope and optimism. Through the pro-labor policies of the National War Labor Board, the support of Woodrow Wilson's administration, and the favorable wartime economic environment, workers experienced significant gains. The twelve-hour workday, once the norm in many industries, became a relic of the past as more and more workers came to enjoy the benefits of an eight-hour workday. By 1918, the majority of American workers toiled a forty-eight-hour workweek, a significant departure from the prewar era. Wages experienced similar gains despite restrictions imposed by the Wilson administration, uplifting the economic status of many workers. And through it all, the labor movement witnessed significant growth as increasing numbers of workers fought for and received union recognition. Whereas about 3 million workers belonged to labor unions before the war, by 1920 union membership in the United States stood at over 5.1 million workers, among the highest levels in the nation's history. Given labor's growing strength, many observers believed that the cooperative relationships forged between labor leaders and industrialists during the war era would carry over into the postwar period, bringing with it continued economic growth and improvements in working conditions for both union and nonunion workers. Yet union officials soon learned that they badly misjudged the situation, overestimating the willingness of employers to accept unionization among their workers and overvaluing the extent to which political leaders embraced organized labor.

For workers, the central workplace issue after the war centered on wages. Though World War I brought higher wages, workers also faced significant economic problems. Wage controls imposed by the government in order to prevent inflation from overtaking the economy put a brake on the economic growth workers enjoyed during the war. In what was a "seller's market" for labor, workers suddenly found themselves unable to realize the full extent of their earning potential. Although many workers recognized the government's wage policies as a necessary sacrifice for the good of the war effort, the policy remained a source of contention. What proved particularly bothersome to many was that while the government placed restrictions on workers' wages, there was no cap imposed on corporate profits or employers' salaries. The disparity created a clear sense of inequity when it came to the government's wartime policies. The war helped mitigate the problem, often offering longer work hours and in some cases overtime pay, thus permitting workers to earn extra money and offset the hourly wage restrictions. However, the problem quickly leapt to the surface when the war ended and defense production dried up. With manufacturers scaling back operations, workers suddenly found themselves earning significantly less. Worse, many more found themselves unemployed as companies shut their doors in order to retool as they began the process of shifting from defense to peacetime production. As unemployment increased, workers saw their wartime savings whittled away in a struggling postwar economy.

The labor situation deteriorated rapidly in the months following the armistice. With companies unwilling or unable to address the workers' economic grievances, workers responded by taking action into their own hands. Beginning in 1919, labor disturbances rocked the industrial landscape. In Seattle, over sixty thousand workers from across the city staged a general strike, shutting down the city for five days. In Boston, police officers seeking better wages and improved working conditions went on strike, setting off a crime spree across the city. In September, 365,000 steelworkers walked off their jobs, engaging in a strike that lasted over three months. Less than two months later, over 400,000 coal miners went on strike to protest unfair wages. Nationwide, over 4 million workers—about 20 percent of America's industrial labor force—participated in a strike in 1919.

The working-class militancy that emerged in 1919 was met by a swift wave of repression. Painting the strikes as communist-inspired and the strikers as radicals, employers and the press tapped into latent xenophobic fears that flourished after World War I. Armed with the support of public opinion, manufacturers and government agencies beat back the threat of the so-called Reds. One by one the strikes were defeated. For workers and the labor movement, the defeat of the postwar insurgency produced lasting consequences. In the wake of their victory, manufacturers unleashed a powerful counterattack. Intent on regaining control over the labor situation, manufacturers embraced an open-shop movement during the 1920s. The goal of the open-shop campaign was to keep unions out of America's factories and keep strikes to a minimum. Leading the way in the battle was the National Association of Manufacturers (NAM), a national advocacy group for American business. Formed in 1895, NAM became a fervent opponent to organized labor equating unionization with "despotism, tyranny, and slavery." In the 1920s, NAM leaders encouraged employers to adopt what came to be known as "the American Plan." The strategy linked unionism with bolshevism, instead promoting union-free "open shops" where workers were discouraged strongly from joining a labor union. Faced with such incessant hostility and the inability to counteract the employer offensive, the gains organized labor enjoyed during World War I collapsed in the 1920s. By 1929 union membership shrank to 3.6 million members nationwide, a decline of 1.5 million members from 1920.

With organized labor in retreat, some employers stepped forward to fill the void. The 1920s brought forward a proliferation of what became known came as welfare capitalism programs. The idea behind welfare capitalism was to win over worker loyalty and dissuade unionization. While the programs varied from corporation to corporation, they followed general patterns of offering noneconomic inducements to foster worker loyalty. Under such plans workers found themselves treated to a host of social programs such as factory-sponsored bowling leagues, baseball and softball teams, and an array of other sports activities. Model-building clubs, book groups, or chess clubs might be mixed in for those not interested in athletics. Summer picnics, holiday festivals, dances, or other seasonal events might be held for workers and their families. By dispensing auxiliary benefits companies sought to nurture a paternalistic form of labor relations in which workers became invested in the "corporate family." Rarely did corporate welfare programs address the economic status of workers. In cases where economic inducements such as profit-sharing plans were offered, employers manipulated plans to ensure productivity and profitability while creating a bond with the workers. Many of the welfare capitalism schemes in the 1920s also witnessed the propagation of company unions. Employee Representation Plans (ERP), as they came to be known, did little in actually representing the workforce. The goal was to create a guise of collective bargaining through company-chosen leaders. In more autocratic companies, "union dues" were demanded of employees for their "participation" in the ERPs. In turn, the compulsory dues were used to offset the cost of maintaining the social programs offered under welfare capitalism. Seldom did ERPs promote the interests of workers or protect their rights on the factory floors.

The assault on labor throughout the Roaring Twenties also hindered the economic progress of America's working class. Even though wages in the 1920s were higher than the prewar era, wages for many workers began to level off and stagnate by 1923. Many American workers struggled to find security and provide for themselves and their loved ones' basic needs. According to one estimate, as much as 40 percent of the population was poor. Poverty proved to be a particularly difficult problem for low-wage, unskilled workers in mass production industries. Few indulged in the so-called affluence of the era. What material success they enjoyed was acquired through the availability of credit and finance purchasing plans that permitted workers to live beyond their means and enjoy the growing consumerism of the 1920s. In all, it was a false sense of prosperity. The simple truth was that the so-called Era of Prosperity eluded most American workers during the decade. Worse, after the crash, workers with little savings quickly found themselves susceptible to the calamities of the Great Depression. Spiraling unemployment and massive wage cuts exposed the limitations of corporate loyalty. The welfare capitalism schemes that companies trumpeted as an alternative to unionization disappeared, hastily receding into the background as employers looking to cut costs jettisoned any and all social programs. With no safety net to fall back on, conditions deteriorated rapidly for the majority of American workers in the aftermath of the stock market crash.

When Franklin Roosevelt brought forward the National Industrial Recovery Act (NIRA) in 1933, the goal was simply to "put people back to work." It was never Roosevelt's intent to spur unionization, let alone create a mass labor movement. Eschewing Herbert Hoover's laissez-faire approach of volunteerism in favor of direct action, Roosevelt harnessed the authority of the federal government to help stimulate economic development. Under the NIRA the president afforded business opportunities to essentially plan the economy by removing the threat of anti-trust violations. The belief was that by doing so, manufacturers could eliminate waste and inefficiency and retreat from the often cutthroat business practices that had plagued earlier recovery efforts. What Roosevelt proposed was not entirely unique. Woodrow Wilson through the War Industries Board encouraged a similar approach when confronting the economic demands created by World War I. The policy also bore a striking resemblance to the pro-business practices embraced by Republican administrations throughout the 1920s. The approach, however, opened the door to potential problems. One of the biggest concerns was the potential for employers to abuse the legislation and use the power proposed under the NIRA against workers and the labor movement. In previous instances when the government suspended or ignored anti-trust prosecution, manufactures seized the opportunity to cut wages, restrict economic gains, and impeded organization. Roosevelt and the authors of the NIRA recognized this potential problem. The president and his supporters also wanted to win over the AFL, believing that getting union leaders to sign on to the measure was vital for helping to ensure the success of the NIRA. Therefore, Roosevelt insisted that the NIRA include provisions to protect organized labor and the working class.

Section 7(a) of the NIRA proposed that workers be given the right to organize and engage in collective bargaining through representatives of their own choosing and free from employer coercion. The measure also tried to circumvent the proliferation of ERPs by prohibiting manufacturers from compelling workers to join a company union as a condition of employment. Furthermore, it required that employers establish maximum hours of work, minimum rates of pay, and other work conditions as approved by the president. The inclusion of Section 7(a) in the NIRA proved contentious. The National Association of Manufacturers and the US Chamber of Commerce both denounced the measure. Henry Ford was so opposed to Section 7(a) that he refused to comply with any aspect of the NIRA, the lone automotive manufacturer to do so. Missouri Senator Bennett Champ Clark, a fellow Democrat, with the backing of business, introduced amendments designed to water down the effectiveness of the legislation, preserving the prerogative of manufacturers in dealing with labor relations. Clark's amendments were defeated, but not without a bitter fight. Ultimately, New York Democrat Robert Wagner and George Norris, an aging progressive Republican from Nebraska, successfully steered the measure through the Senate. On June 16, 1933 Roosevelt signed the NIRA into law, complete with its pro-labor provisions.

Labor leaders immediately grasped the implications of Section 7(a), pouncing on the opportunity offered by the new legislation. The AFL's craft unions rebuilt its moribund organizations. The UMW sent organizers across the country. Informing coal miners that "the president wants you to organize" by 1934, the UMW saw its once depleted ranks swell to over 400,000 miners strong, an increase of over 300,000 members from its pre-NIRA days. The Amalgamated Clothing Workers' union added 60,000 names to its membership rolls, doubling its support to 120,000 members. Meanwhile the membership of the International Ladies' Garment Workers' Union (ILGWU) shot up to over 200,000 workers by 1934, strengthened by a strike in New York City where 70,000 dressmakers walked off the job believing Roosevelt wanted them to go on strike. By 1934 Section 7(a), or "Labor's Magna Carta," as some termed it, reenergized the AFL.

The AFL soon also became caught up in the excitement amid the favorable environment. Since its formation in 1886, the AFL had jealously guarded its craft union structure. Whereas member unions sometimes veered from a stringent craft structure and organized unskilled workers into their respective organizations, the AFL as a whole steadfastly refused to entertain much less sanction the idea of organizing unskilled and semi-skilled workers in the mass production industries. Even though industrial workers represented an ever-growing segment of America's workforce, the AFL tenaciously clung to its traditional craft union structure, viewing itself as the elite of the working class. Section 7(a), however, changed the playing field. With Roosevelt seeming to encourage unionization, or at the very least acknowledge the rights of the workers to organize, a unique opportunity presented itself. The AFL suddenly found itself at a crossroads, left to decide whether to change and adapt to the new environment or maintain the status quo. The man to reconcile this dilemma was the AFL president William Green.

Green intimately understood the orthodoxy of the AFL. The son of English and Welsh immigrants, he entered the coalmines in Coshocton, Ohio, at age sixteen. He soon threw himself into the union movement, becoming secretary of his local union just two years later. Green cut his teeth first in the Progressive Miners Union (PMU) and then later the UMW after it became affiliated with the PMU. The stoic Ohioan steadily ascended the ranks of the UMW, distinguishing himself as a talented and capable administrator. By 1916, Green's skills caught the attention of the AFL, where he was appointed to the union's Executive Council. Over the next eight years, the former coal miner dutifully served the AFL, building an impressive following within the craft union. When Samuel Gompers, the AFL's longtime leader died in 1924, the fifty-one-year-old Green was the consensus choice to replace him as union president.

Although Green recognized the traditional and often dogmatic craft union philosophy that permeated the AFL's hierarchy, the new president was not nearly as rigid in his own beliefs. Green's presidency, in fact, proved to be a departure from the autocratic style of Gompers. Unlike his predecessor,

Green eschewed confrontation, favoring a more collaborative approach to labor relations. Green also placed greater faith in using the political system to improve workers' conditions. This was partly due to Green's background. The new AFL president, in addition to working in the coalmines, also enjoyed a brief dalliance in politics, having served as a state senator in Ohio as well as a bureaucrat for the Wilson administration during the Great War. Most important, Green proved surprisingly receptive to industrial unionism, or at the very least seized the opportunities Roosevelt's New Deal presented the AFL.

Green recognized that the biggest obstacle to organizing the mass production industries centered on the question of jurisdiction. Determining which unions gained organizational rights over the various mass production industries was problematic on a number of fronts. First, while mass production industries relied heavily on unskilled and semi-skilled workers, they also maintained significant numbers of skilled workers. As these workers often fell into a variety of different trades, the thorny question over who should represent them was not so neatly resolved. The thinking among some AFL circles was that the workers should be divided into their respective craft organizations, a process that threatened to weaken the effectiveness of any union movement in mass production industries and potentially alienate the industry's workers. Another line of thought was that jurisdictional rights should be ceded to one of the trades. Unfortunately, this posed a problem in that unions on the losing end of the decision would strongly contest the representation of workers from their craft by another trade. The last solution was to simply organize the workers into one massive union on the basis of their industry. To all sides, however, this was no solution at all. The prospect of establishing new, stronger unions in auto, steel, and rubber industries with high employment numbers appealed to few in the AFL's hierarchy. Doing so raised the potential of new, larger unions that threatened to upset the organization's internal power structure.

The best solution to Green was to simply delay settling the jurisdictional question, at least in the short term. Under the terms of the AFL's constitution, Green and the organization's Executive Council had the authority to create Federal Labor Unions (FLU), which were effectively unions without distinction. FLUs had no direct affiliation with any of the existing unions, and instead came under the direction of the AFL. Essentially, the strategy afforded the AFL the opportunity to organize workers on the basis of their industry and avoid settling the question of jurisdictional control. However, FLUs were only temporary, a condition outlined by the AFL's constitution. For Green this was the necessary compromise. With the blessing of the AFL Executive Council, he could organize mass production workers by bringing them into FLUs. AFL leaders could decide their jurisdictional fate at a later date. The strategy proved successful, at least in the short run. By 1934, the AFL had chartered over 1,400 FLUs. The membership numbers looked even more impressive. Over one hundred thousand workers joined the FLU in the automotive industry. Another ninety thousand workers were organized into an FLU in the steel industry. Over sixty thousand workers in the rubber industries joined an AFL-sponsored FLU. Workers in industries long neglected by the labor movement were jumping at the opportunity to join the AFL. The union movement that limped into the 1930s was in the midst of a renaissance.

For all the progress of the New Deal's early years, the AFL and America's workers continued to face problems, particularly in regard to the NIRA and Section 7(a). Under the NIRA, businesses were allowed wide latitude in organizing their respective sectors of the economy and were given full discretionary power to join together and plan the economy free from anti-trust persecution. To fend off labor's opposition, Roosevelt insisted that workers be allowed to participate in the process. In theory, the code hearings were to jointly bring together workers and employers under government guidance, allowing both sides to peacefully establish standards mutually beneficial to each group. While the idea looked good on paper, there was no denying the fact that by 1934, the NIRA had failed to live up to its expectations. Employers chafed under government oversight, with many jettisoning the codes at the first sign of economic recovery. The seemingly pro-labor provisions were also a source of contention among many companies. Historically resistant to organized labor and pro-worker legislation, the NIRA and Section 7(a) proved anathema to America's business leaders. Particularly troubling for employers was the growing worker militancy that emerged following passage of the legislation.

Between 1933 and 1934, an estimated 1.5 million workers went on strike. Workers in auto and steel walked off their jobs. Longshoremen shut down the wharfs in San Francisco. In August 1934, over five hundred thousand textile workers manned picket lines in twenty states, including over one hundred thousand strikers in Massachusetts. While many of the strikes were initiated with an eye toward improving economic conditions, approximately one-third of the walkouts were organized to win union recognition, a provision supposedly guaranteed under the NIRA. Equally troubling, as the number of strikes grew, so too did the violence. In May 1934, fighting erupted in the streets of Toledo, Ohio, as over six thousand striking workers from the Electric Auto-Lite Company battled thirteen hundred members of the Ohio National Guard. Guardsmen fired into the crowd, killing two protestors. In the ensuing melee over two hundred guardsmen and strikers were injured. Just weeks later in Minneapolis, police opened fire on striking Teamsters, killing two workers and wounding sixty-seven more. Far from bringing stability to labor relations, the NIRA led to growing industrial conflict.

With labor disturbances emerging across the industrial landscape, business hostility grew for Roosevelt's NIRA. Business leaders, however, were not the only constituency upset with the legislation. Both workers and labor unions were equally frustrated over the New Deal's inadequate industrial program. The Labor Advisory Boards, intended to protect workers' interests, often failed to materialize, giving workers no voice during code hearings and allowing for code agreements to be established that negatively impacted workers. In cases where the boards were created, they were often staffed with bureaucrats who had little connection to the industry to which they were assigned or possessed no understanding of the conditions or issues facing the workers they were to represent. Steadily workers saw codes established that failed to adequately address their situations or, worse, hindered their ability to realize the fullest potential of the NIRA. For example, the code established in the automobile industry called for acknowledgement of worker seniority—a standard provision the White House wanted guaranteed in all code hearings. However, with weak and ineffective labor counsel, the Labor Advisory Board for the auto hearings allowed company officials to create loopholes that rendered the provision meaningless, permitting employers the luxury to invoke "merit" as the primary means for retaining, promoting, and hiring all personnel. With similar measures established across industries, rather than shoring up workers, the NIRA often proved a weak and ineffective voice for America's labor force.

The NIRA's structure also failed to provide a vehicle for workers to address grievances that might emerge over the codes. Without an effective police force, the legislation invited employer abuse. Companies continued to discourage employees from joining labor unions, with several firms going so far as to dismiss workers who did—despite the fact that such actions were a clear contradiction to the spirit of Section 7(a). Meanwhile, company unions flourished under the legislation. Even though Section 7(a) intended to prohibit such a development, the vague legislation and lack of oversight allowed the company-controlled organizations to grow. Although employers no longer required worker participation in such organizations, they used every means at their disposal to make it "advisable" for workers to participate. With no recourse in sight, between 1933 and 1934, the number of workers belonging to company unions more than doubled, going from 1.2 million to 2.5 million employees nationwide.

By 1935, Roosevelt's NIRA was under assault from both business and labor. The Supreme Court's Schechter decision in May declaring the measure unconstitutional was the final nail in the coffin for the controversial piece of legislation. For his part, Roosevelt came to recognize the shortcomings of the NIRA. In 1935, he turned to Senator Robert Wagner for help. Wagner, a Democrat from New York, had also realized the weaknesses in the NIRA, particularly as it related to Section 7(a). By 1934 he had already begun to prepare legislation to put teeth into the measure's weak labor provisions. At Roosevelt's urging, however, Wagner held back on his legislation. At the time Roosevelt wanted to see how the NIRA fully played out before making any changes. Finally, by 1935 the president saw the writing on the wall and gave the New York senator his blessing to bring forward the new bill. The National Labor Relations Act (NLRA), or the Wagner Act, as it came to be known, was introduced to the Senate in April 1935, eleven days before the Supreme Court took up arguments in the *Schechter* case.

Wagner had been one of Roosevelt's closest advisers in the early days of the administration, eventually going on to play a key role in crafting not only the NLRA but also the Social Security Act. The German-born immigrant came of age politically in turn-of-the-century New York City. His parents, struggling financially and disillusioned with America, returned to Germany in 1895. Wagner remained behind, eventually working his way through law school. In 1904, the twenty-seven year old was elected to the New York State Senate. He soon aligned himself with pro-labor progressives and began championing working-class causes. While in Albany, he led the fight to establish workmen's compensation legislation. Following the tragic Triangle Shirtwaist fire in 1911, Wagner steered through several pro-worker measures, including legislation calling for greater workplace safety regulation. He also played an instrumental role in passing legislation granting legal recognition to labor unions in the Empire State.

Serving in the Senate, Wagner continued to side with working-class causes, leading the fight for measures protecting and advancing the rights of workers. This philosophy carried through with the NLRA. Operating as Roosevelt's point man, the NLRA was guided by the basic principle that the federal government needed to protect workers' right to organize. Previously workers had no such rights, as industrial relations clearly tilted in favor of business. Employers were free to intimidate, punish, fire, and blacklist without recrimination anyone that associated with unions. Workers remained powerless as the legal system permitted business to dominate all aspects of labor relations. Wagner, in effect, countered this arrangement, viewing his legislation as a means to level the playing field between labor and capital. By protecting the rights of workers to organize, the New York senator hoped to craft an arrangement that permitted workers to counter the enormity and vast resources of business. Only when competing on equal terms could workers and employers effectively forge a relationship that acknowledged the rights and interests of each party.

On July 5, 1935, Roosevelt signed into law the NLRA, a far-reaching measure that significantly altered how employers conducted business with workers. Under the act, employers could no longer coerce employees from exercising their rights to unionize. They could not intimidate workers to keep them from joining a labor union, nor could they discriminate against any workers who exercised their right to organize. In addition, companies could not make financial contributions to any employee organization, a provision designed to stop the company union movement. The act also regulated the relationship between business and labor by encouraging the practice of collective bargaining. In fact, employers had a duty to bargain with workers collectively if they established a union. To ensure compliance, the Wagner Act also called for the establishment of the National Labor Relations Board (NLRB). The NLRB served as a judicial board overseeing the measure. Workers looking to establish a union could appeal to the NLRB, which would then step in and determine the exact bargaining unit, conduct a representation election to determine if the workforce wanted a union or not, and then issue an outcome of the election, free of any coercion from either employers or labor unions. Finally, employers, unions, and workers could come before the NLRB and file complaints over any perceived violation of the act. The three-member committee would then investigate the matter and issue a ruling, which both sides were compelled to abide by.

The Wagner Act sparked an immediate firestorm of controversy. Political opponents derided it as a gross expansion of federal power. Many believed the measure to be overtly pro-worker, at the expense of business and industry. Business leaders likewise voiced opposition to the act. The American Liberty League, a group of conservative businessmen and politicians, took the lead in attacking the measure. Formed in 1934 to counter Roosevelt's New Deal, the group denounced the NLRA as "socialistic" and called on businesses to openly defy the law. Employers were encouraged to seek court injunctions as a means to tie up the courts and prevent the NLRB from functioning. League resistance went on nearly two years until 1937, when the Supreme Court took up the issue in the case of the *NLRB v. Jones & Laughlin Steel Corporation.* The case originated when Jones & Laughlin Steel fired ten workers at its Aliquippa, Pennsylvania, factory for suspicion of union involvement. The NLRB declared the actions a violation of the Wagner Act and ordered Jones & Laughlin management to reinstate the men with back pay. In a 5-to-4 ruling the Supreme Court sided with the Roosevelt administration and the NLRA, declaring it constitutional and forcing Jones & Laughlin to abide by the NLRB's rulings. The decision signaled an end to the court's assault on Roosevelt's chief economic programs and solidified the government's role in protecting the rights of workers.

Just as Roosevelt's New Deal was altering the relationship between workers and the state, AFL leaders experienced a sudden crisis of will. The AFL's enthusiasm for organizing the mass production industries began to subside by 1934. William Green's initiative to bring unskilled workers into the craft union by way of the FLUs was never fully embraced by some segments of the AFL hierarchy. Many AFL leaders continued to voice strong opposition to organizing mass productions workers. The FLU union structure also evoked controversy as union leaders continued to fight over the jurisdictional rights of the new unions. Rather than avoid disagreement, Green's use of the temporary union structure acted as a lightening rod, dividing the AFL hierarchy. Meanwhile, the newly organized workers also expressed dissatisfaction over the structure. Workers in auto, steel, and rubber industries desired to organize mass production unions that represented the entire workforce. The thought of being divided into a variety of craft unions held little appeal for these workers. When they voiced their opposition, preferring instead to establish industrial unions, they encountered fierce resistance from AFL leaders. In the aircraft industry, for example, the AFL created a federal union for production workers, a workforce that had a blend of both unskilled and skilled laborers. As AFL unions representing welders, machinists, carpenters, and others tried to hash out jurisdictional claims over the industry's workforce, FLU no. 18286 made inroads into several of the leading aircraft firms, claiming to represent workers at Curtiss-Wright, Consolidate Aircraft, Boeing, Glenn Martin, and Sikorsky, to name a few. As the FLU grew, local leaders looked to turn the temporary organization into a national union representing all aircraft workers, leading to the formation of the Aeronautical Workers Union (AWU) in late 1933. AFL leaders quickly pushed back, stripping the union of all financial and organizational support, while working behind the scenes with employers and workers to undermine the effectiveness of the new union. The AFL's opposition ultimately doomed the AWU, which existed only on paper by late 1934.

Equally worrisome to AFL officials was the growing working-class militancy that arose in the wake of the NIRA. Historically, the AFL was not one to shy away from confrontation. However, the 1934 strike wave was different. The sheer enormity of the strikes troubled AFL officials, particularly as the number of violent episodes escalated. In some AFL quarters there existed a belief that the unorganized masses were not only "unorganizeable" but also prone to violence. The strike wave of 1934 only confirmed these fears, engendering concerns that the violent outbursts would tarnish the AFL's reputation as a responsible union in the valuable arena of public opinion. Others expressed misgivings over the practicality of the walkouts. Green believed the FLUs were too weak, lacking both the resources and leadership needed to sustain the strikes. The strikes, he feared, only served to jeopardize the AFL's organizing efforts. Still, the most troubling concern for the AFL by far centered on the strikers' emerging leaders. A group of young, militant, and increasingly radical leaders surfaced at the head of the movement. In April 1934, the nearly six thousand striking workers at the Electric Auto-Lite plant in Toledo, Ohio, were lead by the Dutch-born minister A. J. Muste, a noted pacifist and Marxist whose newly established American Workers' Party searched to find an American approach to Marxism. The longshoremen strike that erupted on the San Francisco docks in May 1934 and shut down the city's waterfront was led by Harry Bridges, a thirty-three-year-old Australian-born labor leader who was a former member of the Industrial Workers of the World and current member of the Communist Party of the United States. The Teamster strike that engulfed Minneapolis and came on the heels of the longshoremen's strike just one week later was led by the Dunne brothers (Ray, Miles, and Grant) and Farrell Dobbs, members of the Communist League of America. With the likes of Muste, Bridges, and the Dunne brothers leading the way, the old, traditionally conservative AFL leadership feared risking its reputation by associating with such radicals.

When the AFL gathered for its annual convention in San Francisco in October 1934, an unsettling pall cast a shadow over the union. The unnerving events of the previous year led many within the union's hierarchy to reevaluate Green and the AFL's policies. Yet, just as purists wanted to retreat back to the comfort of the AFL's traditional craft approach, there were those who desired to break from the past and aggressively chart a new path for the organization. Chief among the reformers was John L. Lewis. Lewis was born in 1880 in Cleveland, Iowa, the son of Welsh immigrants. At age fifteen the future labor leader followed in the footsteps of his father, finding work in the coalmines of central Illinois. Though Lewis spent most of his life associated with the sooty black rock, he turned to the occupation grudgingly, trying his hand at a variety of jobs including farming, construction, storeowner, local politics, and even the theater, all in an effort to escape his predestined fate. After each failure, however, Lewis found himself back in the mines digging coal.

In 1906, Lewis joined the UMW, a move that transformed his life. That same year he was elected local delegate to the UMW's national convention, and three years later was chosen as president of his local union. Steadily, Lewis rose through the ranks of the union, going from field organizer for the AFL to statistician, and eventually to UMW president in 1920. In terms of personality there were few who were Lewis's equal. Bombastic, combative, despotic, vindictive, and egoistical are all adjectives that adequately describe Lewis's temperament. In 1940, for example, according to several accounts, when Roosevelt shunned the union leader in choosing his vice presidential running mate, Lewis openly challenged Roosevelt, calling on American voters to oust the two-term president. He went so far as to inform the public across the nation's radio airwaves that should they reelect Roosevelt, Lewis would interpret it as a sign that they opposed his leadership of the CIO and would resign his position. When Roosevelt won the third term, true to his word Lewis quit his post, taking with him valuable organizers and pulling out UMW resources from the CIO in an effort to destroy the union he had worked so hard to form only five years earlier. Still, despite such pettiness, Lewis was a visionary who possessed the foresight to see the changing times afforded to the American worker and the labor movement by the Roosevelt administration. And more than any other AFL leader, he looked to seize those opportunities.

Lewis came to the AFL's convention in San Francisco resolute in his determination to build on the momentum the union enjoyed in the months after passage of the NIRA. Where other union leaders saw radicals and chaotic working-class violence, Lewis saw opportunity. He extracted from the AFL's hierarchy a pledge embracing industrial unionism. Lewis's vision, a drastic turn for the conservative craft union, called for the union to begin organizing in earnest semi-skilled and unskilled workers in mass production industries such as steel, automobile, and rubber. Despite the pledge, however, the campaign never began. The AFL's Old Guard continued to harbor deep misgivings over the plan. In January, the union's Executive Council rejected a massive organizing drive in steel. Green, meanwhile, refused to press the leadership. Instead, the AFL president did nothing, declining to provide leadership and resources for the organizing drive, thus dooming the campaign before it began. The AFL's reticence infuriated Lewis. Compounding his anger, when the AFL came together in November 1935 at its convention in Atlantic City, the union's leadership dismissed its failure to act on the San Francisco pledge, attributing it to poor timing given the Supreme Court's decision striking down the NIRA in May.

Lewis was not buying the AFL's excuses. In the wake of his showdown with Big Bill Hutchinson, a symbol of the craft union's stagnant ways, Lewis mobilized his supporters. After the conclusion of the convention, Lewis brought together the heads of seven AFL unions: Sidney Hillman (Amalgamated Clothing Workers' of America), Charles Howard (International Typographical Union), David Dubinsky (International Ladies' Garment Workers' Union), Thomas McMahon (United Textile Workers' Union), John Sheridan (Mine, Mill, and Smelter Workers' Union), Harvey Fremming (Oil Workers Union), and Max Zaritsky (Hatters, Cap, and Millinery Workers). Together, the men forged plans to carry out their own organizing drive. To coordinate their efforts they established the Committee for Industrial Organizations (CIO). Lewis went to great lengths to make clear that the CIO was not a new or separate union, nor were the eight unions involved in the group leaving the AFL. Rather, as Lewis explained, they continued to remain part of the AFL. The CIO would be operated as an appendage of the AFL, serving as an organizing committee under the auspices of the eight craft unions committed to taking advantage of the New Deal's pro-labor atmosphere. Still, what Lewis was really doing was splitting hairs, and the former coal miner recognized as much. The decision to keep the CIO as part of the AFL was purely pragmatic, done to appease several of the dissident union leaders who were not prepared to abandon the old craft union. Lewis, in fact, had made an intellectual break with the AFL, resigning from the federation two weeks after the boardwalk gathering, and eventually pulling out the UMW from the AFL months later. Even so, Lewis recognized that the other union heads were not ready for such drastic action. Though they willingly supported industrial unionism and the CIO initiative, they were not prepared to jump ship and forge a new union movement. AFL leaders, however, refused to accept that distinction. In their eyes, Lewis and his followers were not only defying the AFL, but they were also establishing a rival organization, a cardinal sin that ultimately led the craft union's Executive Council to expel the unions involved with the CIO in 1938. With the expulsion the CIO became the Congress of Industrial Organizations, officially marking its break from the AFL.

Lewis represented the driving force behind the CIO. He not only provided the inspiration for the group, but he and the UMW were also the very lifeblood of the CIO in its early years. Lewis threw all the resources of his miners' union behind the CIO, providing the nascent industrial union with financial support, organizers, and leadership. He formulated plans for aggressive organizing campaigns in auto, rubber, radio, and steel industries. Lewis clearly looked to make a mark for the CIO, talking of plans to organize all the major mass production industries. In Lewis's estimation, however, one industry stood head and shoulders above the rest, and that industry was steel. For Lewis, the decision to concentrate CIO organizing activities on the steel industry was partly driven by self-interest. The steel industry, which controlled and operated its own coalfields, refused to deal with the UMW. With the so-called captive mines remaining nonunion, other coal operators resisted the efforts of Lewis and the UMW to address working conditions, arguing that any concessions made to the miners' union provided a competitive advantage for the steel industry. As long as the steel industry and the captive mines remained nonunion, Lewis faced obstruction in the coal industry. Therefore, in organizing steel, and by extension the captive mines, Lewis hoped to open up opportunities for his union. Yet there was more to Lewis's strategy than simply advancing his own union's agenda.

John Lewis recognized the psychological symbol of the steel industry. Steel towered over America's urban, industrial landscape. Dating back to the days of Andrew Carnegie and J. P. Morgan, the steel industry cultivated a reputation as a pioneer, a driving force behind the nation's industrial revolution—and as one of the most powerful and ruthless anti-union industries. Steel companies turned to intimidation, private police forces, violence, and eventually company unions, all as a means to hinder the growth of organized labor within their factory gates. Workers, meanwhile, labored in dangerous and unsafe conditions, working long hours for low pay. Failed union efforts at Homestead in 1892, US Steel in 1901, and an abortive national steel strike in 1919, created an aura of invincibility for steel manufacturers. Steel was the Holy Grail for the American labor movement, and Lewis recognized as much. It was a big gamble for Lewis and the CIO. But with big risks came big rewards, and Lewis knew if the CIO found victory in steel, it would set the tone for the CIO and the whole of the labor movement. So, in typical fashion, Lewis threw himself fully into organizing steel.

In June 1936, Lewis announced the formation of the Steel Workers' Organizing Campaign (SWOC), the vehicle by which the CIO intended to organize the steel mills. To head the campaign Lewis tabbed his old friend and UMW vice president Phillip Murray. He provided the Scottish-born coal miner with a stable of thirty-six organizers, soon to expand to two hundred, and an operating budget of $500,000. Now all Murray had to do was deliver the roughly four hundred thousand steelworkers scattered across the United States to the CIO. While SWOC organizers spanned out across steel mills in Pittsburgh, Chicago, Youngstown, and Buffalo, Lewis and the CIO leaders waited with baited breath for news of success. Oddly, the first significant CIO victory did not come in steel. Instead, it came in the automotive industry.

Wyndham Mortimer and a handful of other union organizers made their way to General Motors in Flint, Michigan, in summer 1936. The men represented the United Automobile Workers' Union (UAW). Formed in 1935, the UAW was an outgrowth of the AFL's federal labor union policy. Beginning in 1933, the AFL organized autoworkers into FLUs. The efforts floundered under the weight of poor national leadership and open resistance from auto manufacturers. By 1934, the FLU initiative failed to produce much beyond a handful of locals in such locations as Cleveland, Toledo, and Kansas City. Detroit and the Big Three automotive manufacturers—Ford, General Motors, and Chrysler—remained virtually untouched by the AFL's organizing efforts. Still, within the FLUs a group of young, defiant, and impatient leaders were emerging. In August 1935, determined to see an independent, industrial union for automobile workers, they convinced William Green and the AFL to charter the UAW, an organization separated from the existing craft organizations. The marriage between the two organizations never went smoothly. AFL leaders continued to voice displeasure over the auto union's infringement on the jurisdictional rights of several craft unions that laid claims to segments of the automotive workforce. They also expressed concern over the divisive and factional leadership emerging within the UAW, seeing the organization as incapable of running its own affairs. Meanwhile, UAW leaders balked at what they saw as obstruction on the part of the AFL and its refusal to sanction a nationwide organizing campaign in the auto industry. In May 1936, frustrations boiled over when UAW abandoned the AFL and took up with the upstart CIO.

Mortimer was a central figure in the UAW's formation. A fifty-two-year-old autoworker from Cleveland, Mortimer was one of the most experienced UAW officials, serving as the auto union's vice president. Committed to industrial unionism, Mortimer fought hard for UAW independence. Forceful, determined, and principled, he endeared himself to workers. Drawing heavily on his experience working in the coal, steel, railroad, and auto industries, Mortimer could relate to workers on a personal level. In 1936, after agreeing to head the General Motors organizing campaign, Mortimer realized the formidable obstacles facing the UAW. Though a local UAW had been chartered in Flint, it had little more than a nominal presence at the auto giant and lacked any real power. Mortimer discovered that of the approximately forty-five thousand workers in GM's Flint facilities, only about one hundred workers belonged to the UAW. The lack of internal support spoke to auto union's weak and tenuous presence. However, it also spoke to the domineering influence exercised by General Motors. The auto manufacturer controlled Flint with an iron fist. Company spies circulated freely in and out of the factory gates reporting any suspicious activity to management. Workers deemed a potential threat were dismissed immediately. Outsiders to Flint were cast under of a web of suspicion and subjected to intimidation and violence. General Motors operated with impunity as city officials willingly did the bidding of the auto company. The net effect produced an environment of fear in which workers lived and worked under the ever-watchful eye of GM. Mortimer, facing such daunting circumstances, concluded quickly that organizing needed to be done discreetly. Eschewing open meetings and mass leafleting outside the factory gates, Mortimer and UAW organizers instead visited workers at their homes late in the evening. With a tap on the window or a knock on a back alley door, they quietly introduced themselves to the GM workers, never meeting with more than a small handful of employees at a time and always taking great care to avoid detection from company spies. Steadily, the UAW built a base within the sprawling Flint factories, a fact that did not go unnoticed by company officials.

In late December, responding to the UAW's efforts, General Motors' management decided to move the huge dies used for making its car bodies out of its Fisher no. 1 factory and place them in factories where the auto union had less support. If successful, the move threatened to severely sap the UAW's influence by permitting the company to move its production work elsewhere. Timing of the news proved problematic for the UAW. Even though union organizers had started formulating plans for a strike, targeting Fisher no. 1, they were not prepared for a showdown. Also, they feared that an early walkout before January might put at risk the workers' year-end production bonuses, money workers counted on to help get them through the lean winter months when auto production slowed down. However, faced with GM's threat to move out the dies, UAW leaders rushed into action. The next day, shortly after lunch, workers at Fisher no. 1 launched a sit-down strike. They took possession of the factory, thus preventing GM from removing the dies, and with them the workers' jobs. The sit-down tactic used by the Flint workers was not altogether new. The Industrial Workers of the World first utilized it in 1906 in its battle with General Electric, taking control of the company's Schenectady, New York, factory for ten days. European unionists also found varying degrees of success with the method in the 1920s. Even autoworkers in Cleveland and Toledo turned to sit-down strikes as recently as 1934 and 1935. Still, while the strategy was used before, previous episodes failed to reach the intensity of what unfolded during the Flint sit-down.

Workers quickly mobilized within the factory, electing committees to oversee such activities as security, exercise, and even entertainment. Strikers established strict rules for discipline, determined to ensure that no damage was done to company property. Outside the factory Bob Travis, the Reuther brothers (Walter, Victor, and Roy), and other UAW officials sprung into action, soliciting donations to help feed and supply the sit-downers. Pickets were staged outside the gates, as the UAW called on GM workers, family members, and local supporters to take up the cause. As expected, GM officials responded angrily, determined to dislodge the protestors. Heat to the factory was turned off in an effort to freeze out the strikers. Local newspapers, openly sympathetic to GM, viciously attacked the UAW in the press, denouncing the sit-down as the work of communists and radicals and a threat to private property. And behind the scenes company officials worked diligently to extricate the strikers. In January, GM lawyers won a court order, calling for the sit-downers to leave the premises. However, UAW officials discovered that the judge issuing the order was actually a GM stockholder, holding shares valued at an estimated $200,000, thus forcing the order to be vacated because of the obvious conflict of interest. Frustrated by the lack of success, GM looked to break the stalemate. On the morning of January 11, Flint police stormed the factory in an attempt to remove the sit-downers. Tear gas was launched into the facility. Local bystanders, in a show of support, quickly came to the sit-downers' aid, smashing factory windows to allow the gas to escape. When patrolmen charged the factory, strikers repelled the assault, using fire hoses and hurling bolts, screws, and other car parts from the factory rooftops. After six hours and three failed assaults, local authorities retreated, giving victory to the UAW and the sit-downers in what came to be known as the "Battle of Running Bulls."

As the confrontation between General Motors and the UAW played out, both the federal and state government chose not to intervene, instead insisting that the parties resolve the matter on their own. GM officials refused to negotiate, however, leading the sit-down to drag on through January. On February 1, seeking to compel GM officials to the bargaining table, the UAW struck at a second Flint factory. Seeing no end in sight, GM finally agreed to negotiate, meeting with John Lewis and a delegation of UAW and CIO officials. A settlement was finally reached ten days later. After forty-two days in the Flint factory, strikers emerged victorious. GM agreed to recognize the UAW as the exclusive bargaining agent for its workers for a period of six months. It also agreed that the workers who participated in the sit-down would not be subject to retaliation.

On the surface, the settlement did not look significant. The document contained no references to wages, hours of work, or even work conditions. In fact, the agreement seemed to offer little in the way of immediate day-to-day improvements for GM workers. However, in terms of the bigger picture, the agreement was momentous. First, the accord with GM gave legitimacy to the UAW and, by extension, the CIO. Membership shot up in the auto union as workers saw an organization that could stand up for its members and defeat the strongest of corporations. Second, the Flint sit-down served as a catalyst to empower the working class. In the days, weeks, and months that followed, workers across the nation turned to the sit-down as a means to gain control over their work lives. Coffin makers, rubber workers, and textile workers all staged sit-downs following the Flint strike. Waitresses at Woolworth's in Detroit and de Met's Tea Room in Chicago sat down and refused to serve customers. Garbage workers in Amsterdam, New York, staged protests sitting in their trucks. By one estimate as many as four hundred thousand workers staged some 477 sit-down strikes in the wake of Flint. In Chicago, over 60 sit-ins took place in March alone. And in perhaps the strangest incident, a housewife in Bloomington, Indiana, staged her own sit-in protest against her husband. With the victory in Flint, workers found the strength and inspiration to stand up for themselves. Still, all that paled in comparison to what followed.

On March 2, 1937, less than three weeks after the conclusion of the UAW-GM settlement, John Lewis went on the nation's airwaves and made a stunning announcement. Lewis informed listeners he had personally concluded an agreement with Myron Taylor of US Steel, in which the steel giant agreed to recognize SWOC as the bargaining agent for its workers. The agreement also brought US Steel workers a significant wage increase, an eight-hour day and forty-hour workweek, seniority rights for workers, and a grievance procedure to settle disputes between workers and the company. In less than one month, the CIO accomplished what AFL leaders once deemed impossible, toppling two of the largest anti-union citadels in the nation. Success at General Motors and US Steel quickly propelled the upstart industrial organization to the forefront of the labor movement. Membership in the CIO soared; the industrial union claimed over four million members by the time of its national convention in October 1937. Yet in spite of the union's spectacular success, problems persisted.

Many employers continued to resist Roosevelt's NLRA, opposing unionization at their factories whether it came through the CIO or the AFL. The most visible signs of employer resistance came from the "Little Steel" companies, a term referring to the smaller, nonunion steel manufacturers. When Myron Taylor signed his historic agreement with Lewis and SWOC, the Little Steel companies dug in and fiercely refused to follow the lead of US Steel. Perhaps no one symbolized the vitriolic opposition to unionization among the Little Steel companies more than Tom Girdler. The head of Republic Steel, Girdler openly loathed organized labor. He once reportedly quipped that he would rather quit steel and grow apples than sign a labor contract with the CIO and SWOC. Faced with such determined opposition, nearly ninety thousand workers at four of the principal Little Steel companies across eight states—Republic Steel, Bethlehem Steel, Youngstown Sheet and Tube, and Inland Steel—went on strike in May 1937. The strikers demanded better wages, improved work conditions, and recognition of SWOC as there bargaining agent. Company officials, however, refused to even meet with workers, much less negotiate. Violent confrontations began almost immediately. In South Chicago on May 30, just four days after the start of the strike, police attacked Republic Steel workers as they approached the factory gates. When the battle ended, ten protestors lay dead from gunshot wounds, including several who were shot in the back. Another one hundred suffered injuries from being beaten by police clubs. Three weeks later, a second confrontation erupted, this time at the Youngstown Sheet and Tube Company in Ohio. The melee resulted in the death of two strikers. Facing such brutal opposition, the strike eventually ended without resolution. Demoralized and defeated, workers slowly returned to the mills in July. Success would eventually be theirs, however. In 1938 the NLRB ruled that the Little Steel companies had violated the NLRA. The companies were ordered to reinstate all workers who had been fired for their participation in the walkout. The board also ordered a union representation election to be held at the factories. However, in a final act of defiance, the Little Steel companies delayed compliance with the NLRB decision until 1942, when they finally recognized the union and extended collective bargaining rights to its workers.

In December 1937, a United States Senate Subcommittee chaired by Wisconsin Senator Robert La Follette investigated the state of labor relations between 1933 and 1937. What the hearing revealed was shocking. According to committee reports, during the five-year period over 2,500 companies relied on the use of labor spies, including the Pinkerton Detective Agency and the Williams Burns Detective Agency, to infiltrate labor organizations. Employers spent nearly $10 million for various anti-union activities, including the use of strikebreakers and munitions to combat labor unions. The findings from the Little Steel strike were even more revealing. For the strike, Youngstown Sheet and Tube purchased 8 machine guns, 369 rifles, 190 shotguns, and 450 revolvers to go with over 9,000 rounds of ammunition. It also secured 109 gas guns with 3,000 rounds of tear gas ammunition. Republic Steel purchased similar equipment and spent $80,000 on tear and sickening gas. The La Follette Committee revealed the depth of hostility employers continued to harbor toward labor during the "pro-labor" Roosevelt years.

As disturbing as the findings of the La Follette Committee were, they spoke to a bygone era of labor relations. The days of open, industrial warfare were ending, a throwback to the early years of industrialization. Roosevelt's New Deal legislation, with its emphasis on protecting the rights of the working class and the ensuing rise of the CIO, brought industrial America into a new era that emphasized collective bargaining. Sensing the writing on the wall, even the American Federation of Labor began to change, finally abandoning its narrow craft union orientation in favor of an industrial approach. The shift proved to be a boon for American workers. Unskilled industrial workers, long ignored by the labor movement, now enjoyed the benefits of protection. Now with two labor organizations openly courting mass production workers, unionization grew significantly. By 1940 union membership in the United States reached nearly nine million workers, accounting for approximately 27 percent of the industrial workforce. Steadily conditions improved and wages grew, expanding to include all ranks of society, regardless of class, race, or gender. By the eve of World War II, unionization and collective bargaining were firmly ensconced in America. The war contributed to the continued growth of labor, further improving the economic status of the American working class. By the end of World War II, the position of labor was so solidified that even in the face of a postwar anti-union assault, organized labor was strong enough to persevere. The gains made during the 1930s permitted the working class to gradually make the transition into America's middle class.

The 1930s also brought a greater cohesiveness to the American working class. Unlike European nations, the working class in America was divided. Fiercely contested racial, gender, ethnic, geographic, and even occupational differences exacerbated the divisions separating America's working class. The divisions continued well beyond the 1930s and remain evident even today. In the 1930s, however, cultural ties, along with common economic experiences, produced a cohesion that transcended the various divisions separating the working class. The shift was perhaps most evident in America's ethnic communities.

Beginning in the late nineteenth century a tremendous surge of immigration occurred in America. The wave was the product of rapidly declining conditions in Europe and improving economic opportunities in the United States—opportunities produced by the nation's rapid industrialization. Unlike previous eras of immigration, these refugees came largely from eastern and southern Europe, regions of the world to which Americans had little cultural connection or familiarity. The Italians, Poles, Russians, Greeks, Hungarians, and other "new immigrants" stood out from the native-born population in language, customs, and in some cases religion. Many American citizens looked at these strangers with revulsion, seeing their differences as signs of inferiority. For the immigrants, life in the United States represented an alien experience that few could comprehend. Coming from impoverished peasant villages, the sheer size of America's urban landscape and the enormity of the industrial edifices in which they labored bore little connection to their previous lives. With few appreciable skills to transfer to America's budding industrial economy, they typically found low-wage, unskilled work in the many factories popping up across the nation. Poverty was the one constant in their experience connecting them to the old world from which they came.

As the new immigrants settled in America, one of the ways in which they coped with changing conditions was to established ethnic enclaves. "Little Italys" sprang up in New York City, Buffalo, Cleveland, Boston's

North End, and even Altoona, Pennsylvania, to name just a few cities. Pittsburgh had a "Polish Hill," Brooklyn had "Little Poland," and Detroit boasted a "Poletown." Everywhere the new immigrants went they tended to settle in communities organized along their respective ethnic lines. These communities served a multitude of purposes for America's new inhabitants. First and foremost, they offered immigrants a degree of familiarity, helping to ease their transition to the United States. In these ethnic communities immigrants found people who spoke their language and shared their customs. The enclaves offered comfort for many trying to make sense of their strange new environment. Second, the communities allowed immigrants a way of maintaining their ethnic heritage and identities. Though they moved to America in search of jobs and freedom, most resisted full-scale assimilation, instead looking to preserve their ethnic culture and values. They established schools to instill their traditions and customs in younger generations. Neighborhood stores and shops afforded shoppers a recognizable face and a familiar dialect and allowed customers to buy native foods prepared in traditional ways. The multitude of mutual aid societies, fraternal organizations, and communal clubs provided social outlets, drawing together immigrants and their families and permitting them to celebrate cultural holidays and festivals as communities. Finally, ethnic neighborhoods provided a means of self-preservation. To the native-born population, the waves of new immigrants flooding America's shores after 1890 were viewed with a mixture of revulsion and disdain. Convinced that immigrants contributed to America's deteriorating urban conditions, politicians, civic leaders, and journalists tried to shut the nation's doors to immigration. Immigration restriction laws were passed in 1921 and again in 1924 to discourage and exclude eastern and southern European transplants from entering the land of liberty. Labor unions, particularly the AFL, discouraged affiliates from organizing immigrants, convinced the low-wage ethnic workers threatened unionization and ultimately the well-being of the working class. In this environment, ethnic communities served as a sanctuary for residents, an escape from the unreceptive and often antagonistic society in which they moved.

The ethnic enclaves enabled residents to wall themselves off from their new urban settings, if only temporarily, and create communities that suited their needs. Collective identities were forged in these neighborhoods along ethnic lines, and most immigrants continued to cling tenaciously to these identities, proudly viewing themselves as Poles, Russians, Greeks, Italians, or other ethnicities. Gradually, however, they found themselves unable to resist the tide of Americanization. Steadily, American culture made inroads into ethnic communities, gaining momentum among second and third generations that had little familiarity or connection to their family's place of origin.

Thomas Bell's autobiographical novel *Out of This Furnace* describes America's rapidly changing ethnic environment. Written in 1941, it vividly illustrates the evolution occurring within immigrant communities from the late nineteenth century to the thirties by looking at the lives of three generations of Slovak immigrants. The novel begins with the story of Djuro Kracha, a Slovak who travels from Austria-Hungary to the United States in 1881. Kracha eventually finds work in the steel mills of Braddock, Pennsylvania. Life in the mills is hard and marked by low wages, dangerous conditions, and irregular work. Yet Kracha does not see unionization as a means to improve his life. He has little interest in the comings and goings of the labor movement. When the Homestead Steel strike unfolds in 1892, he is barely aware of it. Rather than join the picket line, Kracha sees little sense in the walkout and views the affair as a day of lost work and wages. Kracha's world revolves around his close-knit ethnic community, which offers friendship, camaraderie, and a means of survival. The ethnic enclave offers support and stability in Kracha's otherwise tumultuous life.

As the novel progresses, the transition from Slovak to American slowly begins in Kracha's family. His daughter Mary settles down and marries a fellow "Hunky," Mike Dobrejcak. Mike, like Kracha, comes from Slovakia and embraces all that America has to offer. Though he remains rooted in the ethnic community, Mike learns to speak English, participates in the political process, and aspires to earn his citizenship. The effects of Americanization are also evident in Mary's life. Unlike Kracha, who takes a wife out of necessity, Mary and Mike's relationship is based on love. Similarly, Bell depicts the changing ethnic community; this younger generation interacts more and more with the "outside" American world. Their ties to the ethnic enclave are not as entrenched. Yet, while Bell shows the positive changes occurring in the young couple's life, the novel also presents the perils facing low-wage ethnic workers. For all the hope Mike pins on his new country, he grows increasingly frustrated by his inability to provide for his family and by the need to call on Mary to work. Helplessness and anger overcome Mike, who eventually dies inside the steel mill, the victim of an industrial accident that was due to the company's refusal to improve dangerous working conditions. With the family imperiled and the ethnic community no longer the cohesive unit it once was, Mary is forced to live on the fringes of society until her family is eventually broken up.

The transformation in Kracha's family from Slovak to American is complete by the third generation. Mike and Mary's son Dobie is contrasted with the elderly Kracha. Whereas Kracha continues to hang on to his ethnic ways and Mary struggles to find her identity in a mixed American and Slovak world, Dobie is fully American. Beyond the Dobrejcak last name, there is little that remains ethnic in Dobie's identity. The Slovak world of Kracha is completely lost on Dobie, except for the old stories and tales he hears from his grandfather. Indeed, Dobie has no roots in the old ethnic community, a fact accentuated by his decision to leave Braddock to find employment in Detroit. Having witnessed the hardships endured by Kracha and his father, Dobie endeavors to gain control over his life. However, unlike his ancestors, the young Dobrejcak does not find solace in an extended ethnic community. Instead, Dobie finds support and strength in a resurgent union movement in the 1930s. Not content to be a victim, Dobie sees the union as the means to improve his lifestyle and provide stability for him and his soon to be family. Unlike Kracha, Mike, and Mary, Dobie's identity is working class, rooted in a union movement rather than an ethnic community.

The changes in the life of Thomas Bell's characters occurred from the late nineteenth century into the 1930s. Though workers still maintained their ethnic, racial, and gender identities, the rigidness of these identities was lessening by the 1930s. In their place a new working-class unity was forged by the common experience of the economic upheaval of the Great Depression. The industrial union movement beginning with the CIO and eventually encompassing the AFL reoriented the working class away from their old insular identities. And whereas other organizations had tried before, and failed, a degree of success was found during the 1930s. Drawn together unlike never before by a common set of circumstances, workers started to forge a collective working-class identity. The Depression offered a degree of unity that crossed divisions once separating workers. Franklin Roosevelt and his New Deal agenda further solidified the emerging identity, crafting a unified political base around America's working class by the end of the decade. Still, the working-class identity of the 1930s would prove short lived. As increasing numbers of workers made their way into the middle class after World War II, riding the wave of pro-labor policies and pro-worker economic programs established by the union movement, the unity that brought workers together began to collapse. Far from lasting, the working-class identity of the 1930s lacked significant staying power and was replaced by a new middle-class identity that at times found itself in conflict with the very values and policies emanating from the Great Depression Era.

Suggested Readings

Irving Bernstein's *The Turbulent Years: A History of the American Worker, 1933–1941* (Boston: Houghton Mifflin, 1970), remains one of the most detailed and readable accounts of labor relations in the 1930s. Robert Zeiger's *The CIO, 1933–1935* (Chapel Hill: University of North Carolina Press, 1997), provides a thorough examination of the history of the industrial union movement in the 1930s. *John L. Lewis: A Biography* (Chicago: University of Illinois Press, 1986), by Melvyn Dubofsky and Warren Van Tine, offers the most comprehensive study of the controversial CIO leader. Henry Kraus, *The Many and the Few: A Chronicle of the Dynamic Auto Workers* (Chicago: University of Illinois, 1947) gives readers a detailed firsthand account of the formation of the UAW and the Flint sit-down strike. Lisabeth Cohen, *Making a New Deal: Industrial Workers in Chicago, 1919–1939* (New York: Cambridge University Press, 1990), is an insightful examination of the transformations occurring in working-class communities with the rise of Franklin Roosevelt and the New Deal.

7

Gender

"Have You Met Miss Jones?"
—Joy Hodges and Austin Marshall, 1937

AMELIA EARHART was one of the most famous and recognizable women of the 1930s, perhaps second only to Eleanor Roosevelt in notoriety. Internationally renowned, Earhart had a positive attitude and an intrepid spirit that came to the forefront during her seventeen-year career as a pilot. In the twenties Earhart carved out a reputation as a trailblazer. The press took to calling her "Lady Lindy" after she served as a crewmember on a successful transatlantic flight in 1928, an event that earned her the distinction of being the first woman to fly across the Atlantic Ocean. Trading on her sudden fame, Earhart quickly became a media darling, publishing books and articles on aviation, giving lectures, and serving as a spokesperson for a variety of consumer products ranging from luggage to women's sportswear to Lucky Strike cigarettes. Earhart's stature continued to grow as the decade wore on. So too did her aviation exploits as she set several speed records in competitive women's air racing. By the 1930s, "The Queen of the Air," as the United Press dubbed her, was the most noted woman pilot in the world, a reputation that was cemented when she became the first person to fly solo across the Atlantic and back in 1932. Three years later, Earhart became the first person to fly from Honolulu, Hawaii, to Oakland, California. She followed up the achievement by completing the first nonstop flight from Mexico City to Newark, New Jersey, just four months later.

Earhart's aviation exploits earned her celebrity around the globe. She received the Gold Medal of the National Geographic Society, the Cross of Knight of the Legion of Honor from the French government, and the Distinguished Flying Cross from the United States Congress—the first woman to do so. She also became a visiting faculty member in the Department of Aeronautics at Purdue University. Yet for all her accomplishments, Earhart may be remembered more for her epic end than for her skill and achievement. On June 1, 1937, Earhart took to the air in pursuit of another daring adventure. The goal this time was to circumnavigate the planet. With the navigator Fred Noonan by her side, the pair left Miami, Florida, and headed east. Over the course of the next four weeks the two flew more than 22,000 miles, crossing South America, Africa, India, and Southeast Asia. On July 2, Earhart and Noonan departed from Lae, New Guinea, on the last leg of their journey. However, the two never reached their destination. They vanished somewhere along the equatorial line near Howland Island in the central Pacific.

Earhart's life symbolizes a broad shift in traditional gender roles that emerged in the 1920s as women lifted their hemlines and rejected the conservative values and morals of the Victorian era. The Great Depression would further test gender boundaries as the economic calamities of the thirties called on women to take on new roles in their homes and communities. But women were not the only ones who found their identities transformed by the thirties. The Depression also altered men's conventional identities as they struggled with the challenges posed by losing the one thing that had defined them—their jobs. Men sought satisfaction outside of work by reconnecting with their identities as fathers and the expanding definitions of masculinity. Thus both men and women would spend the 1930s testing and revising the definitions of the terms "man" and "woman." These changes were not always welcomed or embraced. Yet they set in motion important social, cultural, economic, and political changes that continued well beyond the thirties.

The study of home life exposes the hidden lives of women and reveals greater depth in men's experiences. When unemployment hit middle-class families, the husband's world changed radically, but women's work continued more or less undeterred. The Depression impacted families across the board. Marriage, divorce, and birth rates all dropped dramatically after the stock market crash and would not begin to rise again until after 1934. By 1938, as many as 1.5 million couples nationwide were estimated to have postponed marriage. Contraception was more widely available than it had been previously, and though illegal, abortion was tolerated as an alternative to increasing family size. Reports from marriage counselors from the time show that couples also prevented pregnancy by avoiding intimacy. As a consequence of these trends, birth rates fell below replacement levels for the first time in American history. They would not drop to Depression Era levels again until the oil crisis of the 1970s and the 2007–2009 great recession.

Many men could not handle the psychological impact of their changing circumstances. In a 1940 survey, 1.5 million women said their husbands abandoned them. These were not divorces. Some men left to search for work, but many men simply walked out on their families and never returned. Those that did stay were often required to do domestic chores such as sewing, cooking, and housecleaning. "Men's work," which had become increasingly linked with business and industry prior to the stock market crash, did not prepare them for isolating, thankless, and unpaid domestic work. The men who could not accept a role reversal in their homes found it devastating to their already bruised egos. In *Middletown in Transition: A Study in Cultural Conflicts* (1937), the sociologists Robert and Helen Lynd described one man at the breaking point. This man found that "time hung on his hands. In the morning, before she left for work, his wife told him to make the beds. The children, seeing him in this new role, sometimes laughed at him. I came upon a man who, making the beds one day, was so enraged by his son's laughter that he had nearly killed the child." Though rare, some men took to their new role with stoic determination. There are even a few accounts of men who enjoyed the change of pace at home as they watched their wives assume the role of breadwinner.

Certainly some men have always participated in domestic chores and caregiving; however, there is very little data on how many men contributed to housework, what kind of housework they did, and how much time they spent on it—let alone how they felt about it. Even with men pitching in more, there was very little equity in the division of labor in most American households during the 1930s. In 1930, employed husbands contributed about five hours per week to cleaning, cooking, and caring for children, whereas unemployed husbands contributed only about twelve hours. By 1940, those numbers were higher, totaling six and a half hours for employed husbands, and fourteen hours for unemployed husbands. Housework and caregiving improved somewhat thanks to advances in labor saving technology, the proliferation of new household products, and the introduction of convenience foods. Nevertheless, the number of hours spent on housework remained about the same for women—a little more than fifty hours per week. That was for the average homemaker who worked outside the home for fewer than ten hours per week. For the professional married women who was employed full time, the hours spent on housework was about half that, or twenty-five hours per week—twice the amount of time spent by unemployed men.

During the Great Depression, the profile of working women changed significantly. Around the turn of the century, the majority of women working outside the home were under twenty-five, single, poor, and either an immigrant or the child of immigrants. During the 1930s, older women—mostly white, married, and from middle-class households—displaced young, ethnic women in the workforce. Married women represented a third of working women, a 50 percent increase from the 1920s. Working-class women lost jobs and experienced reduced wages like the men in their families; however, they were less likely to receive relief than their fathers, husbands, brothers, and sons. Unemployed single women from both middle-class and working-class homes were especially vulnerable, suffering from homelessness, hunger, and isolation as an invisible underclass. Rural women saw their participation in agricultural production reduced and their vital roles on the farm undermined by advances in technology and changes in farming practices.

Women continued to work both inside the home and in the workforce; however, data on working women can be confusing and contradictory. In 1930, there were over ten million workingwomen, representing about 24 percent of the nation's workforce. By the end of the decade, the number of workingwomen increased to thirteen million, or 25 percent of the workforce. At first glance, these numbers suggest women workers fared well during the Great Depression. A closer look reveals a number of conflicting trends. For example, men dominated heavy industries that were hit hardest by the economic downturn, such as steel, rubber, and chemicals. Women were most often found working in light industries such as manufacturing, which recovered more quickly than heavy industries. This has led some historians to claim that women workers were displaced less often than men after the stock market crash and that they returned to their jobs more quickly than men. Other historians note that women lost more jobs early on, but were able to find replacements in service industries that were unappealing to men. Labor was highly segregated during the decade, and even in factory work women were assigned traditionally gendered work such as sewing or cooking. There were crews of women working for the P. H. Haines Knitting Company in Winston-Salem, North Carolina, and the H. J. Heinz factory in Pittsburgh, Pennsylvania, promoted the quality of pickles produced exclusively by "Heinz Girls." Whether or not women workers suffered less than men, wages for working women were significantly lower than men's and women were less likely to be protected by labor regulations or unions.

Even though women continued to work throughout the Depression, unemployment for women was still high. By 1931, two million women who had been working or seeking work prior to the beginning of the Depression were unemployed. By 1933, there were four million women out of work. In addition, working women faced many frustrating obstacles. Whereas the number of women in the workforce increased during the decade, wages decreased across the spectrum and women's participation in most professions declined. During the Depression—as during much of the twentieth century—professional and skilled jobs were reserved for men. Women made modest gains as doctors and lawyers during the 1930s but lost work as college professors, clergy, dentists, and social workers. Like factory work, women's professional work was informed by gender stereotyping; 75 percent of women worked as schoolteachers or nurses. Incongruously, when men worked as teachers, they earned more than women. In 1939, the average teaching salary for men was $1,953 per year, whereas women earned only $1,394 dollars. When women worked in business, they were tracked into pink-collar jobs as assistants instead of executives, even when they did the same work as men. Adding insult to a series of injuries, women were subject to frequent criticism from the erroneous perception that they were taking jobs away from men who had families to support.

Indeed, women confronted strong currents of public rebuke and discrimination in the workforce. Women were much less likely to abandon their families, and many women entered the workforce to save families from hunger and homelessness. Even though up to half of women wage earners were the sole income providers for their families, women were accused of abandoning their caregiving responsibilities and threatening the fabric of society. Criticism came from all quarters. In 1932, the director of the Free Employment Agency in New York City, Edward C. Rybicki, publicly stated that workingwomen were weakening home life and neglecting children at the same time as they played a significant role in causing the city's unemployment problems. Upon realizing that the number of gainfully employed women in 1939 equaled about the national unemployment total, the political journalist Norman Cousins wrote, "Simply fire the women, who shouldn't be working anyway, and hire the men. Presto! No unemployment. No relief rolls. No Depression." In response to public opinion, twenty-six state and local governments across the United States considered legislation to bar married women from government work. In 1932, discrimination against married women in the workforce was essentially legitimized by the Federal Economy Act, which dictated that only one spouse could work in government service at a time. Most agencies interpreted the Act by giving preference to employed men. Married women who were already working in public institutions were fired and government agencies refused to hire them for open positions. A wide range of businesses followed suit by discriminating against married women in their employment practices. More than 75 percent of school districts voluntarily banned the employment of married women as teachers, whether their husbands were teachers or not.

Conditions for single women were even worse, in part because single women were a diverse and largely invisible population. Images of the "forgotten man" were everywhere, and public controversy concerning married women kept them in public view. Single women did not share a group identity that garnered attention, sympathy, or support. "Unattached women," as they were sometimes called, lived outside of families for a variety of predictable reasons. Some were daughters of middle-class and working-class families who could not support them, and some were from families abandoned by fathers. Others were deserted or widowed by husbands. Many young people put off marriage during the Depression, and for some that delay would become permanent. Finally, there have always been women who remained single by choice. As a group, single women could be young, middle aged, or elderly. They were typically urban, white, and not included among the habitually dispossessed.

There are few reliable records on the number of single women who had to fend for themselves during the Depression, but there is compelling evidence of their presence and suffering. In *Holding Their Own: American Women in the 1930s*, Susan Ware notes the proportion of single women between the ages of twenty-five and thirty was 30 percent higher in 1935 than a similar cohort in 1930. Another source suggests that single women accounted for about 10 percent of the urban homeless population during the decade. Although they may have been independent, even successful, prior to the stock market crash (and as long as their luck or savings lasted afterward), single women had little economic power and no political voice. Just as working husbands were expected to support married women, it was assumed that a father supported single women. As a result, single women received little attention from the public and rarely qualified for support from relief agencies.

The first wave of feminism had ebbed and the independent, irreverent flappers had vanished by the end of the 1920s. Ideas about women's roles in society became more conservative and resistant to change during the Great Depression and there was little tolerance, let alone consideration, for a "modern women" who was single, without a family, and formerly self-sufficient. Already on the margins, single women who lost their jobs were only a few short steps away from hunger, homelessness, exploitation, and violence. News coverage, primary documents, and images in the media bear this out. In 1933, the *New Republic* reporter Emily Hahn was among the first to draw attention to the growing and underserved population of single women. Letters from single women to the president and first lady resound with crushed pride, frustrated hope, fear, and despair. Val Lewton's 1932 novel *No Bed of Her Own* emphasized the shame-filled, perilous conditions for women who chose hustling over starvation after losing decent jobs and an independent life. Vulnerable, single women appear in Hollywood films, but their presence is more likely to advance the plot than raise awareness about the conditions such women faced. Ann Darrow (Fay Wray) is recruited to join the adventure in *King Kong* (1933) when she is caught stealing fruit because she is hungry, and in his masterpiece *Modern Times* (1936), Charlie Chaplin's Little Tramp falls for a homeless urchin credited only as the Gamin (Paulette Goddard). Since both Darrow and the Gamin are brought under the protection of men during the film, they may have ultimately undercut concern about actual homeless single women.

Meridel Le Sueur's "Women Are Hungry," which preceded "Cows and Horses Are Hungry" in *The American Mercury* (March 1934), recounts the conditions faced by women across the social spectrum, from urban working-class mothers and elderly widows to rural farm women, from a middle-class teacher to homeless teenage girls. In the piece, Le Sueur makes an ominous comparison between the situation for poor men and single women. She writes, a "man can always get drunk, or talk to other men, no matter how broken he is in body and spirit; but a woman, ten to one, will starve alone in a hall bed-room until she is thrown out, and then she will sleep alone in some alley until she is picked up." An independent woman born to middle-class, educated, socialist parents in Murray, Iowa, in 1900, Le Sueur was well prepared to witness the harrowing conditions faced by single women in Depression Era America. As a child, she enjoyed lively debates and political activism, which she continued as an adult by embracing the great social and political movements of her time. Le Sueur nurtured a deep interest in working-class consciousness, midwestern farmers impacted by dust bowl storms, and the struggles of women and those living in poverty. She studied drama in Chicago, worked as an actress and stuntwoman in Hollywood, and for a time lived in Emma Goldman's commune in New York City. By 1927, she was publishing political commentaries and short stories in newspapers and magazines. In much of the reportage writing she published in the 1930s, she depicted women struggling to negotiate desperate needs for food and shelter as they sought to shield themselves from abuse.

Relief and protection were slow in coming, and inadequate once available. Government relief focused on families and dependent children, at the exclusion of single women. Charities were more likely to provide emotional and spiritual support rather than the financial and material assistance single women needed. In most cities, the "forgotten man" could find a free place to stay overnight and food in soup kitchens or bread lines, but such services were either unavailable or unappealing to single women. As early as 1932, one assistant director of the Emergency Work Bureau in New York City admitted that the Depression was affecting an unprecedented number of women, yet many cities failed to offer emergency plans or designate municipal resources to help them. That same year, New York City's newly organized Emergency Relief Committee predicted thirty thousand unemployed and homeless women needed help to survive the coming winter, but the city was unprepared to offer assistance. In Cleveland, thirty-three thousand out of one hundred thousand workingwomen who were unemployed faced similar conditions. Chicago had only one free women's lodging house with accommodations for one hundred to serve a metropolitan population of three million. In 1933 the Federal Emergency Relief Act (FERA) director Harry Hopkins acknowledged that all classes and all groups—including single women—were victims of the Depression, and in 1934 unattached women became legally eligible for home relief.

As married or single workers, wives, mothers, sisters, and daughters of workingmen, women supported workers and participated in the labor movement. Mostly support was provided through membership in the women's auxiliaries affiliated with labor unions. The first big sit-down strike of women workers occurred in cigar manufacturing in Detroit in 1937 when 2,500 mostly Polish-speaking women demanded higher wages, better working conditions, and union representation. The strike occurred in six cigar factories occupying a 4-square-mile area bordered by Milwaukee, Grandy, St. Aubin, and Warren Avenues, where 4,000 women manufactured R. D. Dunn cigars. After the stock market crash, the women's wages had been cut 35 to 50 percent, becoming among the lowest wages for workingwomen in Detroit. Poor ventilation ensured that toxic tobacco dust was always in the air, and sexual harassment by foremen was a frequent occurrence. Furthermore, factory owners provided neither soap nor hot water in lavatories, and toilets were too few and often primitive, dirty, and broken.

Motivated by successful sit-down strikes at General Motors plants in Flint and Detroit, workers at the Websten-Eisenlohr cigar factory sat down on February 16. In a matter of days, workers from Mazer-Cressman, Essex Cigar, Bernard Schwartz, Tegge-Jackson, and General Cigar joined the strike. Unfortunately, labor unions had a poor record of supporting workingwomen. The conservative, craft-based American Federation of Labor (AFL) Cigar Workers Union had ignored their pleas. So the women turned to the United Auto Workers (UAW), which successfully directed the Flint sit-down strike days earlier. The UAW had a better record for supporting women workers and responded by sending Stanley Nowak, head of the Polish Trade Union Committee, to provide leadership. Additional support came from local businesses and residents that provided food for workers as well as support for husbands, brothers, and sons of striking workers left to deal with the unfamiliar burden of domestic work and caregiving.

Lasting for two months, the strike proved women were not immune from police violence against striking workers. Following orders from Detroit Mayor Frank Couzens, police stormed Bernard Schwartz and removed the women using any means necessary, bruising arms, tearing clothes, and dragging them out by their hair. They used clubs to beat sympathetic bystanders and even threw a pregnant woman off her porch. Three days later, two hundred thousand protestors, including the women's auxiliary of the UAW dressed in bright green overalls and green berets and nearly two thousand out-of-town supporters, marched five abreast through downtown Detroit to a rally in Cadillac Square, where they listened to passionate speeches by the UAW's Walter Reuther, the Detroit Federation of Labor's Frank Martel, and the Congress of Industrial Organizations' (CIO) Leo Krzycki. Rally organizers even provided a fifty-piece UAW band for the event. On April 22, more than two months into the strike, representatives from management met with the strikers in Michigan Governor Frank Murphy's office. The strike ended the following day with an agreement and the formation of Cigar Workers Union Local 24, affiliated with the CIO. The success inspired women workers in Detroit to strike at Ferry-Morse Seed, Yale and Towne Locke, and Woolworth's, where the union for Hotel Employees and Restaurant Employees (HERE) would yield benefits for women workers in the region and nationwide.

The situation for rural women differed significantly from that of urban women. Rather than the separation of roles found in middle-class households in which the husband was the breadwinner and the wife was in charge of home life, farm families operated as a unit with much overlap between the roles for men and women. This is not to say there were no gender divisions in farm families, but there was more equity in farm work. Women's work included domestic chores such as cooking, cleaning, and caregiving, as well as raising chickens and milking cows. They also operated tractors, drove trucks, and cared for livestock. In fact, rural women pitched in on the farm wherever they were needed, often providing essential labor or generating indispensable income. Many rural women even preferred agricultural work to housework, as it was less tedious and repetitive, if not less labor intensive. Because there was little or no conflict between their role as mothers and their value as farm hands, rural women were welcome participants in actions by agricultural workers. Some even rose to leadership positions.

In 1932, sharecroppers in Arkansas organized the Southern Tenant Farmers Union, which included men and women farmers of both white and black races, and women union members played a major role in organizing the 1935 successful strike of five thousand cotton pickers. In San Antonio, Texas, Emma Tenayuca led twelve thousand Mexican American women pecan shellers and members of the International Pecan Sellers Union No. 172—affiliated with the United Cannery and Agricultural Packing and Allied Workers of American (UCAPAWA), a CIO union—to strike on January 31, 1938. An early advocate for social justice, Tenayuca was an active organizer throughout the 1930s. Idealistic, compassionate, and community minded, she was raised by grandparents who sensitized her to working-class issues affecting families on both sides of the border by taking her to listen to political speeches in the town square when she was seven. In high school, she read Karl Marx and Leo Tolstoy in a student group and continued to cultivate an interest in social and economic justice. Soon after, she began to act: first joining the Finck Cigar Strike in 1933, and then helping to establish a local chapter of the Ladies Garment Workers' Union in 1934. By the time she became involved with the pecan shellers, Tenayuca was a seasoned organizer and a capable, energetic, and informed labor leader. After three months and over a thousand arrests (including Tenayuca's), the union emerged victorious, winning increased wages and better working conditions. Satisfaction was short lived, however, when the pecan growers opted to mechanize production, thereby eliminating the need for most workers.

Early in his presidency, Franklin Roosevelt recognized the national importance of solving the problems facing farmers. He introduced legislation and regulation that impacted every aspect of life on the farm. As indicated by letters and articles in *The Farmer's Wife* and their participation in farm movements, rural women responded to the changes imposed on them—for better and worse. One of the most popular and radical movements was the Farmers Holiday Association (FHA). Most active between 1932 and 1937, the FHA was a national organization of Midwest and Great Plains farmers and ranchers in Iowa, Nebraska, Minnesota, Wisconsin, and the Dakotas. Emerging from the National Farmers Union, the FHA supported the economic well-being and traditional lifestyles of farmers by storming foreclosures and staging farm strikes. When a bank was to foreclose on a farm, the FHA would organize farmers to circumvent the auction by bidding pennies on the dollar for property before returning the property to the original owner. Farm strikes, or "holidays," called for farmers to refuse to sell, buy, or trade goods and forgo paying taxes until they received recognition and fair compensation. Innumerable women participated and three prominent white women rose from the ranks to achieve success as leaders of the FHA: Edith Pearson, Josie Hallquist, and Effie Kjorstad.

Pearson and Hallquist lived in adjoining counties in western Nebraska, whereas Kjorstad was from northwestern North Dakota. All three women were militant, energetic, and effective organizers who received a lot of press for their work. A charismatic speaker and determined leader, Pearson was responsible for organizing several demonstrations against foreclosures. Both she and Hallquist occupied leadership positions in their local FHA chapters and both were elected to the state board of the Madison County Plan group in 1933. Kjorstand came from a family of farm activists within a community that supported radical rural women, including Ella Reeve "Mother" Bloor, Lavina Amsberry, and the Huss sisters. Nevertheless, as the climate worsened for family farmers, rural women saw their roles change and status decline. Even though many women continued to contribute unpaid labor on family farms and gardens, the number of women working in agriculture declined significantly during the 1930s. By the end of the decade, all three FHA leaders would abandon their farm actions for participation in other social issues, including antiwar movements for Pearson and Hallquist and a bid for public office by Kjorstad. Tenayuca would also leave her radicalism behind as violence and death threats pursued her. She returned to San Antonio to work as a schoolteacher after living for many years in anonymity in San Francisco.

President Roosevelt's New Deal programs were a mixed bag for working women, whether urban or rural. Beneficial programs included the National Recovery Administration (NRA), which helped raise some women's wages modestly to 3 percent above pre-Depression levels and ensured that some workers achieved a forty-hour workweek. The NRA and Wagner Act's support of organized labor helped improve women's collective bargaining efforts, encouraged women to organize in industries populated primarily by women, and improved women's participation in labor unions dominated by men. By the end of the decade, three times as many women belonged to a union as had at the beginning. The Works Progress Administration (WPA) created government jobs for women to cook, sew, clean, can foods, and care for children, while the Social Security Program initiated monthly payments to widows, women with disabled husbands, and single mothers.

In addition, Roosevelt appointed women to prominent positions in his administration, including Frances Perkins, the first woman to serve as the secretary of labor, and Mary McLeod Bethune, who was the highest-ranking African American as the director for Negro Affairs in the National Youth Association. Having had a longstanding career advocating civil rights for African Americans and women, Bethune founded the National Council of Negro Women in 1935. Molly Dewson and Ellen Sullivan Woodward were both members of the Social Security Board and participated in the development of WPA programs. The former Wyoming governor Nellie Tayloe Ross became the first woman to head the US Mint in 1933; she would work there until her retirement in 1953. Though courageous and accomplished, most women in politics avoided the limelight and rarely received coverage in the press.

By far, the most prominent woman serving the administration was First Lady Eleanor Roosevelt. One of the most highly visible, widely known, and greatly admired women of her time, Anna Eleanor Roosevelt Roosevelt

(1884–1962) continues to be an American icon, having inspired countless articles, books, and films. Viewed by one historian as the "conscience of the administration," and compared with the likes of Jesus, Gandhi, and Buddha by a recent best-selling author, Eleanor was intelligent, kindhearted, sincere, and principled. She was an excellent political partner to Franklin, supporting his career and their shared goals with hard work, dedication, and zeal. A prolific communicator who left an impressive collection of speeches, letters, and articles, Eleanor also exhibited a high degree of media savvy, holding regular press conferences, acquiring her own press corps (women reporters only), delivering addresses, and writing a nationally syndicated column. As a result, Eleanor seemed more accessible than previous first ladies and won a large following of loyal fans who considered her one of their intimate acquaintances. Many historians have cited her among the reasons for Franklin's extraordinary popularity, and by the end of the decade her popularity actually exceeded his in the polls.

Born into an affluent New York dynasty, Eleanor was a beneficiary of the Progressive Era. Even as a young woman, she embraced reform movements and first-wave feminist concerns about the rights of women, people of color, and workers. She taught dance and exercise at a Settlement House in New York City before volunteering with the National Consumer League to improve living conditions for sweatshop workers and their families. Though not a "feminist" as modern readers would understand the term, Eleanor promoted a liberal political agenda of her own that was considerably more left-leaning than her husband's. In addition, she earned an income that would, by the end of the decade, match his, although she donated her earnings to charity—a practice she continued throughout her tenure in the White House from 1933 and 1945. She was outspoken and conveyed both gentle courage and matronly pluck. Still, she was sensible and her progressive views had limits. In her support of labor, she stopped short of militancy, and in spite of her affirmation of women, she was opposed to the Equal Rights Amendment. As an indispensable political asset, Franklin tolerated her agenda, valued the minority support she brought him, and shut down those within his administration who criticized her.

Although she left an extensive public record, the details of her inner life remain largely hidden. In many ways, the conditions faced by women during the Great Depression are reflected in what we do know about her life. Since childhood, Eleanor made the best of a series of bad situations. Her early years were marked by tragedy and loneliness that revisited her throughout her life. When she was a naïve twenty year old, Eleanor accepted Franklin and unwittingly entered into a marriage with rules she had not agreed to. His infidelity and reluctance to support her against his mother caused a great deal of distress during their marriage. After producing six children—five of whom would survive—and following a decade when she endured the overbearing supervision of a controlling mother-in-law, Eleanor emerged as a national heroine who exerted considerable independence and influence behind the scenes. Though publicly hailed as a nurturing matriarch, Eleanor exhibited ambivalence toward domestic life and motherhood, instead choosing an ambitious schedule that required nonstop travel. She was criticized by the public for meddling in public affairs, for advocating on behalf of African Americans, for letting work keep her away from her family, and for not measuring up to the standards of beauty of the time.

Ordinary American women looked to Eleanor for inspiration as a role model. Letters to the first lady brim with admiration and often confidential requests for help. Caring and compassionate, Eleanor could empathize with much of the suffering women were experiencing, but of course her family roots and proximity to the presidency provided opportunities that made her life exceptional. She had access to resources and could make choices that were unavailable to most women. Unlike many women in the 1930s, Eleanor could—and did—opt for freedom from domestic work. Whereas married women in the workforce were reviled and persecuted, Eleanor earned substantial wealth from her own efforts. She and Franklin lived separately for much of the time he was in office. Even when together, they were rarely alone, instead preferring to share their home with the company of a large network of extended family and friends—an arrangement they both apparently enjoyed. Like her husband, she would find satisfaction outside of her marriage, first in work, and then in intimate relationships with others. Though it would be several generations before women would enjoy similar liberation from double standards in marriage and work, women of the 1930s strongly identified with Eleanor's private suffering and greatly admired her public achievements.

Although the Roosevelt administration had a number of high-profile women in important positions and although the New Deal included polices that helped some women, most workingwomen were negatively impacted during the Great Depression. NRA wage and hour codes applied to industries dominated by men and helped only a small percentage of women. In fact, one quarter of NRA codes set lower minimum wages for women than for men performing the same jobs, and the majority of women working in agriculture, domestic work, clerical work, and even professions such as teaching and nursing were exempt from the codes. Furthermore, the NRA did not recognize or protect women who worked from home. Cottage industries represented an important way for women to contribute to the household income without sacrificing time rearing children, caring for a disabled spouse, or tending to elderly parents. Urban or rural women who took in sewing or laundry, or sold homemade goods and crafts from home, were vulnerable to exploitation and had no recourse when customers failed to pay.

Much of the work that became available through New Deal agencies was considered unsuitable for women. As a result, women represented only a small minority of those who were employed by the agencies, and when included, they were assigned clerical and domestic work. Though only too happy to have the work, such jobs prepared them for little else but low-paying jobs and housewifery. Only 15 percent of the workers hired by the WPA were women and of the 4 million workers hired by the Civil Works Administration (CWA), only 300,000 were women. The Civilian Conservation Corps (CCC) offered young people the opportunity to earn a wage doing educational work while providing housing, food, and mentoring supervision to participants. A meager 8,500 women enjoyed these benefits, compared with 2.5 million men. Finally, in spite of progressive ideals, the administration of New Deal programs was plagued by sexism and racism, complicated by the prevailing belief that married women should be prohibited from working.

Women faced significant challenges in the workforce during the hard times of the Depression, but they recaptured and revitalized their vital role in the home when a nineteenth-century, sentimental ideal of motherhood reemerged as a powerful cultural force. It explains, in part, the hostility married women faced in the workforce: a majority of Americans—both men and women of all races—believed a woman's most solemn vocation and inviolate obligation was to be a mother. The ideal of "mother love" that resurfaced during the 1930s was conceived prior to the Civil War by America's embryonic middle class. It was further shaped by the rigid social codes of the Victorian era. This maternal ideal linked domestic and public life by promoting motherhood as a noble and necessary civic duty. Social stability required strong, unified families; women were the "keepers of the hearth" and "angels of the house" who nurtured future generations of robust and patriotic nation builders. By the turn of the twentieth century, motherhood had become a venerated institution and virtuous mothers symbolized the best of an honorable nation.

The "cult of domesticity" that shaped attitudes about motherhood during the 1930s no longer holds sway in American culture. Evidence of the symbolic relationship between mother and nation remains, however, in the still common expression associating Americanism with mom, baseball, and apple pie. As a result of second-wave feminism and the women's movement, the maternal model has changed significantly, and today motherhood is understood as a personal choice, not a civic obligation. The situation for women in the 1930s was complicated because modern ideas about women's role in society had begun to appear in American culture after the turn of the century. Beginning with the abolition and temperance movements in the mid-nineteenth century, first-wave feminists used their purview over the home to propel them into public life. Women protested against slavery on the grounds that it destroyed families in two fundamental ways. First, slavery separated slave children from their mothers, and second, white men created children with slaves outside of marriage. Later in the century as problems associated with alcoholism among workingmen began to cause trouble in the home, women joined the debate on temperance and organized public actions to restrict access to alcohol. The prohibition they helped achieve lasted from 1920 to 1933. Suffrage would be the issue that carried an increasingly modern woman into the twentieth century.

The impact of the modern age on attitudes concerning women's role in American society reached a critical mass in the 1920s. Achieving the vote in 1920 inspired women to imagine new destinies for themselves. After Margaret Sanger founded the American Birth Control League in 1921, the promise of reliable contraception and sex education offered women heretofore unavailable opportunities to manage reproduction. Later, Sanger would change the name to the Planned Parenthood Federation of America and begin offering services to poor, primarily immigrant women in New York City. As private lives changed, women began to reconsider their public lives. They embraced their newfound political voice with zeal, but that does not mean society was ready to listen. Alice Paul introduced an Equal Rights Amendment (ERA) to the US Constitution in 1923. The amendment, which simply states that women must be treated as equal to men, did not pass. Instead of realizing their newly imagined potential, anxieties about modern life, concerns about family values, and fear of change made progress for women slow in the 1920s and stagnate—perhaps even regress—in the 1930s.

The daughters and granddaughters of first-wave feminists enjoyed increased political agency and personal freedom, but the cultural shift that could accommodate them would not occur until the second wave of feminism in the sixties and seventies. Like feminists today, no clear consensus existed about the modern woman—what she did, how she behaved, where she fit in. Whereas images of the modern woman were common in 1920s media, traditional gender roles returned in the 1930s. Gone was the "new woman" with her bare knees, jiving in speakeasies, speaking her mind, and smoking in public. No more were the independent debs in straight-line dresses designed to erase feminine curves. They were all replaced by public images of women yielding to the will of husbands in marriage and putting motherhood above all else—including themselves. The proliferation of conservative images of women in the media stands in contrast to the fact that more real women than ever before were asserting themselves—through choice and need—in public and economic life. Unfortunately, competing views of women in society during the 1920s led to a growing intolerance for independent women in the 1930s.

Popular culture provides the most visible evidence of the ambivalence toward women during the Great Depression. Films from Hollywood during the period reinforced traditional values and undermined women's independence and liberation. Women in 1930s films who seek independence find that it brings them sorrow or worse. Happiness can only be achieved through passive acceptance and submission to men. At the same time, such roles were played by a generation of strong, ambitious, and self-assured women including Mae West, Greta Garbo, Joan Crawford, and Bette Davis. Even though these actors imbued their performances with confidence and determination, the subordination of their characters was inevitable.

George Cukor's film *The Women* (1939) is an interesting example that clearly demonstrates the paradox facing women during the period. Written by Clare Boothe Luce, *The Women* was a successful Broadway play before Cukor adapted it for the silver screen. Cukor was known in Hollywood as "the women's director," and this film gave expression to the enormous creative energy of talented women by featuring women prominently on both sides of the camera—even the leopard that makes a brief cameo was female. The story follows Mary Haines (Norma Shearer) as she divorces her husband after the discovery of his affair, only to return to remarry him after determining that pride is "a luxury a woman in love can't afford." Along the way, she is berated as a coward for abandoning her husband, no matter what he did, criticized for holding onto a schoolgirl's naïve wishes about love and marriage, and advised—by her mother, no less—that happy marriages require wives to ignore gossip and evidence of infidelity. The message to audiences was plain: good wives had better shut up and suck it up if they wanted the security of marriage.

These themes are reinforced and deepened in the title story of Tess Slessinger's popular collection of short stories *On Being Told That Her Second Husband Has Taken His First Lover* (1932). Written as an internal monologue as Cornelia Graham reels from her second husband Jimsie's confession, the narrator vacillates between crushing disappointment, self-loathing, and uncertainty about the future, all the while maintaining the pretense that she is the perfect wife—calm, clever, and an unflappable good sport. The character's disassociation is evident as she bounces between first-, second-, and third-person narration. After Jimsie has the "gall to ask you whether you feel 'through' with him now," her response is telling, because she uses the analogy of chronic disease to describe serial infidelity: "No, you answer, the thing has been going on right along and I've been happy enough. I'm not one to look back now that I know I've always had t.b. and say God how I have always suffered." Mixing period slang with civilized formality, Cornelia contemplates her options. "Certainly, you think, you have a legalistic right to go out and get even. . . ." But it's different with men, explains her husband, so "no gents for you, my girl, one gent and [we are] through." Unlike Cukor's film, the consequence of such stoic reckoning is excruciatingly evident, as the story ends with Jimsie leaving to meet his lover. Slessinger writes, "in a minute now the pain will go tearing through the veil, drop the curtain on the polished comedy," but before it does, Cornelia stops him to fix his tie, "tweak, tweak, like an idiot" because remember, she tells him, "everything you do reflects on me." Slessinger and her readers were clearly concerned about the impossible double standard women had to negotiate and the suffering it caused.

The most common roles for women in mass media were superficial and tangential, and their influence generally restricted to domestic life and caregiving. Independent women were often portrayed as heartless and cruel, but films venerating motherhood remained popular. For example, Frank Capra's 1933 *Lady for a Day* shows both trends, and makes sense only within the complicated context of 1930s gender relations. Apple Annie (May Robson) is a wretched, white haired, alcoholic street vender who receives the support of other peddlers, impoverished indigents, a disabled panhandler, and a band of gangsters who mutually conspire to help her maintain a lie she's been telling her daughter. Of illegitimate birth, Louise (Jean Parker) has been in a convent in Spain since infancy. To protect Louise from being stigmatized by her mistakes (and to sooth her own conscience), Annie invents a life in high society that she communicates to her daughter in letters. The lie is threatened with exposure when Louise, her fiancé, and his father, Count Romero (Walter Connolly) set sail for American to meet the mother of the bride and ensure Louise's pedigree.

The farce that follows was reassuring, heartfelt, and entertaining to 1930s viewers, but may seem perplexing to modern viewers. Crime boss Dave the Dude (Warren William), who only enters into business deals after buying a good luck apple from Annie, becomes her champion, bankrolling an expensive charade that includes significant makeovers, a fancy hotel suite, and recruiting a suitable stepfather for Louise. Annie is successfully transformed into a sympathetic matron while her co-conspirators from the streets struggle to become high society guests at a reception to seal the marriage deal in the final scene. Glenda Farrell plays Missouri Martin, Dude's brassy, fast-talking, platinum-blonde showgirl squeeze. She can go toe-to-toe with the Dude's thugs, but reveals a heart of gold by helping to pull off the elaborate scam. It works only because everyone understands how important it is to maintain a mother's love. Women like Missouri are marginal, as is made clear when one of Dude's henchmen is advised to get a "dizzy dame" out of his head, to which he replies, not to worry, "I don't think about her during the day." Adding legitimacy to the ploy, the Dude convinces law enforcement, the mayor, and a governor to join them in winning over the count and ensuring Louise's marriage. Mother love is preserved, although no thought is given to the circumstances that brought about Annie's fall, her destitution, or what will become of her after her daughter returns to Spain.

To navigate a social terrain of competing gender codes, women drew from both traditional and modern trends. Housewives' leagues had first appeared in American communities prior to World War I as a means for reform-minded women to combat the high cost of living, improve food safety laws, and raise the status of housewives as consumers. A resurgence of housewives' leagues occurred during the 1930s in both white and black neighborhoods where women organized boycotts, participated in negotiations with aid agencies, and canvassed for support of their initiatives. Women organized to control rent and food prices, and worked together to procure relief from government and social agencies. Neighborhood groups protested evictions and petitioned for additional unemployment benefits. Women were responsible for the household's daily spending. As the average housewife had only $20 to $25 per week to cover all domestic expenses, women became experts at frugal management. Women ran consumer cooperatives to keep the price of goods low. Even in urban settings, women kept chickens and gardened more to trim the family budget. Mass-produced clothes were increasingly available and affordable, but many women opted to make their own or mend the clothes they had. They purchased day-old bread and practiced energy-saving measures in the home. Collectively, these efforts contributed significantly to the family's quality of life and economic well-being.

Women were a powerful force in the economy as consumers during the Great Depression. Women became more involved in consumer advocacy as well, pressuring grocers to establish grades for perishables and insisting on standards of hygiene. Consumer cooperatives organized by women, run by women volunteers, and frequented by women shoppers thrived during the 1930s. For a time, consumer cooperatives outpaced the proliferation of chain stores that had erupted during the 1920s. For the first time, women shopped in supermarkets such as A&P and Kroger, where their input helped establish trends in grocery shopping that remain standards today. Supermarkets were often regional chains that provided consistent, no-frills, one-stop shopping. They brought together complementary foods that had previously been sold by discrete butchers, bakers, small markets, and neighborhood grocers. Supermarkets leveraged volume to offer consumers lower costs and offered self-serve, wide-aisled shopping that reduced labor costs and added convenience.

Through polls, surveys, and other marketing strategies, women shaped the development of consumer culture and transformed the American diet. Products such as Bisquick and Birdseye frozen vegetables joined Kraft macaroni and cheese, Hormel SPAM, and Wonder bread on shelves for the first time. Gerber baby cereal followed the strained baby foods that had been available since 1928. New categories of snack foods including Snickers and Twinkies were developed and sold. As an additional advantage for the supermarket culture, shoppers could park in adjacent lots free of charge. They carried their purchases in their own cloth bags or baskets until wheeled shopping carts were introduced in 1937. In the final analysis, these conveniences were more novel distraction than time saving or health giving; however, they permitted women to participate in consumer culture, exercise choice, and assert greater economic power.

Informed by Western traditions, American society is patriarchal, which means that both public and private institutions are organized hierarchically under the rule of fathers or father figures. Whether referring to the founding fathers, God the father, the fathers of churches, the fathers of industry, or the fathers in households, men have occupied positions of leadership, power, and authority in American history and therefore have preoccupied both the written record of the time and—until recently—the scholarship that chronicles the past. Following the stock market crash that threatened men's roles as providers and protectors of families, and exacerbated by changing attitudes from and about women, men struggled to come to terms with traditional roles as they contemplated new ones. Franklin Roosevelt, whose photograph hung on the wall in many American homes during the Great Depression, exemplified the most obvious symbolic representation of a patriarch during the 1930s. He cultivated a reassuring, fatherly appeal when addressing the public during his radio broadcasts. His governmental programs became de facto "father-providers" for families whose primary breadwinner was absent or unable to work. The idea that public institutions could replace the father figure extended government beyond its basic functions, and to this day remains a source of contention between liberals, who believe in Roosevelt's vision of an active government, and conservatives, who argue for a more limited role of government.

The media promoted traditional father figures in radio shows such as the drama *One Man's Family*, which debuted in 1932 and endured with few changes until 1959. The show offered weekly insights into the fictional Barbour family, which was led by Henry, a character who provided moral and practical advice to his sons and daughters. Audiences learned about family life from idealized but accessible scripted media families like the Barbours. According to the announcer, the show was dedicated to "mothers and fathers of the younger generation and to their bewildering offspring." In movies, the popular Andy Hardy series, which began in 1937 with Mickey Rooney in the title role, featured Andy's white-haired, honorable, and patient father, Judge Hardy (Lewis Stone), bestowing wisdom and guidance to the young Hardy as he negotiated pitfalls and triumphs on the road to adulthood. The films featured father-and-son talks that always put Andy back on the right path.

Media culture was also rife with symbolic fathers such as Dr. Kildare, a popular character created by Frederick Schiller Faust (pen name Max Brand). James Kildare was a noble doctor who dispensed wisdom as he healed sick and injured patients in a series of films in the late 1930s and early 1940s, in a radio series in the early 1950s, in two television series in the 1960s and 1970s, and in a comic book based on the TV show. Even Tarzan the apeman settled into fatherhood by the end of the decade when he adopts a son in *Tarzan Finds a Son* (1939), the fourth of eleven films starring Johnny Weissmuller. For children without fathers, characters like the Lone Ranger filled in, offering fatherly advice and preaching a moral code to young radio listeners. Composed, competent, and caring fathers in the media reinforced traditional values and provided comfort for audiences. They also offered an assuring image to shore up men broken down by the Depression.

Perhaps the most visible and sympathetic father during the 1930s was the internationally famed aviator Charles Lindbergh. Lindbergh's conservative and isolationist politics and early support of Adolf Hitler's regime has tainted his reputation in the twenty-first century; however, he was known as a daring, record-breaking pilot during the 1920s. Handsome and athletic, with a confident, penetrating gaze, "Lucky Lindy" had achieved fame, married well, and by the 1930s appeared to be living the American Dream. The decade was only in its second year when what journalists dubbed "the crime of the century" occurred near Hopewell, New Jersey, on March 1, 1932. Charles Augustus Lindbergh, Jr., the twenty-month-old son of Lindbergh and his wife, the writer and poet Anne Morrow Lindbergh, had been reported abducted from his crib at the family home. New Jersey police responded to Lindbergh's call and discovered mud inside the bedroom, footprints under the window, a carpenter's chisel, and two sections of a homemade extension ladder. No other evidence was found, except for a poorly written ransom note addressing Lindbergh alone:

> Dear Sir!
>
> Have 50,000$ redy 2500$ in 20$ bills 1500$ in 10$ bills and 1000$ in 5$ bills. After 2-2 days we will inform you were to deliver the Mony. We warn you for making anyding public or for notify the polise the child is in gute care. Indication for all letters are signature and 3 holes.

The apparent agony that Lindbergh, America's hero, displayed over his missing son added even more drama to the story. Daily dispatches from New Jersey, written by reporters with an eye toward the crime's unfolding drama, built suspense for the public. Newsreels of an anxious father using every means at his disposal to restore his family kept people riveted. The Federal Bureau of Investigation, headed by its first director, J. Edgar Hoover, lent its assistance even though it did not have jurisdiction in kidnapping cases. Even President Herbert Hoover pledged his support and help in finding the hero's child.

Unfortunately, on May 12, 1932, after a series of gripping twists and turns, including false leads, opportunistic grifters, and a cat-and-mouse exchange of letters and meetings between an earnest schoolteacher and the potential kidnapper, a passerby found Charles Jr.'s decomposing body half buried along a highway, just four and a half miles from his home. The coroner declared the toddler had died from a blow to the head shortly after his abduction. The next day, President Hoover put the FBI—and all federal agencies—on the case. Two years later, police arrested Bruno Richard Hauptmann on September 18, 1934. He was an ideal suspect. Rootless, rudderless, foreign born, and without family, the thirty-five year old, after several failed attempts, had illegally entered the county in July 1923 aboard an ocean-liner from Germany. He married in 1925, but remained childless. Although he worked as a carpenter and as a stock trader, he had a criminal past, having been charged with extortion in New York and murder in New Jersey. When he was arrested, he had on him a $20 gold certificate that had been part of the ransom money.

According to the Newseum, the museum of news in Washington, DC, William Randolph Hearst's International News Service transmitted fifty thousand words on the crime the day the baby was kidnapped alone. The wire service supplied stories to newspapers across the country, further fueling a nationwide interest in the case. Millions of readers followed the coverage like one might tune in to the storyline of a favorite soap opera. The attention from media, law enforcement, and government to the Lindbergh kidnapping cannot be accounted for wholly by sympathy, morbid curiosity, or because of Lindbergh's celebrity. Other famous people had suffered terrible misfortunes or been the victims of violent crimes. The kidnapping fascinated Americans for several reasons. Everyone could sympathize with the Lindbergh family over the grief caused by the tragic loss of their baby. Some felt sorry that a powerful and heroic man could be rendered so helpless by forces outside his control. Others coveted the look inside the lives of the rich and famous. More than anything, Americans rooted for a father willing to do anything to restore his family.

Fathers were to protect families from harm. In society, the job of protection is assigned to law enforcement, and popular images of police and government agents reveal another example of paternal masculinity common to the culture of the 1930s. Radio shows such as *Gangbusters* (1936–1957) dramatized so-called real cases of upstanding and unstoppable law enforcement officers who took down underworld criminals. The hope was that these examples would provide young people with an alternative to the glamorous image of actual bootleggers and bank robbers that newspapers and movies presented in great detail. J. Edgar Hoover understood the importance of image and took every step possible to ensure the public saw the FBI agent, or G-man, as a superman above reproach who was the last line of defense between good and bad. Hoover had agents in Hollywood closely monitor film production as well as the lives of filmmakers. He was not above using political influence, and even blackmail, to ensure positive portrayals of law enforcement.

The Hoover biographer Richard Hack writes that Hoover was not pleased when James Cagney portrayed criminals—which the actor did in a number of blockbusters. Hoover gave this advice to the actor: "Get killed by the end . . . make sure you're dead because I don't want to see any crooks living." In 1935, Cagney played a heroic FBI agent in *G-Men*, a film directed by William Keighley. Soon the production became Hoover's pet project. He loaned out FBI agents to consult on set as well as to appear on-screen. Surprisingly, Cagney's FBI agent character, Brick Davis, was as defiant and volatile as any gangster—only this time the actor didn't have to die in a hail of lead in the film's closing scene. The film's commanding tone gratified Hoover and moviegoers alike, and it became one of Warner Brothers' biggest hits. It was so popular that Warner Brothers released it again in 1949.

The image of actual and symbolic fathers appealed to Americans looking to regain a sense of order and stability. Yet Americans have always had a sweet spot for outsiders, underdogs, and rebels who disrupt the status quo with explosive energy. Gangster films became one of the biggest crowd-pleasers during the 1930s, with stories of dangerous men who lived the high life dressed in fancy clothes and driving flashy cars, all the while thumbing their noses at the law. The representation of gangsters in the media provides another popular model for masculinity in the 1930s, but their allure was antiheroic. Antiheroes lack conventional heroic attributes; they may ultimately do good, but their motives are questionable and their methods dubious. Antiheroes prospered during the period because they showed what was possible when venerated traits associated with rugged individualism went too far. Instead of courage and fortitude, antiheroes of the 1930s displayed ruthless grit and brutal determination. Americans didn't have to search far for a real-life example of a gangster antihero. They had only to look at the front page of their newspaper or listen to a radio newscast to learn about the daring exploits of John Dillinger.

Though law enforcement deemed him "Public Enemy no. 1," the public seemed to admire Dillinger, perhaps because he earned a reputation for robbing banks that were foreclosing on homeowners during the Great Depression, and since then he has come to epitomize bad-boy appeal. Dillinger had only a fourteen-month crime spree before eating lead from a federal agent's pistol outside a Chicago movie theater, but his handsome looks and wisecracking flair captivated newspaper readers, radio audiences, and newsreel viewers all over America. He gained fame during the 1930s as he changed the image of the criminal from petty thug to charismatic rogue. Today, Dillinger continues to have strong public appeal and remains the subject of books, documentaries, and movies such as the 2009 film *Public Enemies* starring Johnny Depp. That same year, the *Wall Street Journal* included him on a list of "Ten People Who Got Rich during the Depression," alongside Babe Ruth, Gene Autry, Howard Hughes, and J. Paul Getty.

Dillinger was characteristically charming and falsely modest when he explained to a reporter in 1933, "I don't smoke much, and I drink very little. I guess my only bad habit is robbing banks." In fact, he had been wild since adolescence. He was like many men coming of age in the 1920s: for them wealth was visible, tantalizing, and mostly out of reach. The 1920s may have been prosperous for some, but for Dillinger and men like him on the opposite end of the fiscal spectrum, times were hard and jobs were scarce. Precipitated by a growing sense of restlessness, many young men hit the road or rode the rails in search of opportunity and adventure—something, anything. Dillinger was among a growing number of young men whose frustrated ambition turned to criminal volatility. In 1924, he found himself in jail at the age of twenty after he and an accomplice assaulted and robbed a grocery store owner of $50 in Dillinger's hometown of Mooresville, Indiana.

Dillinger had just deserted the United States Navy and married a sixteen-year-old girl. He had trouble finding work. The Roaring Twenties ended for Dillinger when the town's minister recognized him fleeing the scene of the grocery store robbery and tipped off the police. They arrested him the next day. His father, believing the judge would be lenient if his son was penitent, urged Dillinger to plead guilty, which he did. To the shock of father and son, Dillinger received harsh joint sentences of two to fourteen years and ten to twenty years in the Indiana state penitentiary. The experience left him bitter and angry, and cost him his marriage. Four and a half years into his sentence, Dillinger's father had collected enough signatures on a petition to request parole for his son and on May 10, 1933, Dillinger regained his freedom.

The America Dillinger reentered as a free man dramatically differed from the one he had left nearly a decade before. If the prosperity of the 1920s had been an illusion, the Great Depression was a nightmare. The Depression had an iron hold over the US economy and millions of people struggled to survive. In 1933, thirteen million people were unemployed and some workers with jobs were not getting paychecks. The federal government seemed incapable of stopping the fiscal hemorrhaging. Once on the outside, Dillinger returned to crime, though now he was older and smarter. While in prison, he learned the tricks of the criminal trade from experts in bank robbery. His focused on banks, figuring police were too dumb and bank employees wouldn't mind. Dillinger's explanation in an interview added to his folk-hero appeal: "The people who work in the banks have got a lot of relations who lost money in banks. I bet some people who work in banks would be glad to see us. And anyway, it ain't their money."

Dillinger's crime spree was marked by bold and daring capers that added to his magnetism and distinguished him from most criminals of the period. It is believed he robbed a bank in Daleville, Indiana, on July 17, 1933. He planned on busting out his friends from the penitentiary. Dillinger's clever scheme involved shipping a crate loaded with guns, ammunition, and money to a contact inside from a thread factory that supplied the prison laundry. He sent word to his friend that he should open the crate marked with a splash of black paint. For Dillinger, law-breaking offered the best way for someone to help themselves. It had worked for criminals such as Al Capone, who bootlegged his way to become a Robin Hood-like hero for the people of Prohibition Era Chicago. It worked, at least until the federal government put Capone in prison on tax evasion charges in 1931.

In spite of his chosen vocation, Dillinger demonstrated considerable professionalism, expertise, and hard work. While waiting for the jailbreak, he and fellow ex-con Homer Van Meter spent August 4, 1933 casing a bank in Montpelier, Indiana. Dillinger devised a detailed plan that calculated how long they could remain inside the bank and which direction—and at what speed—he needed to drive his fast new getaway car. He noted the distance between the police station and the bank, the time it took for the traffic light to change, and the number of cars clogging the streets. They robbed it the next day. Newspapers described the robbery as thorough and efficient. According to one witness, the gunmen left behind only 40 cents. Dillinger's next bank job came on August 14 in Bluffton, Ohio. Again, a well-executed plan allowed the gang to rob the bank and escape without apprehension by police. The *Lima County News* wrote that the men were well organized and well dressed. Dillinger's fourth and biggest score came three weeks after the Ohio bank job with the robbery of the State Bank of Massachusetts Avenue in Indianapolis. The robberies were well-choreographed affairs and the last heist netted the Dillinger gang $25,000.

Elliot J. Gorn writes in *Dillinger's Wild Ride* that the Midwest was a great place to be a bank robber in the midthirties. Although government officials blamed bad parenting and the corrupting influence of movies for the rise in crime, the facts point to state government cutbacks on law-enforcement spending. Police in the East had the latest technology: faster cars, better communications, and automatic weapons. They were also well paid and better educated. But criminals outfitted with Tommy guns, money for bribes, and cars with V8 engines could outshoot and outrun any police officer or sheriff in the Midwest. The federal government could do little. The Bureau of Investigation (BOI), the precursor of the FBI, offered help to local police in identifying bank robbers and distributing information, but bank robbery did not fall under its jurisdiction. Except that their business was criminal, Dillinger and outlaws like him were a lot like the robber barons a generation before—J. D. Rockefeller in oil, Andrew Carnegie in steel, and Jay Gould in railroads. They were hardworking, coolheaded, brilliant strategists who routinely exploited weaknesses in the system as a means to guarantee success in their antiheroic careers.

Dillinger's status with the public angered law enforcement officers who were tired of looking like fools for their inability to bring him to justice. Efforts to capture him increased until police busted Dillinger without incident on September 22. He took the arrest nonchalantly and with typical bravado told police, "You've won this hand. But you can bet I'll win the next one." Newspapers began publishing Dillinger's name, and his legend grew in an America desperate for depictions of self-made men, even if they found their success at the point of a gun. More robberies, another arrest, another escape, two dead guards, and a dead sheriff later, Dillinger and his gang continued their high-profile rampage. They robbed banks across Indiana and even raided a police department arsenal where they made off with guns, ammo, and bulletproof vests. By November 1933, Dillinger was wanted in two states and by the federal government. Newspapers nicknamed his band "the Terror Gang." It is estimated that the robberies netted Dillinger and his gang about $127,000.

Law enforcement eventually caught up with Dillinger in Chicago on July 22, 1934, and this time there was no escape. Dillinger's death by gunfire outside of a crowded theater ended his crime spree and ensured that increasing public fascination with gangsters would continue. Gangsters such as Dillinger aspired to the good life as it was depicted in much of the print, film, and radio media of the day. The Great Depression touched fewer wealthy men than it did middle- and working-class men, and they spent their time and money, as they had during the Roaring Twenties, on leisure pursuits and luxury items such as clothes, cars, and mansions. The interests of the wealthy and powerful gradually informed a new cultural aesthetic that would change ideas about masculinity for all Americans. More and more, appearance and possession, not vocation or deed, would literally make the man.

Consider the significant changes in menswear from the previous decade. Men's fashion shook off the starched conformity of 1920s style in favor of more personal expression. The men of "café society" began dictating new rules of dress in place of traditions inherited from bygone generations. The changes in style trickled down to men in the underclasses as new looks took hold, and the 1930s would become the most important decade in menswear. The fashion expert Alan Flusser said that it was money and a sense of security that inspired men to innovate and break fashion rules. For Flusser, new styles for men, or different ways of "rigging out an old one," and their appeal across social classes was never more apparent than during the 1930s. Movies stars such as Cary Grant and Fred Astaire, along with fashionable world leaders such as the Duke of Windsor, showed the world new ways of looking good in formal and casual dress.

The significance of this shift in style should not be underestimated. Since the middle ages, everything one needed to know about a man—whether tanner, baker, soldier, cleric, farmer, or aristocrat—could be gleaned from his outfit. Compelled into being by images of men in the media as much as by new technologies of mass production and distribution, a new era in masculinity began in the 1930s that transcended formerly impenetrable class and race differences. The influence of stylish men accelerated and broadened out during the 1930s with the publication *Esquire* (1933) and *Apparel Arts* (1931). Two of the most influential men's fashion magazines ever, *Esquire* and *Apparel Arts* featured full-color illustrations of fresh clothing trends, bold combinations, and a bevy of new products. Both magazines became arbiters of style and remain in print today, although *Apparel Arts* changed its name to *Gentlemen's Quarterly* (*GQ*) in 1957. *Esquire* chronicled a lifestyle that was not affordable to its target audience of middle-class readers. Nevertheless, wish fulfillment worked, because the slick, sophisticated *Esquire* grew from a quarterly to a monthly publication in less than a year. Circulation doubled each month from 1934 to 1935 in spite of its steep 50-cent cover price.

First sold only in men's stores, *Esquire* targeted "that class just below knighthood—the cream of that great middle class between the nobility and the peasantry." It not only offered clothing advice but also presented an overall lifestyle for men to emulate. In October 1933, the founder Arnold Gingrich wrote in the first issue about the leisure time that many men now had—either by choice or as a result of unemployment. He called them "the new leisure class" and described their enjoyment of recreational sports such as golf and tennis. The magazine showcased what would be called "the good life" today and covered dominant trends in sophisticated entertainment—in the arts, in books, on stage, and at the movies. American luminaries and icons of modern masculinity such as F. Scott Fitzgerald, Ernest Hemingway, Ezra Pound, and John Dos Passos published early works in the glossy, oversized pages of *Esquire*. Those pages also contained full-color advertisements for cars and cocktails to complete the high-class image its readers sought. The magazine offered a chance to see how "the other half lived," though for many readers the image was just a fantasy.

At the same time that the cultivation of individual style was encouraged, mass production of cheap clothing, accessories, and other consumer goods increased. The Great Depression took its toll on tailors, just as it had on other professions. "Bespoke" tailoring, whereby clothes were made to fit individual customers, declined. In 1933, *Esquire* reported that double-breasted suits with fuller-cut trousers were in style. The "London cut," featuring softer materials and more flexible cuts, became the rage. Its nipped waist and folds flattered most men more than the confining, highly formal suits of the previous decade. Stylish Hollywood trendsetters such as Grant and Astaire adopted the look, which also added to its popularity. Metal zippers, invented in 1851 but not perfected until 1913, were promoted in the 1930s for use in children's clothes. Zippers went into wider use in men's clothes during the 1930s, adding convenience and a modern technical feel while further diminishing the visual distinction between the classes.

Even hats, which continued to be associated with the kind of work men did because they were mass produced and distributed nationwide, yielded to changing trends in men's fashion. In 1929, the National Association of Merchant Tailors announced that a properly dressed man needs "a dozen hats" to coordinate with his suits, the weather, and the proper occasion. In almost every photograph of men outdoors during the 1930s, they appear in hats—whether attending a baseball game or knee deep in a trout stream. Boys and laborers wore a flat cap, or "newsboy." Upper-class gents sported beaver fur fedoras or straw boaters, depending on the time of year. If an event required semi-formality, there was the homburg or bowler. In *Hatless Jack*, Neil Steinberg writes that a man without a hat could be ridiculed and "risked being hissed at by strangers and insulted by hatcheck girls." Failure to don the correct headgear was such a fashion crime that men might be killed "for wearing a straw hat out of season," according to Steinberg. That may be an exaggeration; however, a study of men's hats from the decade suggests that mass-produced hats allowed men both individual expression and group affiliation.

Why study natty threads for men, grocery shopping for women, images of fathers and mothers, women in the workforce, men in domestic life? Because remembering the forgotten lives of women from the 1930s helps us better understand the successes and failures of social and institutional responses to public suffering. Recovering the hidden lives of men helps us appreciate how social identities shape our experience as individuals. Studying representations of gender in the culture and media of the 1930s provides insight into the institutions of an era that continue to inform our modern life; for example, the media continue to shape and influence personal identity and lifestyle choices. Such a study also sheds light on the different ways Americans have responded to conflicts between individuals and groups in society. Screwball comedies—a genre utterly unique to the 1930s—perfectly captured many of the elements that made film popular during the Great Depression and provided important opportunities to work out the tension between representations of masculinity and femininity. They are curiously irreverent and elegantly disruptive of the norms common to the era. Screwball comedies were popular with audiences in the thirties, and whereas modern audiences continue to enjoy the originals, the genre barely outlived the decade.

Although actually a subgenre, screwball comedies were favored by two of the smaller studios, Columbia and RKO. Screwball themes and storylines reflected the public's desire to level the playing field between men and women and see the upper classes ridiculed or brought down a few notches at the same time. Screwball comedies provided desperately needed cathartic release through laughter. Studio executives, wealthy men themselves, thought this purging of emotion was better in the theater than in reality with women demanding equal rights in the workplace or the poor rising up in a class war. These glamorous, farcical films were crazy, escapist love stories in which sassy women assumed the lead and otherwise self-possessed men were happy to follow. The term "screwball" refers to a baseball thrown in a way that the hitter cannot predict its erratic path. The analogy works perfectly when trying to follow the plot of a screwball comedy. While there were many variations in screwballs, most shared a reversal of the familiar "boy-meets-girl" formula. Often a madcap heiress pursues a potential boyfriend or errant husband. Powerful men may be pushed off balance and scramble to keep up with her wacky and unconventional machinations. In the end, love triumphs and order is restored—at least for the moment.

In screwballs, if not in life, the reconciliation of class differences and the resolution of gender wars was reached without violence, and temporary frustration replaced pain and strife. Screwball heroes, such as Cary Grant and William Powell, were chic, sophisticated, and sardonic men whose masculinity is apparent without the need to prove it through physical exploits, as they did in other genres. Rather than relying on their hands or their brawn, these characters excel in a modern world that is urban, refined, and dominated by society events and nightlife. Similarly, screwball heroines defy the traditional and restrictive roles for women that resurfaced during the 1930s. They are valued for their wit, vitality, and beauty, not their motherly instincts. Like the men, they are preoccupied with social life, not political life or radical agendas, which makes their playful disruption of cultural norms acceptable, amusing, and even gleeful. Both women and men dress in cutting-edge styles, speak well, and carry themselves with confidence and grace. The film critic Andrew Sarris called screwballs "sex comedies without the sex." They allowed studios to continue to sell glamour and romance while showing the public the well-to-do as inept and unable to function like "normal" people.

Screwball comedies relied on witty verbal dialogue delivered at a rapid-fire pace, which took full advantage of new sound technologies. Grant launched his career in screwballs—a genre he himself didn't "get" in the beginning. The dashing actor would finally set the standard for this type of comedy with such films as *Topper* (1937) with Constance Bennett and *The Awful Truth* (1937) with Irene Dunne. *Bringing Up Baby* (1938) with Grant and Katherine Hepburn is considered one of the greatest screwball comedies ever made, even though it bombed with audiences upon its release. Other films that would become classics were commercially successful, including the Academy Award winning *It Happened One Night* (1934) with Clark Gable and Claudette Colbert, *Twentieth Century* (1934) with John Barrymore and Carole Lombard, and *My Man Godfrey* (1936) with Lombard and William Powell.

This style of comedy, although still influencing movies today, became less popular as America entered World War II and the Great Depression ended. With the national desire to present a unified front, laughing at zany, over-the-top rich people and the innuendo-laden scrapple between genders in screwball comedies became less appealing. Americans already keened to hard times, dug deep to confront war. Women benefited from less competition as they entered the workforce without the public opposition they faced during the 1930s. For men, a return to the traditional role of soldier and two-fisted champion replaced the urbane, light-hearted screwball lead. This unique brand of comedy and social critique would be replaced by traditional romantic comedies such as *Woman of the Year* (1942), *The More the Merrier* (1943), and *Good News* (1947). Nevertheless, many film historians believe that the screwball comedy is a classical American art form, and it accounts for some of the most memorable and distinct films of the 1930s. What was lost at the end of the era of screwball comedies was a valve to release the pressure of changing roles for women and men. For a while, World War II would serve as another kind of distraction until rigid divisions between men and women resurfaced in the 1950s and lead to the second wave of feminism and the women's liberation movement of the 1960s and 1970s.

Suggested Readings

Susan Ware's *Holding Their Own: American Women in the 1930s* (Boston: Twayne Publishers, 1982) remains the most comprehensive study of women's experience during the decade. Sarah Jane Deutsch and Nancy F. Cott's *From Ballots to Breadlines: American Women, 1920–1940* (Oxford: Oxford University Press, 1998) also provide a broad overview of women's experience, focusing on the evolution from rebellious Progressive Era feminists and flappers in the twenties to their vital and enthusiastic participation in the workforce in the forties. Many studies of women in the 1930s focus on specific demographic groups or particular vocations. Rebecca Jo Plant's *Mom: The Transformation of Motherhood in Modern America* (Chicago: University of Chicago Press, 2010) provides a historical context for the evolution of motherhood as a social identity, including a chapter on the tensions resulting from conflicting norms during the 1930s. Ruth Feldstein's *Motherhood in Black and White: Race and Sex in American Liberalism, 1930–1965* (Ithaca: Cornell University Press, 2000) includes the interaction of race and gender in the construction of motherhood beginning in the 1930s. Sarah Berry's *Screen Style: Fashion and Femininity in 1930s Hollywood* (Minneapolis: University of Minnesota Press, 2000) and Rebecca Arnold's *The American Look: Sportswear, Fashion, and the Image of Women in 1930s and 1940s New York* (London: I. B. Tauris, 2009) explore visible trends in the media that influenced women's roles in society. Finally, Constance Coiner's *Better Red: The Writing and Resistance of Tillie Olsen and Meridel Le Sueur* (Oxford University Press, 1998) reveals important insights into the lives of workingwomen, rural women, and immigrant women during the very worst of hard times.

For further discussion on crime and gangsters, see Bryan Burrough, *Public Enemies: America's Greatest Crime Wave and the Birth of the FBI, 1933–1934* (New York: Penguin Press, 2004); and Eliot Gorn, *Dillinger's Wild Ride: The Year That Made America's Public Enemy Number One* (New York: Oxford University Press, 2009). Jim Fisher's *The Lindberg Case* (New Jersey: Reuters University Press, 1987) offers a detailed look at the case that captured the nation's attention. For an interesting look at male culture in the 1930s, see Alan Flusser, *Dressing the Man: Mastering the Art of Permanent Fashion* (New York: Harper Collins, 2002); and Randy McBee, "'He Likes Women More Than He Likes Drink and That Is Quite Unusual': Working-Class Social Clubs, Male Culture, and Heterosocial Relations in the United States, 1920s–1930s," *Gender & History* 11, no. 1 (1999): 84–112.

8

Media

"Wrap Your Troubles in Dreams"
—Harry Barris, Ted Koehler,
and Billy Moll, 1931

PICTURE THIS. Four men in a small stateroom on a transatlantic ship heading for New York. A man wearing a fitted suit and tie with heavy greasepaint eyebrows, glasses, and a signature chevron mustache huddles with another man in peasant clothes and a Tyrolean hat as the first man agrees to harbor three stowaways. A third man with blonde curls, a top hat, and shabby clothes lies asleep on the narrow cabin bed, while the fourth, a young and handsome character, looms silently in the background. A knock at the door interrupts the conversation between Otis B. Driftwood (Groucho Marx) and Fiorello (Chico Marx), and two maids arrive to make up the room. Sleepy Tomasso (Harpo Marx) is pulled off the bed and falls over the women. With wandering hands, he puts one of the maids into a wrestling hold instead of the passionate embrace that seemed imminent. Another knock and an engineer enters the room, followed moments later by a burly assistant, a comely manicurist, a fellow passenger looking for her Aunt Minnie, a maid to "mop up," and finally four stewards with enormous trays of food. In total, fifteen people crowd into the tiny room. Otis offers the hilarious understatement, "is it just my imagination, or is it getting crowded in here?" Then the door opens and everyone topples out in a pile in front of Otis's love interest who has arrived expecting a discreet romantic interlude.

This scene from the Marx Brothers' 1935 movie *A Night at the Opera* runs less than 4 minutes and remains one of the funniest sketches in movie history. The absurd, controlled chaos exemplifies the style that made the Marx Brothers among the most memorable and popular box office attractions during the 1930s. Groucho, Chico, Harpo, and sometimes Zeppo seamlessly blended sharp, witty dialogue filled with innuendo with impeccably timed physical comedy against straight-faced foils. Although scenes seem to flow spontaneously, creating these classic movies required the hard work and expertise of seasoned professionals. The stateroom scene took two weeks to rehearse before it was immortalized on film. The characters played by the Marx Brothers are irreverent, antiestablishment, and gleeful miscreants, and no one was immune from their biting jocularity. The anarchy that reigned in Marx Brothers' comedies reflected the instability Americans felt following the 1929 stock market crash. Their films provided opportunities to laugh in the face of utter despair and hopelessness.

Indeed, Marx Brothers films reveal much about the preferences and preoccupations of Depression Era moviegoers. Groucho, who had himself suffered a major setback after investing heavily in stocks during the 1920s, perfectly punctured both stuffed shirts and social norms with his verbal darts in the 1930s. He demonstrated that no matter the circumstances, he would act as his own man and speak his mind. The Marx Brothers screwball, rapid-fire assault on rich, upper-class society types appealed to Great Depression audiences; however, the wealthy were not the quartet's only targets. The Marx Brothers ridiculed higher education in *Horse Feathers* (1932), gangsters in *Monkey Business* (1931), and even war and patriotism in *Duck Soup* (1933). Neither the individual nor the institution was safe from their barbs, and this formula worked for nearly all of their Hollywood films.

A study of Marx Brothers' films also shows that one cannot pigeonhole the media of the 1930s as simply providing escapist fare for audiences—as is so often the case. To look at mass media in the thirties through such a narrow lens underestimates the influence and distorts the legacy of the period when mass media came of age. The mastery of new technologies like sound and the surge of creativity that rose in response to increased regulation helped create a series of "golden ages" during the 1930s that are the direct progenitors of the modern media audiences enjoy today. For instance, radio and film, two media that were seen as novelties in the 1920s, transformed into major industries that Americans integrated into their daily lives. Print also changed to reflect an emerging culture of celebrity in glossy fan magazines and newspaper gossip columns. A majority of Americans in the 1930s—across gender, race, generational, and class differences—were united as the first to see mass media as a necessity, not just a luxury, during a time when luxuries were few and far between. Of course, mass media provided entertainment and distraction during the 1930s, but more important, it established a strong and powerful presence in American homes that shaped an increasingly mainstream, national American identity.

Perhaps the most democratic of media, radios were played in public places where everyone could listen. By the end of the 1930s, nearly every home had at least one radio, and into the 1940s, loudspeakers in public squares and mounted on trucks broadcast important programs so that even people without a radio could keep up with current events and popular trends. Radio programs were delivered free of charge, thanks to advertisers who promoted products and services on the shows. Companies worked with radio networks to sponsor certain programs and link products to popular radio characters. For instance, *Little Orphan Annie* became a pitch character for the fortified chocolate drink Ovaltine, and the mysterious crime fighter in the program *The Shadow* appeared in advertisements and brochures for the anthracite coal company Blue Coal. Sponsorships were not just for children's programming. One of the most popular variety shows was named for its sponsor, the Chase and Sanborn coffee company. Advertising even generated a new phrase to describe the melodramatic shows broadcast during the day for housewives. "Soap operas" were thus named because soap companies such as Lux and Proctor & Gamble sponsored them. According to one study, expenditures for radio advertising went from $4.8 million in 1927 to $215.6 million by 1939, highlighting the power and reach radio had during the decade. This is an extraordinary increase considering the context of the Great Depression.

In print media, a new form of journalism emerged alongside a new generation of journalists ready to deliver all sorts of information to satisfy a growing hunger for news and commentary. As American culture moved further away from Victorian-era repressiveness, the public wanted stories about salacious topics such as sex, scandal, and crime. "Tabloid journalism" filled the desire for prurient stories, as did the rise of the personal columnist. Many of these men and women gained power and fame by reporting celebrity gossip, a subject that remains popular with many entertainment consumers today. Newspapers promoted columnists who dispensed with the journalistic principle of objectivity and wrote their own opinions about movies stars, politicians, business leaders, and other public figures. Walter Winchell was among the first to become popular with readers starting in the late 1920s. His "On Broadway" column in the *New York Daily Mirror* reflected Winchell's unique writing style that favored short phrases set off by ellipses, slang, and innuendo to make his point. "Gossip," Winchell once said, "is the art of saying nothing in a way that leaves practically nothing unsaid." Winchell's column became a "must read" in New York City and soon was syndicated to two thousand newspapers around the world.

Those who lacked power loved Winchell. Working people such as waiters and waitresses, cabbies, and doormen provided Winchell with much of the juicy gossip he used to his benefit. By 1932, Winchell's fame spread to a larger audience. He was given his own radio show that was essentially an extension of his newspaper column. With his distinctive delivery of short bursts of words, Winchell sounded like a human machine gun backed by the clacking sound of a teletype. His dispatches reeked of big-city urgency and importance. Winchell skewered the rich and famous, much to the delight of his audience, and his popularity—and power—spread. Winchell had his own table at the Stork Club, an elite and upscale establishment in Manhattan where the most powerful people in New York, whether elected officials or mobsters, visited in the hopes of remaining in his good graces. Many lived in fear that Winchell would destroy their reputations and careers with a clever but cruel line in his column or on the radio. As testament to his celebrity and influence, President Roosevelt invited Winchell to the White House following his election.

One of the best examples of celebrity making the news was the trial of Bruno Richard Hauptmann for the kidnapping and murder of Charles Lindbergh, Jr., son of the famed aviator Charles Lindbergh, Sr. and the well-known writer Anne Morrow Lindbergh. The trial began January 3, 1935, lasted five weeks, and cost the state of New Jersey a million dollars.

All available media—newspapers, magazines, newsreels, and radio—covered the dramatic proceedings with a frenzy never before seen. Reporters snuck in microphones and cameras to record testimony. Celebrities came to watch. People sold souvenirs. The general public packed the courtroom in the Hunterdon County courthouse in Flemington, New Jersey, each day as a series of witnesses took the stand. The reporter and social critic H. L. Mencken called it "the biggest story since the Resurrection." Hyperbole like Mencken's is typical of the new sensationalism in journalism that would become a standard in news reporting.

Across the nation and around the world, people followed the trial as it unfolded in the media. Americans read reports of the dramatic testimony of Amandus Hockmuth, the eighty-seven-year-old man who lived on the road leading to the Lindbergh estate. Hockmuth told the court he saw a man driving a green car pass his house and go toward the Lindbergh home. Hockmuth remembered that the man glared at him and that the car had a ladder in it. This was significant because everyone already new that a ladder had been found at the scene. A few weeks into the trial, the defense attorney Edward J. Reilly made an unprecedented direct appeal on the radio, pleading for witnesses to come forward, but most of the people who did were described as "loonies." Throughout, images of the bereaved parents Anne and Charles Lindbergh appeared in newspapers and on the big screen. Although there had been sensational trials before, the Hauptmann trial is the one that earned the title "Trial of the Century," and for good reason.

Media coverage of the trial would shape audience expectations of court reporting from then on, with implications for all news reporting. The media's unruly behavior during the Hauptmann trial forced journalism to change. A two-year study of trial coverage resulted in the American Bar Association recommending that cameras and broadcasting equipment be limited—or banned—from court proceedings. States turned those recommendations into laws, many of which still stand today, despite challenges by journalists and news organizations. Finally, coverage and public discussion of the Lindbergh case demonstrates a growing body of shared knowledge among Americans that transcended their local communities. More and more, people were pulled into national discussions about significant events, social trends, and even personal perspectives on public figures—journalists, politicians, and celebrities—whom they counted among their intimate acquaintances. This body of shared knowledge would, perhaps more than anything else, shape American culture in the age of mass consumption.

As the old saying goes, the more people learn, the more they understand how little they know. Although the media had the power to inform, it also produced considerable uncertainty and confusion. After the jury returned its guilty verdict on February 13, 1935, a *New York Times* reporter described Hauptmann, handcuffed, silent, and still between two guards, "his face ashen white and terror in his deep-set eyes, while he heard the jury state its verdict and the judge pronounce sentence." Ironically, his death by electric chair on April 3, 1936 provided little closure in the case. Everyone had heard the same story, and still there was no consensus as to Hauptman's guilt. In the March 1936 issue of *Forum Magazine*, the attorney Richard A. Knight argued that Hauptmann had been unfairly tried. A 1938 article in *Liberty* magazine even went so far as to claim that the baby found along the road was not the Lindbergh baby. These articles flew in the face of much of the media coverage that had been biased against Hauptmann from the start of the trial. After all, Lindbergh was one of the most photographed, interviewed, and admired men in the United States at the time.

The speculation continues today with books, TV shows, and websites devoted to the case. Many theories abound, including that anti-German sentiment at the time caused police to frame Hauptmann, a native-born German. It has also been speculated that one of the Lindberghs may have accidently killed the child and concocted a phony kidnapping as a cover-up. In 1987, the former FBI special agent and criminologist Jim Fischer published *The Lindbergh Case*, which exhaustively looked at the evidence and the trial. He concluded that Hauptmann did kidnap and kill the Lindbergh baby in cold blood for the ransom money. He wrote a follow-up, *The Ghosts of Hopewell*, in 2006. Neither book has put to rest the rampant debate, and speculation continues.

The power of media to influence public opinion, attitudes, and actions can be observed in every aspect of life during the 1930s. Both Franklin and Eleanor Roosevelt had pronounced media acumen and used print and radio resources to forever transform the relationship between the White House and the citizens of Main Street. Roosevelt used radio to great effect, talking directly to voters as the governor of New York. As president, he used the medium brilliantly to create a new kind of political and social power. Between 1933 and 1944, he broadcast thirty radio addresses from the White House, which were known as the "fireside chats." In the inaugural program aired at the end of his first week as president, Roosevelt explained America's banking crisis to the American people. He was concerned a panic would ensue if he did not address the matter. On air, Roosevelt's delivery matched his message. In clear terms and a comforting tone, he assured the public that banks would reopen the next day, following a bank holiday. The *New York Times* covered Roosevelt's unprecedented informal chat and concluded: "When millions of people can hear the president speak to them directly in their own homes, we get a new meaning for the old phrase about a public man 'going to the country.'" People listened and responded. As a result, there were actually more deposits than withdrawals in the days following the address.

As first lady, Eleanor Roosevelt continued her established career as a writer and public speaker at the same time as she cultivated her persona as a media celebrity. Like her husband, Eleanor utilized the media to advance her mission to educate, advocate, and promote dialogue on important issues. Also like her husband, she had nearly ten years of experience on radio prior to becoming first lady. Following the 1932 election, Eleanor began a series of twelve radio news commentaries sponsored by Pond's cold cream company. She donated the proceeds to charity—a practice she continued during her tenure in the White House from 1933 to 1945. She broadcast for a series of sponsors after Pond's as a freelance host and on contract with NBC. Her audience was primarily women, but she counted a surprising number of men among her listeners. The same would be true of the readers of her published writing.

At the end of 1935, Eleanor began her popular syndicated newspaper column *My Day.* She wrote it six days a week, every week, until her death in 1962. Within three years, *My Day* was syndicated in sixty-two daily newspapers and read by over four million nationwide. Over the course of thirty years, Eleanor would produce an amazing 8,112 installments of *My Day.* The subjects for early columns included amusing observations or touching sketches inspired in her daily life as wife and mother. It would not be long before she began to use the column to address larger public issues and encourage dialogue on the controversies she deemed important. For example, she announced her resignation from the Daughters of the American Revolution because of the organization's refusal to lease its auditorium for a concert by the African American contralto Marian Anderson.

In addition to writing short pieces, Eleanor wrote lengthy magazine articles on issues she felt especially committed to—everything from deep reflections on moral debates to commentary on social and political issues. As a freelance writer, she enjoyed the freedom to choose particular venues to reach target audiences and wrote for magazines as diverse as *The Saturday Evening Post*, *McCall's*, *The New Republic*, *Women's Day*, *House & Garden*, and even the *Harvard Law Review*. In addition to freelance work, Eleanor entered into several extended contracts with monthly magazines including *Women's Home Companion* and *Ladies Home Journal*. The "I Want You to Write to Me" column that began in August 1933 was a typical format for Eleanor, and one that set the stage for the kind of personal access and mutual interaction modern citizens expect from public figures. The response at the time was overwhelming; approximately three hundred thousand individuals wrote to her within the first five months.

Thirties audiences turned to the media for more than just news or to catch up with their favorite public personalities. People of all ages could find common ground and shared enjoyment at the movies. Of the many "golden ages" associated with the 1930s, none carry more long-term impact than the golden age of film. The stars and films of the era are still revered by critics, academics, and fans alike. *Grand Hotel* (1932), starring Greta Garbo, John Barrymore, Lionel Barrymore, and Joan Crawford; *Top Hat* (1935), starring Fred Astaire and Ginger Rogers; and *Petrified Forest* (1936), starring Leslie Howard, Bette Davis, and Humphrey Bogart, are considered classics. The year 1939 remains Hollywood's greatest for movies. The Academy Awards had to expand its "best picture" category in 1940 to honor the ten best movies made during "Hollywood's greatest year," including *Mr. Smith Goes to Washington*, *Love Affair*, *Wuthering Heights*, *Wizard of Oz*, *Goodbye, Mr. Chips*, *Ninotchka*, *Stagecoach*, *Of Mice and Men*, and the winner, *Gone with the Wind*. Hollywood offered moviegoers of the Great Depression feelings of hope, an escape from daily hardships, and a peek at the good life that was increasingly available for purchase. Many theaters had been built during the

1920s and looked like opulent palaces; celebrities on the silver screen were venerated as royalty.

The medium of film has been a ubiquitous part of everyday life for the average American since the 1930s; however, none of the glitz, glamour, entertainment, or escape we often associate with the period would have been possible without major advances in technology. The change that revolutionized filmmaking forever is the introduction of sound. Of course, films had never been truly silent. Once they became mainstream entertainment, movies were always accompanied by music, whether from a single upright piano, a full orchestra, or audio recording. Musical scores influenced how people reacted to what they saw on screen. The music heightened the tension of a hero's derring-do, punctuated a comedic gag, or moved viewers to tears in a dramatic scene. The so-called talking pictures added audible dialog that drastically changed the popular aesthetic of film, and it altered significantly the techniques used by the performers who appeared in them. Radical changes in technology required enormous investments of time and lots and lots of money.

When people talk about the advent of talking pictures, they are referring to synchronized sound, or the words, music, and audio effects that match on-screen movements consistently and at a pleasing level. Synchronized sound had always been the goal since the earliest days of film; however, no one could invent a commercially viable process that provided perfect synchronization every time a film was projected. Even the genius who invented the motion-picture camera, Thomas Edison, failed to devise a sound system. Some filmmakers—Charlie Chaplin in particular—firmly believed that film was a visual medium and speech should be left to the legitimate stage. After some highly publicized failures that left the public dismissive of sound, studios reduced their research and development funds into synchronized sound technology. The public heard the earliest example of synchronized sound in 1926 with the premiere of *Don Juan*. The film had been shot as a silent movie but was screened by playing prerecorded synchronized music and sound effects.

By 1927, a technological breakthrough made it possible to synchronize sound with film, although the technique was mostly reserved for short or experimental films. On October 6 of that year, the public tide turned in favor of talking pictures when the superstar Al Jolson faced the camera and boldly proclaimed, "Wait a minute. Wait a minute. You ain't heard nothin' yet!" In *The Jazz Singer*, Warner Brothers released the first full-length motion picture that combined a fictional storyline with synchronized sound. The studio called its "sound-on-disc" system Vitaphone, after the New York-based experimental sound studio they had purchased in 1925. *The Jazz Singer* was well conceived to bridge the divide between silent and talking films. It showcased the lyrics to songs, but still relied on intertitles, the plates that communicate dialogue to the audience in silent films. It was the moments of Jolson singing on camera that captured the enthusiastic support of moviegoers, and henceforth everyone wanted "talking pictures."

Some filmmakers switched from silent to sound during or even after production. In 1930, Howard Hughes had half finished filming *Hell's Angels*, a silent World War I aviation epic that featured some of the most amazing flying sequences ever captured on film. Upon learning the public wanted sound, Hughes fired the female lead, Greta Nissen, because she spoke with an accent, and hired the then unknown Jean Harlow. He also changed directors; Edmund Golding was dismissed and the newcomer James Whale was hired to reshoot dialog scenes for the film. These were costly moves that delayed the film's release, but Hughes bankrolled the production himself and the gamble paid off. Though it received mixed reviews from critics, audiences loved *Hell's Angels*; the film has been hailed by film historians as an American classic and the first talking blockbuster.

Hollywood continued to produce silent films until the end of 1931 as the major studios scrambled to embrace the new technology and switch to sound. The smaller, independent studios couldn't afford to make the change, and some artists, most notably Chaplin, just didn't want to. Although audiences quickly took to the new technology and demanded more and more talking pictures, Chaplin believed that talking pictures lacked the artistry of silent films. In addition, he feared that if his world-famous character, the "Little Tramp," spoke in English, it might limit his global appeal. He eschewed sound for his 1931 masterpiece, *City Lights*. Chaplin even mocked the use of sound in his critique of industry, *Modern Times* (1936). Since he owned his own production and distribution companies, he could decide if—and when—he would adopt sound. Twelve years after sound became standard in Hollywood, Chaplin would use it to successfully parody Nazi Germany in *The Great Dictator* (1940). Chaplin's final speech in the movie warns of fascism and carried great impact with audiences because his voice could be heard for the first time in theaters.

Most studios had neither the artistic integrity of Chaplin nor the financial clout of Hughes and had no choice but to put their financial futures at risk by borrowing money to make the transition to sound. For actors, the change was even more stark and unpredictable. If they spoke with a heavy accent or a weak-sounding voice, their careers could be over. The same was true if actors' voices did not match the fickle expectations of audiences. Studio executives used sound as an excuse to get rid of troublesome or expensive talent. People behind the cameras also had to adapt or quit. Directors, who formerly yelled directions to actors from behind the camera, now had to find different ways to elicit the actions or emotions they wanted in a scene. Still, some in the industry prospered by the change. Speech coaches and Broadway performers who were skilled in reciting dialog now found those skills in big demand.

The widespread use of sound in the thirties resulted in the expansion of many film genres and the creation of a few new ones. Westerns, comedies, and drama had all been represented during the silent era. Sound gave filmmakers an opportunity to reimagine those genres and to explore new ones, such as screwball comedies and musicals. Fast-paced screwball comedies filled with quick wit and wordplay could have flourished only in a film with sound. While advances in technology propelled film production, filmmakers of the 1930s were not experimental in terms of narrative, and innovation did not always extend to source material. Some of the most popular films drew inspiration from stories and characters from classic literature, folklore, and mythology. The studios produced films that followed predictable formulas, allowing them to exchange actors, sets, and locations while capitalizing on winning and popular themes. Most of those would inform a growing mainstream (white, middle-class) American identity that promoted individual initiative, had faith in a just society, and believed that anyone who worked hard enough could transcend social class.

No other type of film benefited from the advancement of sound technology more than the musical. Musicals were popular on the stage before appearing on the silver screen and were a favored remedy for audiences looking for sheer spectacle and escape from the real world. These films are considered "pure Hollywood" today, but early 1930s musicals were often hampered by the restrictive formats directors took from stage musicals and fixed cameras. Increased experience behind the camera and improved technologies on the sets allowed studios to create some of the most memorable hits of the decade. Already known for its gangster films, Warner Brothers released "backstage" musicals such as *42nd Street* (1933), which invigorated the genre. The Broadway choreographer Busby Berkeley gave Warner musicals a distinctive look and style with overhead camera angles that displayed glamorous showgirls dancing synchronically. The songwriting team of Harry Warren and Al Dubin provided catchy songs such as "You're Getting to Be a Habit with Me" and "Shuffle Off to Buffalo." Audiences were entranced by glamour and sympathetic to the melodramatic stories of show people. Other musicals from Warner Brothers include *Gold Diggers of 1933* (1933), *Gold Diggers of 1935* (1935), *Footlight Parade* (1933), and *Dames* (1934).

With their tuneful "rags-to-riches" storylines, these movies acted as fantasy fulfillment for Depression Era audiences. Musical numbers such as "We're in the Money" from *Gold Diggers of 1933* promised audiences that better days were ahead. Ironically, their influences outlived their popularity because when better days arrived, audience interest in "backstage" musicals waned. The public no longer cared for the clichéd plots and increasingly overwrought dance numbers. For the rest of the century, Broadway musical theater would prove more resilient than over-the-top Hollywood productions. Although musicals resurfaced in cycles for the rest of the twentieth century, including a significant comeback by MGM during the 1950s, musicals would never again touch the public the way they did during the 1930s.

Warner Brothers was not the only studio in the song-and-dance movie game. Depression Era audiences could also count on musicals from RKO to give them a lift. What the small studio lacked in financial power it made up for in a series of sophisticated and elegant musicals starring Fred Astaire and Ginger Rogers that were set in a dreamlike world with luxurious art deco sets and costumes. The music, from America's greatest composers such as Jerome Kern, Irving Berlin, and George and Ira Gershwin, set the perfect modern romantic tone. Together, Astaire and Rogers would light up the screen in ten musicals between 1933 and 1949, the most famous being *Top Hat* (1935) and *Swing Time* (1936), which set record ticket sales on the opening days at Radio City Music Hall. The Astaire-Rogers musicals transported Depression audiences into the dream realm of tuxedos and gowns, swanky nightclubs, and elegant rooftop cafes in Venice and Monte Carlo, where romance was just a song and dance away. Although the sets and storylines were pure soundstage fantasy, these movies conveyed the sense that love was far more important than money, a theme that resonated powerfully with Depression Era audiences.

Not everyone in Hollywood was interested in portraying splendid romances or providing idealized visions of the world. Some filmmakers used images to dramatically convey social and political issues. One example is Warner Brothers' *I Am a Fugitive from a Chain Gang* (1932), which was based on the real-life experiences of Robert Elliott Burns. In the gritty film, Paul Muni stars as James Allen, an unemployed World War I veteran who finds himself disenfranchised, unemployed, impoverished, and finally entangled in a robbery. He is arrested and forced to do hard labor in a Southern prison under a cruel and vicious warden. Allen escapes and establishes himself as a productive and respectable member of society in Chicago, only to have his success threatened when he is exposed as a fugitive. No amount of hard work or good intention can erase the past, and all hope for redemption is lost as Allen disappears into the shadows as a broken man in the final scene. There is no escape. The film, which premiered at the lowest point of the Great Depression, challenged the accessibility of the American Dream and called into question America's penal system. It even helped mobilize a political movement that changed the treatment of Southern prison inmates.

With the rise of the media came early concerns about its role in society. One notorious incident that got everyone in America talking occurred on Halloween Eve, October 30, 1938, when a young actor-writer-director dramatized H. G. Wells's classic 1898 science fiction novel *The War of the Worlds* for his CBS radio show *Mercury Theater on the Air.* Orson Welles, a twenty-two-year-old wunderkind, opened the broadcast acknowledging that *The War of The Worlds* had no further significance than the holiday offering it was intended to be. According to Welles, it was "the Mercury Theater's own radio version of dressing up in a sheet and jumping out of a bush and saying Boo!" Following this disclaimer, the broadcast continued with a fictional dance program before a series of radio news bulletins from Grover's Mills, New Jersey, interrupted. The news announcements segued into highly descriptive "live remotes" from a reporter (played by Frank Readick) who described the aliens for listeners:

> Good heavens, something's wriggling out of the shadow like a gray snake. Now it's another one, and another. They look like tentacles to me. There, I can see the thing's body. It's large, large as a bear and it glistens like wet leather. But that face, it. . . . Ladies and gentlemen, it's indescribable. I can hardly force myself to keep looking at it. The eyes are black and gleam like a serpent. The mouth is V-shaped with saliva dripping from its rimless lips that seem to quiver and pulsate.

More and more saucers arrive and the aliens begin destroying the human armies attempting to turn back the invaders. The story continues to be told in the form of "emergency bulletins" and reports "from the field." The aliens use poison gas on people as they march toward New York City. Five of the monstrous killing machines lay waste to the Big Apple before the program breaks for a commercial and a reminder that the story is fictional.

Such was the power of radio and so compelling was the work of Welles and his company that many listeners missed these clues and believed the invasion from Mars was real rather than a well-produced Halloween prank. Millions of listeners did not wait around for the third act of the drama, choosing instead to flee the Martian invasion. This was unfortunate because the final third of the performance is delivered as a more traditional narrative by one of the survivors, who speaks in an extended monologue. On the show's tenth anniversary in 1948, Welles's colleague and Mercury Theater player John Housemen described how the show impacted people. He recalled millions of American citizens, mostly on the East Coast, who "milled about the streets, clung sobbing to one another, or drove wildly in all directions to avoid asphyxiation and flaming death." Houseman noted that approximately one-half were in fear of Martians—not of "Germans, Japanese, or unknown enemies." Intuitively or intentionally, Welles had tapped into the undercurrent of terror generated by the war in Europe.

Overall, the incident vividly exposed the media's growing influence as a mediator of truth and its ability to give shape to ideas and beliefs as well as perceptions and behaviors. In an early example of the self-spiraling media spectacle modern audiences are well acquainted with, newsmakers hyped the scope of the panic. Some newspapers accused Welles of intentionally starting a panic. Print media had always had a love-hate relationship with radio and the *War of the Worlds* broadcast provided an opportunity to accuse radio people of reckless and irresponsible conduct. A major scholarly work by Dr. Hadley Cantril in 1940, *The Invasion from Mars, a Study in the Psychology of Panic*, estimated that about six million people heard the broadcast and only about one million of them thought it real. Of those who believed the drama, the majority had tuned in to the program late. The Mercury Theater program aired opposite the more popular NBC variety show *The Chase and Sanborn Hour*, starring the ventriloquist Edgar Bergen and his puppet partner Charlie McCarthy. Listeners who had turned the dial after Bergen and McCarthy's opening sketch missed Welles's disclaimer, hearing only the "breaking news" bulletins. Welles also skipped an announcement that reminded the audience that what they were hearing was not actually occurring. Cantril's report asserted that tuning in to *War of the Worlds* twelve minutes late helped spark the panic, especially among people with little education.

The radio, or "the wireless," as some called it, became a dominant force in almost every household during the decade. For the first time, people of all economic levels received the same news, sports, and entertainment programming. Thanks to readily available installment payment plans, even those struggling to pay their bills could afford a radio. Production increased to meet demand, and in just four years the average price of a radio dropped from $139 in 1929 to $47 by 1933, and the number of American households owning a radio climbed to 60 percent. Cars, which were also increasingly accessible with consumer credit, started rolling off the assembly line equipped with radios. By the end of the decade, twenty-eight million people were spending an average of four and a half hours per day listening to radio. The modern era of personal electronic entertainment had begun, transforming family time and establishing new social rituals. People ate dinner near the radio so as not to miss their favorite programs. Families stared at the radio console's lighted dial, mesmerized by the pictures they "saw" in their own imaginations. Coworkers, friends, and neighbors exchanges their views on what had happened on last night's shows.

The types of programs on the airwaves during the 1930s would be familiar to anyone who watches current broadcast television. The original TV networks—NBC, ABC, and CBS—started out as radio networks. Radio writers, producers, and performers perfected all of the entertainment formats enjoyed today such as comedy, drama, science fiction, soap operas, Westerns, and police shows. From shows featuring news and political commentary to entertaining family dramas and talent shows, radio programming had something for everyone. Many of the popular children's comic strips of the day were brought to life on radio, including *Little Orphan Annie*, *Dick Tracy*, *Superman*, and *Popeye*. Music and variety shows inspired trends and fads and helped define a new generation of teens. Comedy shows featured popular vaudeville entertainers who cheered up Depression Era listeners. Vaudeville, a traveling stage show featuring a variety of acts from acrobats to comedians, was America's most popular form of entertainment until the advent of radio and film. Many vaudevillians, such as Jack Benny, George Burns, Gracie Allen, Edgar Bergen, Fanny Brice, Bob Hope, Eddie Cantor, and the Marx Brothers left the grind of nonstop town-to-town touring for increased fame and wealth in broadcasting. These comedians could reach more people by standing behind a microphone in a New York or Los Angeles studio than they could from countless one-night performances across America.

Like all media productions, radio programs reflected the values and beliefs prevalent at the time. One of the most popular comedy radio shows of the 1930s may seem unfathomable—even offensive—to modern listeners; however, understanding the long-running show as a cultural artifact in historical context provides important clues about the media's role as arbiter of race relations in pre–civil rights America. The Harlem Renaissance had introduced African American culture into mainstream American culture, but authentic representations of African Americans in mass media remained conspicuously absent. As a result of the Great Migration, African Americans had established themselves in the North and East and West while reinventing themselves as best they could in the South. By the end of the 1920s, they were ready for more accurate representations of the black experience in the public domain. What they got in 1928 was *Amos 'n Andy*, a situational comedy-drama about two African American men operating an inner-city cab company; the show was created and performed by two white broadcasters, Charles Correll and Freeman Gosden.

When *Amos 'n Andy* debuted on the radio, it was met with immediate controversy. Although the show represented a dramatic breakthrough in the amount of airtime devoted to black culture, there were no black performers, writers, or technicians on the set. The setting was Harlem and, unlike the majority of the representations of African Americans in the media, Correll and Gosden scripted believable and relevant stories that many listeners struggling to get by during the Depression could identify with. Correll and Gosden followed common practices by relying on caricatures and race-based dialects in the show. Caricatures of African Americans would have been recognizable to audiences and highly visible in advertisements, in film, and on other radio programs. They evolved over the course of 150 years, beginning in the South and figuring largely during the post–Civil War Reconstruction Era. By the turn of the century, caricatures such as the Mammy, Uncle Tom, and Coon could be found everywhere on consumer foods and in the media, from advertisements to great literature. *Amos 'n Andy* simply updated characters types that were already part of a collective heritage.

Based on these underlying conditions, it may seem surprising that by 1931 *Amos 'n Andy* was a nationwide success that, according to some historians, appealed to people of all races. In truth, it is difficult to assess the popularity of the show among African Americans. They were among the hardest hit by the Depression and were less likely than whites to have radios in their homes. They were also less likely to be polled. At the height of its popularity, some theaters submitted to audience demands to play *Amos 'n Andy* through the theater's sound system, delaying the start of the movie. Since most theaters were segregated, this too is an unreliable indicator of its status among African Americans. The most compelling evidence of the show's popularity is its longevity. The *Amos 'n Andy* radio show ran until November 25, 1960. The radio historian John Dunning said that the bitterness Americans felt over the Depression "was relieved by the plights of two commonest of common men." Fans loved the antics of characters who were initially parodies but over time were like old friends. Correll and Gosden each played multiple characters, developing rich, layered performances that transcended the limitations of the radio show format. Something worked because *Amos 'n Andy* outlasted almost all other contemporary radio programs and a short-lived television program that included a cast of talented African Americans and reignited the controversy surrounding the show's premise.

Some modern critics have argued that *Amos 'n Andy* amounted essentially to white performers broadcasting in black face; to be sure, the shows tells us very little about the concerns of African Americans at the time. On the one hand, the script was predicated on embarrassing distortions about African Americans. At best, the result was appropriation. At worst, the show exhibited rampant exploitation. It was certainly not inclusive. On the other hand, the longevity of *Amos 'n Andy* guaranteed a certain amount of interest in African Americans that may have helped them in the long run. White Americans may not have learned anything about the specific conditions faced by African Americans, but some viewers gained a level of tolerance and sensitivity that would lead them to support their rights as citizens. *Amos 'n Andy* may have perpetuated stereotypes about African Americans, but it also built an audience for the many ethnic sitcoms that would be popular later in the century, such as *Sanford and Son*, *Good Times*, and even *The Cosby Show*. The only conclusion that seems beyond dispute is that representations of race continue to be contentious issues in American culture.

The role of the media as a cultural force in the 1930s must be considered alongside the emergence of major media empires that exercised massive economic and political power. Sponsorships and advertising were already time-tested ways for the media to capitalize on its growing influence. Merchandising and direct marketing introduced during the decade would both propel popular culture and boost an emergent fan movement. Among the best examples of successful merchandising and the development of a loyal fan base relates to the most iconic movie star from the 1930s, a six-year-old girl with curly blonde hair and an irrepressible smile named Shirley Temple. In 1932, when she was four, Temple was discovered during a talent search at a Los Angeles dance studio. Temple made short films and brief appearances in feature films until 1934, when she starred in *Bright Eyes*, a feature film developed specifically for her. Temple went on to earn international fame, lifting the spirits of moviegoers in a series of popular musical comedies and dramas until 1938. Her films cost little to make and returned big profits. If box office receipts are the measure of success, Temple was the biggest celebrity, drawing large audiences to movie theaters from 1935 to 1938.

Many of Temple's films involve tempestuous social or personal issues and frequently take place in unavoidably turbulent settings such as the Civil War South. In *Our Little Girl* (1935), Temple's character successfully renews the love between her estranged parents, bringing them back from the brink of divorce and restoring the family unit. In *The Little Princess* (1939), Temple plays Sara Crewe, the good-natured only daughter of a widowed officer fighting in the Boer War. Set in an exclusive private school for girls in class-divided Victorian England, Sara's world comes crashing down when her father is listed as missing in action. Since she has no other family and nowhere else to go, she is moved to the garret and allowed to earn her keep as a maid. This drastic change of circumstance is made worse when she is treated cruelly by the headmistress and ridiculed by the other children.

In spite of her grim circumstances, Sara retains her spirit and optimism. She makes the best of her situation and never gives up hope that her father will return. Over time, she earns the love and devotion of nearly all those around her until eventually she is reunited with her father and returned to her rightful station. One film historian claims that such pure, selfless, healing love comforted the sad, lonely audiences of the Great Depression, and such an explanation makes sense. It also seems likely that Temple's innocent altruism carried an important symbolic message for Depression Era audiences. The extreme promotion of self-sacrificing humanity reinforced ethical and moral values as an alternative to costly New Deal programs. Some audience members saw individual responsibility as the solution to social suffering—whether that meant digging deep and working hard to persevere in hard times or doing charitable work and making voluntary donations. In Temple's films, the sunny disposition and spontaneously offered affection are all it takes to soften the hardest hearts and change the worst of circumstances.

Temple was one of the first stars marketed to the public through a concerted campaign of merchandise tie-ins. The Ideal Toy Company negotiated a contract to manufacture and distribute a variety of Temple-inspired items. A movie fan could buy Shirley Temple coloring books, toys, dishware, soap, clothing, and plastic dolls. In fact, the Shirley Temple doll accounted for one-third of all dolls sales in 1935, and clothes for her dolls cost more than clothes for real girls. Companies such as the breakfast cereal maker Post used her name on food products. Exploiting her image was good for business in more ways than just direct sales. To lure customers, movie theaters and department stores held Temple look-alike contests. The Temple hairstyle also became popular, increasing business for hairdressers. Mothers enrolled their daughters in dance schools. In 1936, Temple earned an estimated $200,000 from royalties and endorsements. Adjusted for inflation, that number would be more than $3.3 million today. Even though her career as a Hollywood celebrity effectively ended by 1940, Shirley Temple collectables continue to be highly sought after.

Media was big business in the 1930s, and like most businesses the Depression brought both challenges and opportunities to the various industries. Radio was among the few media to benefit from the economic downturn. People bought more and more radios and advertisers moved from print to radio to reach larger audiences. Print took major economic blows with shrinking circulations and lower advertising revenues. In many cases, publishers spent their own capital to keep the presses running. Newspapers became more competitive in reporting exclusive stories or publishing popular columnists. In Hollywood, the decade began with anxiety and uncertainty about the future of the industry. The Great Depression hurt ticket sales and new technology came with a steep learning curve for studios, filmmakers, and performers. Movie business profits went up in 1930, thanks to the novelty of "talkies"; however, talking pictures required studios to borrow large sums of money to retrofit soundstages to record sound. They also spent money on vocal coaches to train their once-mute stars to talk in front of a camera. That money would ultimately prove well spent and movie studios stayed in the black during 1931, before 1932 returns revealed another downward trend as the Great Depression took a stronger grip on America.

People with little money did not waste it on entertainment when they could barely keep their families clothed and fed, and profits dropped sharply as the effects of the Depression persisted. Movie attendance declined 56 percent between 1928 and 1932. Attendance numbers would improve, but by the end of the decade one-third of all movie theaters were closed. Salaries and budgets were cut across the board. Four of the eight major movie studios, RKO, Paramount, Universal, and Fox, had financial problems that forced reorganization. Studio founding fathers were ousted by new moneymen who provided fiscal relief in exchange for complete control. Only Warner Brothers, MGM, Columbia, and United Artists survived intact.

Audiences may not have been privy to industry strife and internal power struggles, but they did enjoy the creative measures studios and theater managers developed to improve attendance. For one thing, studios reduced movie ticket prices from an average of 30 cents to 20 cents. Still, that was not enough. When admission hit a new low in 1933, studios resorted to give-aways and contests to help fill the seats. Faithful moviegoers could win everything from dishware to cars, and chances were enhanced if they kept returning to the theater. Concessions improved when theater managers replaced lost ticket sales by marking up the price of popcorn, candy, and soda pop for sale in the lobby. Back then, as today, concession stands represent big money for movie theaters. Saturday afternoon cartoons for children made theaters family friendly and popular serials brought back moviegoers week after week. These proactive steps worked and the movie business began to come back by 1934. By the end of the decade, the film industry would be an unassailable giant wielding enormous economic and political power.

The proliferation of mass communications and advances in new media technologies occurred in rapid succession over a relatively short period of time. In the 1930s, there were few regulations and fewer regulating agencies determining either content or conduct for the mass media. Although this would gradually change for print and broadcast media, the filmmaking industry successfully demonstrated great political influence by choosing to self-regulate. This choice allowed moviemakers to escape government regulation—an anomaly during the era of government oversight fostered by the New Deal. In the early 1930s, many films had been filled with sex, violence, and other risqué activities that filled seats but prompted strident critiques from religious groups. Films such as *The Divorcee* (1930) drew audiences to theaters with scenes filled with titillating parties, drinking, adultery, and betrayal. Although the film alarmed conservative critics, it earned its star, Norma Shearer, an Oscar for Best Actress. In some versions of *Tarzan and His Mate* (1934), a film in the popular series starring Johnny Weissmuller, his love interest Jane (Maureen O'Sullivan) is visibly nude as she swims in a jungle pool. It may have been realistic, but it drove religious groups crazy and they finally took action.

The foundation for film censorship was laid in 1915, when the US Supreme Court ruled that free speech did not extend to movies. Even then, people were concerned about the possibility that media could influence impressionable minds and vulnerable personalities. By the midtwenties, religious and civic leaders began to mobilize against the influence of Hollywood. The Roscoe "Fatty" Arbuckle murder trial and other such scandals damaged the industry's reputation and fueled a national debate over the role of film in society. Many people believed Hollywood was immoral and show business people were degenerates, and no one could deny that movies were influencing every strata of America life. State governments passed laws that allowed the censoring of movies by mandated committees. In some states, self-appointed committees were formed to censor movies based on local standards. These groups would cut scenes, even those that were critical to the plot, because they objected to the presence of nudity, the use of profanity, excessive violence, or the mixing of races.

The power of outside groups to edit or ban films sent chills through Hollywood executives, who were not interested in safeguarding the nation's moral conscience. They were concerned with profits and looked desperately for ways to rehabilitate the industry's image before government agencies intervened any further into their business. In a surprising move, studio executives joined together to create a solution that would placate religious groups while allowing them to continue to deliver films audiences would pay to see. In 1922, the movie industry turned to Will Hays, a former postmaster general under President Warren G. Harding, to clean up Hollywood through self-censorship under the Motion Picture Producers and Distributors of America (MPPDA). This first attempt was ill fated from the beginning. Hays never forgot that the studios paid his salary, and therefore he seemed more like a studio stooge than a moral crusader. Not until 1927 did Hays issue lists of "don'ts" and "be carefuls" for filmmakers to follow.

The list Hays proposed closely followed one created by religious leaders who had met with studio executives about their concerns. All of Hollywood paid lip-service promises to adhere to the guidelines in order to avoid censorship from state boards and condemnation from the Catholic Church. Irrespective of the manner in which they were treated, the list disavowed any use of profanity, including the words "God," "Lord," "Jesus," and "Christ" (unless used reverently in connection with proper religious ceremonies), "hell," "damn," "Gawd" (and every other profane and vulgar expression, however it was spelled); any licentious or suggestive nudity, lechery or licentiousness, inferences of sexual perversion, children's genitals, miscegenation; sex hygiene and venereal diseases; drug trafficking and white slavery; scenes of childbirth; ridicule of the clergy; and willful offense to any nation, race, or creed. The recommendations were to be followed without exception.

The list of "be carefuls" covered even more ground. Filmmakers were cautioned to use special care when treating the subjects on the list and encouraged to emphasize good taste, eliminate vulgarity, and avoid suggestiveness at all times. Without advocating censorship, some "be carefuls" made sense. There was to be no unfavorable representations of other countries' religion, history, institutions, prominent people, and citizenry. Determined to prevent filmmakers from glorifying violence, the list prohibited the depiction of most criminal activities, including theft, robbery, safe-cracking, the dynamiting of trains, mines, buildings, etc. (to prevent influencing "the moron"), arson, the use of drugs, sedition, techniques of committing murder by any method, techniques for smuggling, the deliberate seduction of girls, and rape or attempted rape. Other prohibitions and cautions reflect the values of the time, such as the use of the flag, the attitude toward public characters and institutions, the institution of marriage, the sale of women or a woman selling her virtue, first-night scenes, men and women in bed together, brutality and possible gruesomeness, apparent cruelty to children and animals, sympathy for criminals, and actual hangings or electrocutions as legal punishment for crime. And finally, there are some prohibitions that are simply inexplicable, such as depictions of the use of firearms, surgical operations, titles or scenes having to do with law enforcement or law-enforcing officers, excessive or lustful kissing, particularly when one character or the other is a "heavy."

Because all parties agreed to follow the "don'ts" and "be carefuls" lists in principle, no one gave much consideration to enforcement. Studio Relations, or the Hays Office, as it was commonly called, served an advisory role and did not have any power to police the studios. Censorship at the state level continued and even expanded as many filmmakers simply ignored Hays. Religious leaders renewed their demands that more needed to be done to curb immorality in films. In 1930, the "don'ts" and "be carefuls" lists gave way to the Motion Picture Production Code, also known as the Hays Code. A much longer and more detailed document than the Hays lists, the Hays Code was written by the lay Catholic editor Martin Quigley and Daniel Lord, a Jesuit priest. The Hays Code acknowledged the power films could have over young people and the public in general. It stressed that bad behavior needed to be punished and that audiences should always understand that "evil is wrong and good is right."

The period from 1930 to 1934 is known as the pre-Code era. The Hays Code was in effect, but there was neither incentive nor leverage to compel studios to comply with the new rules. Indeed, few pre-Code filmmakers shied away from using adult material in their films and, as a result, Hollywood produced a slew of box office hits during this time. The Hays Office routinely made official recommendations to change films, but Hollywood mostly conducted business as usual—and it was good business. The 1934 crime caper and comedy *Jewel Robbery* had audiences rolling in the aisle when the lead character William Powell gave his victims marijuana cigarettes to smoke so they would better cooperate during the heist. In *Female* (1934), Ruth Chatterton played Alison Drake, an independent heiress who runs a thriving automobile plant and enjoys all the luxuries and entitlements available to successful men—fast cars, a decadent night life, and a succession of pliant lovers. Drake regularly seduces young men who work for her and abandons them with careless disregard when they begin to bore her. Neither the high life nor her sexual power give her satisfaction, and she ultimately resigns from her job and submits happily to the will of an uncompromising engineer. In spite of this restoration of traditional values at the end of the film, conservative critics bristled at the depiction of an ambitious, professionally successful, and daringly carnal woman. This flagrant disregard for the Code did not sit well with moral crusaders. It could not continue.

Gangster films were among the most egregious offenders of the standards of decency promoted by concerned citizens, yet they were also among the most popular. As a genre, gangster films represent the first truly American contribution to film history, although it is not the version of rugged individualism most Americans identify with openly. Following storylines that had been "ripped from the headlines," American gangsters rejected the wholesome values of hard work, fair play, and loyalty in favor of a rebellious, pessimistic, self-destructiveness that would—at least for a time—help them achieve success in an inherently unfriendly and unfair world. Warner Brothers became the movie studio best known for gangster films, and some of the film industry's greatest directors such as Howard Hawks, William Wellman, and Mervyn LeRoy began their careers directing them. Gangster films introduced audiences to men who succeeded on their own terms by using their wits and strength and never needing a handout from anyone. During the dark days of the Great Depression, these figures were not only entertaining but they also offered vicarious thrills to moviegoers who continued to struggle in a society that failed to provide them with relief. Three films, *Little Caesar* (1931), *The Public Enemy* (1931), and *Scarface* (1932), set the standard for what the public would expect from the genre—dark, gritty scenes of intense violence and the glamorization of crude thugs who disregard the law for their own personal gain. The first two films featured the charismatic, young actors Edward G. Robinson and James Cagney, and the third featured the popular veteran Paul Muni; the actors portrayed men who defied societal norms to achieve short-lived wealth and fame as criminals.

The Public Enemy took only a month to shoot, and despite its fast schedule and low budget, the movie packed a punch that can still be felt today. Cagney's performance is electrifying. In an unscripted gesture that would become one of the most famous scenes in Hollywood history, his character shoves a grapefruit half into his girlfriend's face over breakfast. His volatility is terrifying and Mae Clarke, the uncredited actress who plays Cagney's moll, is as shocked and frightened as audiences must have been. *The Public Enemy* begins as a tight story of two brothers, Tom and Mike (Cagney and Donald Cook), who were raised in poverty by a hard-line father and long-suffering mother in Chicago's inner city. Mike followed the straight and narrow, going to school and enlisting to fight in World War I, whereas Tom began a life of crime as a bootlegger. After the death of their father, the mother tries to hold the two brothers together as their life choices drive them further and further apart. Tom's criminal activities earn him the title "Public Enemy," and finally he is gunned down by police and left to die in the gutter. As a tacit nod to the Hays Production Code Office, most gangster films ended similarly fatalistically.

Warner Brothers released another gangster film destined to be a classic at the same time as *The Public Enemy. Little Caesar* starred the newcomer Edward G. Robinson in a role that would define his career for most of his acting life. The movie tells the story of Caesar Enrico "Rico" Bandello, an Italian immigrant who uses murder and deception to become a top thug in the Chicago underworld. Audiences would have seen the obvious parallels between Rico and the recently arrested Chicago crime lord Al "Scarface" Capone. Both displayed a combination of ruthlessness and vanity as they rose in the ranks of gang life to become crime bosses of a city. Beautiful women, stylish clothes, and ritzy apartments were mandatory for both criminals. Whereas Capone is arrested, tried, and convicted, "Little Caesar" meets a more inglorious end as he pays for his sins in the film's final violent moments.

The third great Warner Brothers gangster film also drew its inspiration from Capone, even going so far as to co-opt the mob boss's nickname. *Scarface* debuted in 1932, the first year of Capone's imprisonment. Actually, *Scarface* had been completed the year before, but studio executives thought it too shocking and violent to release. In the era of weak Code enforcement, they soon got over their squeamishness and released one of the most chilling depictions of gang life ever. The film was produced by Howard Hughes and directed by Howard Hawks, who was known for making lean, hard, masculine films, whether gangster films, Westerns, or comedies. Paul Muni played the title role, a ferocious gangster named Tony Camonte who kills anyone who stands in his way, even his friend and brother-in-law. The film reflected Capone's real-life rise in Chicago as he led his South Side gang in a territory war with the North Side mob. There are no heroes in this stark, brutal film. The police are corrupt and inept. They can't stop the killings and bombings. As Tony becomes more violent and unpredictable, the public demands results. The film ends with a shoot-out between Tony and the police. Tony yields for a moment before making one last attempt to flee, only to be shot dead.

When *Scarface* opened in theaters, it received a positive review from the *New York Times* critic Mordaunt Hall, who compared it to a Shakespearean tragedy. It was rumored that Capone loved the movie so much that he owned his own copy—in those days that meant reels of 16-millimeter celluloid film. However, movie censors at the Hays Office did not approve of the film and its depiction of crime. They demanded cuts be made to the script, but Hughes reportedly told Hawks to ignore the Hays Office and shoot the movie as it was written. In the end, Hawks would make some changes to the final version, including the addition of a subtitle "The Shame of the Nation" and a moralistic opening, all of which Hughes disowned. Nevertheless, the film remains popular today and is often listed as one of the greatest gangster films of all time. It inspired a remake in 1983 by director Brian De Palma and starring Al Pacino. De Palma's version updated the story by substituting Cuban characters for Italians and trading Chicago for Miami. Like the 1932 version, critics saw the remake as excessively violent in its glorification of the criminal life.

In 1932, Roman Catholic bishops founded the Catholic Legion of Decency (CLOD) to combat the lax enforcement of the Code. CLOD professed concern for the moral fiber of America's youth, which they saw as under attack by "vile and unwholesome moving pictures." Members took an oath to battle against such films, especially ones that promoted "sex mania." Protestant and Jewish religious figures joined CLOD and the group changed its name to the National Legion, which better reflected the group's widespread support and made for a less-humorous acronym. The group threatened movie executives with government intervention and widespread boycotts in 1934 if studios did not strictly apply the Code to all films made in Hollywood. The timing of the announcement added leverage to the threat. The year 1933 had been financially disastrous for all the Hollywood studios. The Depression persisted—worsened even—and fewer people were attending movies. Several studios went into receivership and personnel, stars included, took pay cuts. Studios could hardly survive another year in the red. Hays capitulated, and at the behest of the National Legion, appointed one of his lieutenants, Joseph I. Breen, as the head of the newly created Production Code Administration (PCA), or as it was more commonly known, the Breen Office.

Breen, a former newsman and devout Catholic, had secretly been coordinating the protests against Hollywood with the National Legion. As PCA director, he ruled Hollywood with an iron fist from 1934 until he retired in 1954. No film could be released into theaters without his office's seal of approval. Every aspect of filmmaking fell under his moral microscope, from dialog to costumes. He personally reviewed scripts and edited out what he saw as objectionable material. Movie attendance bounced back to pre-Depression numbers, but there is little to indicate that the enforcement of the Code can be credited with the upswing. It may simply have been that after 1935, the iron grip of the Depression on people's pocketbooks began to loosen.

A new generation of critics complained that the Code simply created an alternate reality on screen wherein bad people were always punished and all marriages were happy, even though husbands and wives slept in separate beds. What is beyond dispute is that under Breen's watchful eye and guiding hand, Hollywood films after 1934 helped define an increasingly mainstream American identity that was more and more unified and coherent—and further and further away from the lived experiences of many Americans. In the eyes of some film scholars, however, Breen helped create "the Golden Age of Hollywood" by making sure that entertainment appealed to the greatest number of viewers while offending the fewest possible. Studio executives welcomed the fact that the Code ensured all movies released into theaters would appeal to the widest possible audience. It also streamlined the production process, which, in turn, cut costs.

It is helpful to remember that all films are social documents—even censored or restricted ones. Certainly, much was lost when films no longer represented an individual director's artistic vision. As indicated by the wide range of offerings in the pre-Code era, studios motivated by profit made daring choices as they vied to fill their theaters. As a result of the Code, filmmakers were forced to find creative ways to convey their vision while avoiding censorship. They turned to innuendo and allusion—the turn of a phrase or a meaningful gesture. In seeking to lessen the influence of this powerful medium, moral crusaders inadvertently empowered cinema to represent and redefine issues, values, ideology, and practices, both intimate and public, by appealing to the subconscious through insinuation and inference. Through the rest of the decade, the power of film to describe and prescribe aspects of personal, social, and political life accelerated and amplified.

As unlikely as it seems today, given the trepidation and dread that were ever-present undercurrents during the Great Depression, horror films were all the rage starting in the pre-Code years of the early 1930s. Horror films also parlayed well with the Breen Office, and by the end of the decade they would establish a benchmark that continues to be applied today. Far-fetched premises and fantastic storylines gave audiences an opportunity to escape the difficulties of life, but film historians believe horror films offered more than just escapism. They helped viewers confront fears about the period by reflecting—albeit allegorically—on the most significant and prevailing themes of the day. In any medium, genres provide the comfort of predictable plotlines, characters, and settings, and most horror films followed a similar pattern whereby someone—or something—upsets the natural, peaceful order. Order is restored through the efforts of a heroic character who defeats the monster and wins the girl, who is often the monster's object of desire. Moviemakers ensured catharsis for viewers and satisfied censors when good defeated evil by the closing credits. Horror films benefited from advances in technology, were often drawn from well-known stories, and enjoyed a cross-generational appeal.

Horror films first gained attention in the 1920s with the introduction of characters that are still recognizable today in *Dr. Jekyll and Mr. Hyde* (1920), *The Phantom of the Opera* (1922), and the vampire tale *Nosferatu* (1922). Horror films produced by Universal Studios would define the genre during the 1930s and for much of the century. Universal, one of the smaller studios, became the home of the "monster movie" following the 1931 releases of *Dracula*, starring Bela Lugosi, and *Frankenstein*, starring Boris Karloff. Both characters were familiar to the public, having risen from still-popular nineteenth-century novels. Mary Shelley's *Frankenstein*, in particular, had been adapted for the stage many times during the nineteenth and early twentieth centuries. The string of popular monster movies continued through the darkest days of the Great Depression; thirty horror movies made between 1931 and 1936 by Universal, including such classics as *The Mummy* (1932), *The Invisible Man* (1933), and *Bride of Frankenstein* (1935).

The horror genre was one of several that were fantastic, popular across media, and enjoyed by young and old alike. During the 1930s, stories about superheroes were similarly evocative, rich with symbolism, and readily available on radio, film, and in print. Every month at the local newsstand, criminals were handily dispatched by a multitude of archetypical characters in the pages of cheaply made magazines known as the "pulps." For just one thin dime, readers of all ages could marvel at the exploits of superheroes that knew no fear and were not bound by laws, either man made or natural. They had cool names like Doc Savage, The Shadow, and the Phantom Detective. Unlike their Depression Era readers, pulp heroes traveled the world, sometimes even the galaxy, and readers enjoyed the intrigue and adventure their favorite characters encountered. The 1930s hosted many "golden ages," but none is as exciting or as fantastic as "the golden age of pulp heroes."

Although they were a significant medium during the 1930s, pulp novels were not new. They began in the previous century when the journalist and publisher Frank Munsey began a monthly children's magazine called *Golden Argosy*, and then just *The Argosy*. It became the first official "pulp" magazine in 1896. Munsey chose to target a wide audience that included children and adults, particularly the large working-class population that was increasingly interested in reading but was challenged to find affordable, interesting reading materials in the current marketplace. Magazines at the time were printed on expensive, high-quality glossy paper referred to as "slicks," and they appealed primarily to middle and upper class readers. Magazines such as *The Saturday Evening Post* were 25 cents—more than the cost of a ticket to see a movie. Munsey figured he could maximize profits by using high-speed printing machines and inexpensive, rough, wood-pulp paper. Pulps were not only cheaper to make, but they were also cheaper to mail. Equally important to the success of pulps, Munsey thought that what was printed on the paper was more important than the paper itself. He decided to include only fiction in *The Argosy*.

The scheme worked so well that he sold thousands of copies across America and became a multimillionaire by the early 1900s. Into the 1920s, Munsey published general fiction stories to mass audiences of readers. He died in 1925, just as another publisher was developing the next incarnation of the pulp novel. Using Munsey's model for *The Argosy*, Street & Smith began publishing *Popular Magazine* for children in 1903. Street & Smith included more than just general fiction in their magazines, and they released titles that focused on one particular genre, such as *Western Story* or *Detective*

Story. The popularity of single-themed titles grew as more and more publishers began churning out pulp magazines.

By the 1920s, most pulps shared a similar format no matter the publisher. They were about 128 pages, 7 inches wide and 10 inches high, printed on rough-edged pulpwood, with a coated stock cover. They included no illustrations except for colorful, eye-catching artwork on the covers, designed to lure readers browsing the newsstand. Many contained a half-dozen short stories and one longer piece. Some of the most influential writers of the twentieth century began their careers in pulp magazines. Ray Bradbury, Dashiell Hammett, F. Scott Fitzgerald, and Upton Sinclair are just a few whose early work appeared in pulp magazines. Smith & Street's new formula kept original readers happy while attracting new ones. There were about two-dozen pulp titles in circulation in the early 1920s. By the midthirties, there were over two hundred.

That is not to say that the Great Depression did not put a strain on the pulp magazine market. Like movie attendance, purchasing the "luxury items" enjoyed by working- and middle-class consumers decreased or ceased completely during the 1930s. Yet, even at the worst of times, people continued to purchase pulps featuring great heroes. In an interview with the pulp historian Will Murray, the Street & Smith editor John L. Nanovic said he believed that "character books" saved the pulp magazine during the Depression and helped the industry survive for another twenty years. Heroes in pulps were perfect for Depression Era readers who could lose themselves for hours in thrilling adventures for a modest price. It did not hurt that publishers took note of the movie industry's marketing machine and began to market merchandise from the most successful series. They ensured a new stream of revenue and nourished an emerging fan culture emerging across the nation. At the same time, they introduced characters that have resonated powerfully in the hearts and minds of Americans ever since.

Two heroes in particular, Doc Savage and The Shadow, have withstood the test of time. Their exploits remain in print even today, as new generations discover the breathless prose and wild exploits of the pulps. The characters and storylines may seem corny and old fashioned, but every present-day comic book fan owes a debt of gratitude to the men who created Doc Savage and The Shadow. These two heroes would be transformed by succeeding generations into modern versions of Superman and Batman. Indeed, their influence runs deep in many of the superheroes that swoop across our contemporary movie screens and comic book stores. Surprisingly, the reason these characters appeal to current readers are much the same as their appeal to 1930s fans.

The popularity of The Shadow and Doc Savage storylines also benefited from Street & Smith's decision to market them in multiple media formats. Before 1930, publishers relied primarily on store advertisements to sell their magazines. Street & Smith decided to see what the new medium of radio could offer to promote their products. The company sponsored a drama called *Detective Story Hour*, which tied into a magazine of the same name. It had a narrator that came to be known as The Shadow because of his deep, spooky voice. People wanted to learn more about this mysterious character, so Street & Smith quickly began publishing *The Shadow* magazine, which featured a dark, cloaked crime fighter who could "melt into the shadows." In every issue, his twin 45-caliber pistols gun down evildoers who dared cross the path of The Shadow.

Street & Smith's general manager Henry William Ralston turned to the writer and magician Walter B. Gibson to create *The Shadow*. Gibson had worked as a ghostwriter for the most famous magicians of the day, including Houdini and Blackstone. He wrote newspaper columns about games and tricks as well as stories for pulp magazines. Gibson's ability to crank out the necessary number of words each month made him the perfect candidate for the new publication. He created "a somewhat nebulous figure" dressed in a black slouch hat and cloak who could move easily within the criminal world thanks to his skill with disguises. People who remember the character know that The Shadow had the ability to "cloud men's minds so they could not see him," but Gibson did not assign his character supernatural powers. Those would come later, when The Shadow became a weekly radio fixture.

The Shadow's real identity can be attributed to Gibson, and its appeal for audiences is rooted in cultural experiences that would have been familiar to 1930s fans. Gibson wrote that a downed World War I aviator named Kent Allard became the menacing crime fighter upon his return to America after the war. The idea of a secret identity owes its origins to the classic novel *The Scarlet Pimpernel*, as well as to Johnston McCulley's 1919 pulp magazine hero Zorro. The story of a veteran striving to reinvent himself after war and struggling to find meaning in life is an early manifestation of a character introduced in Sloan Wilson's generational milestone novel from 1955, *The Man in the Gray Flannel Suit.* Although the type did not have a name after World War I, the experience was all too common, and both Gibson and his readers would have witnessed the trials faced by World War I veterans during the 1920s and 1930s.

Gibson's first story, "The Living Shadow," hit newsstands on April 1, 1931. It bore the name of Maxwell Grant as author. Pulp publishers commonly used "house names" for writers so that readers would be none the wiser when writers changed. Writers were on grueling month-to-month deadlines and house names helped when they wanted a break. House names also eased the transition when writers quit or were fired. At the peak of The Shadow's popularity, the magazine was published twice a month. Gibson would write 282 of 325 stories that Street & Smith published in *The Shadow* series. Two other writers, Theodore Tinsely and Bruce Elliot, also provided stories under the Grant pen name. The magazine ceased publication in 1949, but the character lived on in reprints and new adventures, including a 1994 movie version starring Alec Baldwin.

The Shadow radio show is perhaps more widely remembered today than the pulp novels that inspired it. The show signed on the CBS radio network in 1937, and its signature line, "Who knows what evil lurks in the heart of men? The Shadow knows," uttered with a menacing laugh, is still familiar to fans of popular culture. While the basic concept of The Shadow remained the same, several important changes were made for radio. Most notably, the radio Shadow received superpowers and could become invisible. He had only one alter ego, Lamont Cranston, and Cranston had a girlfriend, Margo Lane. Orson Welles narrated the show prior to his headline-making *War of the Worlds* broadcast. In fact, the melodramatic superhero show provided Welles with a steady paycheck as he formed his cutting-edge company The Mercury Theater. He stayed only until the end of *The Shadow's* first season in 1938, but his departure did not mean the end of the radio series, which outlasted the pulp magazine, remaining on the airwaves until 1954.

The other important pulp superhero of the era had neither superpowers nor secret identity. Clark "Doc" Savage, Jr. did not even wear a costume.

A real-life adventurer named Lester Dent created Doc Savage for Street & Smith after the publisher saw the success of *The Shadow*. Dent would write more than a 150 of Doc's 181 adventures, earning him the nickname "the father of the superhero." Nanovic and Ralston also played major roles in the creative process, which would explain the parallels between the two characters. In many ways, Doc was the day to The Shadow's night. The Shadow roamed the inner city, fighting gangsters and corruption. Doc roamed the world, battling fantastic foes bent on destroying the world or enslaving mankind. The Shadow had agents at his command but fought crime essentially alone, whereas Doc had a colorful group of genius sidekicks called "the Fabulous Five." The Shadow had a dark, underground lair. Doc Savage occupied the eighty-sixth floor of the Empire State Building.

Unlike The Shadow, Doc's success did not extend beyond the printed page. Two attempts at a radio show in 1934 and 1943 failed, and it was not until 1975 that Doc made it to the silver screen in *Doc Savage: The Man of Bronze*, directed George Pal and starring former *Tarzan* actor Ron Ely. Aimed at children, the film bombed with critics, audiences, and Doc Savage fans. Further attempts to bring Doc back to film, including one by Arnold Schwarzenegger, have all failed. Doc might have been totally forgotten had Bantam Books not reprinted all the stories in paperback in October 1964. The eye-catching cover art by James Bama helped the books find a new audience of readers who were not alive when Doc began his crime-fighting career.

In March 1933, Street & Smith published the first issue of *Doc Savage Magazine* with an origin story titled "The Man of Bronze." The pulp bore the Street & Smith pseudonym "Kenneth Robeson" and detailed, in what the pop culture expert Ron Goulart described as "breathless, turgid prose," how Doc Savage became the most perfect human specimen on Earth. Doc's fabulously wealthy father arranged for scientists to raise his son. As a result, there was nothing Doc could not master and he became an expert in all areas of study, including aviation and medicine. His nickname, "the Man of Bronze," came from the color of his skin, tanned perfectly under a tropical sun. In future issues, evocative titles like "The Sargasso Ogre," "The Devil Genghis," and "The Czar of Fear" let people know exactly what awaited them after they plunked down their dime.

Dent's writing style would not win him any literary prizes, but he knew how to hold a reader. He made the books easy and fun to read, and before long, sales of Doc Savage adventures topped two hundred thousand copies a month. Since pulp magazines were not illustrated, writers relied on familiar characters and formulaic plots. Sharp, specific details helped readers follow the fast-paced action. The passage from "Red Snow" (February 1935) below is a good example of Dent's terse, quick-cut movie style, which is representative of the writing found in most pulps. The story has Doc battling a grotesque-looking scientist whose evil machine creates red-colored snow that destroys everything it touches.

> Doc Savage put on speed. He came in sight of the basement window just in time to see the golf-hosed legs of his quarry disappearing inside. Then, in the basement, a man saw Doc and bellowed profanely. What might have been a thick-walled steel pipe of small diameter jutted out of the window. Its tip acquired a flickering red spear-point of flame. The weapon was an automatic rifle of military caliber and its roar volleyed through the compound. Doc Savage has rolled behind a palm, which, after the fashion of palms when stunted, was extremely wide at the base. The tree shuddered, and dead leaves loosened and fluttered in the wind. A cupro-nickel-jacketed slug came entirely through the bole. More followed. The bole began to split. The racket was terrific.

The pulp writers were not writing for worldly sophisticates. Their readership was the young teen and the workingman looking for thrills, adventure, and mystery—which Dent and others delivered with consistency and flare.

For readers during the Great Depression the appeal in the outlandish pulp was more than just the escape it offered from the struggles of daily life. Even today, pulp fans say it is more than the nonstop action and colorful plots that keeps them reading. Like most pulp writers, Gibson and Dent used well-worn conventions for assembling their stories. Such narrowly drawn genres are more appealing during turbulent times because they offer clear resolutions to conflicts and the assurance of continuity. Readers might be anxious, titillated, excited, even frightened by what they read, but they were never truly surprised. Readers back then—like film and radio audiences—were more willing to accept heroes who were not cynical, even when there seemed so little to be optimistic about. The pulp heroes promised good would always triumph over evil and they delivered, issue after issue. The characters in pulps emphasized courageous fortitude that inspired hope. A recent resurgence in the popularity of pulp heroes suggests that Americans are responding to the economic downturns and two recessions that have occurred since 2000 with preferences similar to those of pulp fans from the Great Depression.

When *Doc Savage Magazine* stopped publication in March 1949, it marked an unofficial end to the pulp era. World War II had been hard on pulps because of paper rationing. The "golden age of pulps" gave way to the "golden age of comics" as comic book creators took bits and pieces of pulp heroes to build superhero characters that are still popular today. New audiences preferred the colorful superheroes of the comic books, which offered pictures. Two teenagers in Cleveland, Ohio, Jerry Siegel and Joe Shuster, created Superman in 1932, although the character would not appear in print until June 1938. Detective Comics (now DC Comics) published the first Superman story in the first issue of *Action Comics*, officially kicking off the new era. Though "super" in comparison to regular folks, the Superman of 1938 was not the invincible flying superhero that comic books fans enjoy today. He could only "leap tall buildings" and run "faster than a locomotive." It was more appealing for 1930s audiences that Superman fought against those who preyed on the poor and downtrodden. The comic readers of the Great Depression could not get enough of a superhero who championed social causes. The character became an instant success and soon symbolized the virtues of the proud but struggling nation.

In addition to the evolution and expansion of media, the 1930s represent a major turning point in American popular culture at a time when most media were enjoyed by people who had a wide spectrum of experiences and before direct marketing would target specific demographic groups in earnest. Dick Tracy, another fictional crime-fighter who became an enduring cartoon icon beginning in 1931, enjoyed a broad, intergenerational readership. Though he wore no costume and had no secret identity, Dick Tracy fought outrageous villains worthy of his caped counterparts, in a daily newspaper comic strip syndicated by the *Chicago Tribune*. Newspaper comic strips served as a transition for readers between the pulp novel heroes and comic book superheroes. Up until *Dick Tracy*, the "funny pages," or newspaper comic strips, were primarily aimed at children. However, *Dick Tracy* provided hard-hitting action that attracted both young and old. *Dick Tracy* migrated into every kind of media and the character is still fighting crime today in America's newspapers and online.

Chester Gould, who wrote the strip until his death in 1977, created *Dick Tracy*. He originally called this square-jawed, scowling police investigator "Plainclothes" Tracy, but quickly changed the name to "Dick," a commonly used slang term for a detective. Whereas gangster movies frequently lionized criminals, Gould portrayed his villains as monstrous persons with physical deformities that were reflected in their gangland names. Readers would root for Tracy as he fought the foes "Flattop," "Prune-face," and "Mumbles." Inspired by Sherlock Holmes, Gould had Tracy use the latest police procedures and criminal investigation techniques. Despite the focus on scientific police methods and technology, storylines usually ended with a shootout between Tracy and that month's bad guy, reflecting an aspect of the real world readers could find on the front page of their newspapers. The strip became an instant hit as its hero satisfied a desire for justice in a country seemingly awash in crime and violence.

Although much of the media of the 1930s held intergenerational appeal for audiences, music would become an exception as a new style called "swing" became popular with teenagers on radio, in dance halls, and on records. Classical music was a staple of radio broadcasts and concert halls, but media and advertising executives began to recognize the growing power and influence of the younger generation. For the first time, teenagers emerged as a unique and distinctive group in American culture. Prior to the Great Depression, teens routinely dropped out of school to work. After the stock market crash, there was a push by the US government to keep teens out of the labor market so adults faced less competition. While some teens needed to earn money for their families, most were encouraged, and then required, to stay in school. As a result, the high school graduation rates in the United States rose from about 17 percent in the spring of 1920 to 29 percent in spring 1930; graduation rates continued to rise during the decade to just over 50 percent in 1940. Another consequence was that the passage from childhood to adulthood was effectively extended for most American youth. Reinforced by new ideas about human development and maturation, the concept of the "teen" as distinct from either children or adults was born in the 1930s.

In their increasingly unsupervised spare time, teens turned away from the family and toward each other for fun and excitement, giving rise to a separate culture from adults. After school hours, popular culture, sports, and social activities kept teens occupied, out of the workforce, and, it was hoped, out of trouble. Teens began to amuse themselves in ways that parents found disconcerting. For instance, *Time* magazine reported contests in which teens would see how many live goldfish they could swallow. A fascination with "jalopies," spurred by a burgeoning car culture and the availability of cheap used cars, resulted in teenagers obtaining even more independence from their parents. In 1932, a '29 Ford could be had for $57.50 and a '27 Lincoln for $125. That was still a lot of money, but it was possible for thrifty middle-class teens to save enough to buy an old car to fix up. Recognizing a great opportunity, publishers tailored fan magazines to teen tastes. Advertisers began to target them as potential customers. This was the start of a youth movement in the United States, which would lead, over time, to the tastes and interests of the young becoming those of the nation.

Nowhere was the influence of teenagers more prevalent than in music. The 1930s became known as the "Swing era," as teenagers discovered the joys of dancing to big band music. Big bands, which featured seventeen or more instruments, came to prominence when the jazz age became unfashionable at the end of the 1920s. "Sweet" big bands replaced smaller jazz groups and provided more syncopated and "sentimental" sounds. They were also called "society bands" because they played in respectable venues such as upscale hotels and private parties. Rural and provincial adult listeners enjoyed the tame sound of the sweet bands, which usually included a "crooner," a lead singer with a smooth style. A popular band of this type was the Paul Whiteman Orchestra, featuring Bing Crosby as its boy singer. Whiteman was billed as "the king of jass" [*sic*], though his arrangements had little to do with the improvised sound of real jazz music. The fact that Whiteman and his band were white added to their appeal during the racially segregated period.

Bands that favored the more energetic and rhythmic style of jazz were known as "hot" bands. They could be found in all-black or mixed clubs frequented by college-age students. Starting in the 1920s, Kansas City, Missouri, became a focal point for the "hot" movement as jazz musicians—most of them African American—tested their talents against each other in what were known as "cutting sessions." On these nights, musicians displayed their technical proficiency so that they could brag to other musicians that they had beat the competition and to gain a reputation among fans. One of the most popular big bands, the Count Basie Orchestra, came out of the Kansas City music scene. William "Count" Basie worked in a variety of musical jobs, including playing piano for silent movies, before establishing himself as a big band leader. Basie had been part of Benny Moten's big band in Kansas City when Moten died in 1935. Basie and several members of Moten's band formed their own popular jazz band that would eventually become illustrious the Count Basie Orchestra. The Basie sound came from his hard-swinging rhythm section and attracted both jazz fans and dancers. The big band authority William Simon says Basie emphasized the importance of the drummer to drive the band "to do things they never did before." Basie's piano playing also had a percussive "hot" sound that separated him from other jazz pianists of the time.

Although hot jazz was enjoyed within a thriving subculture of nightclubs and speakeasies, it would take a talented white musician to turn it into a national phenomenon and launch one of the earliest teen crazes. Many experts believe the Swing era was born on August 21, 1935. On that date, the Benny Goodman Orchestra, a hot band led by a bespectacled white clarinet player who looked like an accountant, attracted a youthful audience, mollified parents, and sparked a nationwide craze for swinging big band music and wild dances like "the Lindy Hop" and "the Jitterbug." Prior to August, Goodman had been on a disastrous nationwide tour. The low point came in Denver when a number of audience members asked for their money back because the band didn't play waltzes. When Goodman opened at the Palomar Ballroom in Hollywood, he expected the worst. The band played the first few sets without receiving much reaction from the audience. According to the drummer Gene Krupa, Goodman then decided to stop playing it safe and the band roared to life with its new jazz swing arrangements. The mostly young people in the audience went crazy, dancing and shouting for more.

In spite of Goodman's faith in his own talent as a musician and bandleader, he had struggled during the midtwenties, moving from band to band, finding success as a session player, but always dreaming of starting his own jazz orchestra. Like many in the music industry, Goodman recognized immense talents among black jazz musicians such as the arranger and bandleader Fletcher Henderson. In the late 1920s, Henderson led one of the greatest jazz bands in history, featuring many of legendary soloists of jazz such as Coleman Hawkins, Benny Carter, and Louis Armstrong. When the stock market crash wiped out Henderson's savings, Goodman helped him by purchasing his arrangement books. Goodman was unique in his willingness to cultivate partnerships with black musicians such as Henderson, and Henderson would play a vital role in Goodman's band and its meteoric rise to stardom, despite resistance from white club owners and promoters who refused to hire integrated bands in the 1930s.

Goodman was also fortunate in his association with the legendary record producer John Hammond, who helped Goodman when the Great Depression worsened and work became scarce for entertainers. With Hammond's encouragement, Goodman decided to form his own band. Biographers note that the new man in the White House inspired Goodman. As Roosevelt's steady and buoyant confidence began to spread across the country, Goodman figured it could still be possible for a good dance band to make money. After a rocky start, Goodman received the break of his life thanks to the NBC radio network. NBC had trouble selling advertisements on Saturday nights, when few adults were at home listening to the radio. In 1934, NBC began a three-hour "dance party" program, directed at young people, called *Let's Dance.* It featured three different bands playing in three different styles. Goodman and his band auditioned for a coveted spot on the show. After their music was piped into a room full of young NBC staff members, they were unanimously chosen for the "hot band" spot. The show provided national exposure for the band and introduced Goodman directly to the listeners who would enjoy his style of jazz the most—teenagers.

Goodman was twenty-five years old when the *Let's Dance* radio program helped build a following on the West Coast. His segment aired at midnight in the East but, thanks to the time difference, young dancers in the West could tune in during prime time. It wasn't long before Goodman became a household name. He used his popularity to introduce African American jazz musicians such as the pianist Teddy Wilson and the guitarist Charlie Christian to white audiences. Segregation remained in place in hotel ballrooms and restaurant lounges, but on stage, black and white musicians jammed together. Goodman's success helped bring national attention to "hot" jazz big bands led by African Americans such as Count Basie, Edward "Duke" Ellington, Jimmy Lunceford, Chick Webb, and Earl Hines. Ellington is now considered among the greatest American composers, equal to classical composers like George Gershwin and Aaron Copland. Young people were becoming more and more "color blind" while their elders—and many in the music industry—still preferred that the races not mix.

"Sweet" bands like those of Glenn Miller, Guy Lombardo, and Tommy Dorsey found success with older dancers who could not appreciate the frenzy of swing. Swing was popular with teens and young adults, whereas older, upper-class Americans tended to look down their noses at jazz and swing in particular. They did not consider it "high culture." Many complained it was too loud, too fast, and too likely to encourage indecent or immoral behavior. In 1938, Goodman helped change that attitude and won cross-generational appeal with a major concert at Carnegie Hall in New York City. Up to that point, only classical music had been allowed at the prestigious venue that had never before hosted a racially mixed orchestra. With chart-topping hits such as "Sing, Sing, Sing" and "King Porter Stomp," Goodman was at the height of his popularity prior to the concert, yet jazz fans feared he would flop. Instead, tickets sold out in just two weeks, and some seats sold as high as $2.50.

On January 16, Goodman marched into Carnegie Hall with Count Basie, the vibraphonist Lionel Hampton, and members of the Duke Ellington Orchestra. Young people showed up to dance in the aisles, as they had wherever Goodman played. By all accounts, the concert was a success and became known as one of the most important jazz concerts in history. Recordings of the event are still popular seventy-five years later. The Carnegie Hall concert transformed jazz from "lowbrow" music into America's first classical music and it demonstrated that mainstream adult audiences would accept jazz. Unfortunately, the Swing era began to fade not long after Goodman's revolutionary concert, as the upbeat sounds seemed increasingly incompatible with the persistent suffering of a prolonged Depression and the increasing number of military returnees and their stories of the war in Europe. It would officially end in 1946, when the former teen fans who were now soldiers returned from war and turned to more sentimental tunes to get them through. As for the next generation of teen fans, hard-edged be-bop won them over. Nevertheless, Goodman continued to play his unique style of hot jazz until his death in 1984.

Popular entertainment today is also still compared, sometimes unfavorably, with the classics that were produced over seventy years ago. In 2013, both Superman and the Lone Ranger returned to the big screen in big-budget summer blockbusters. There has been talk in Hollywood for the past decade about reviving Doc Savage for film. Even today, any new young actor who portrays characters that are witty, romantic, and sophisticated is immediately compared to Cary Grant. Almost all of the studios that matured into big businesses during the 1930s, such as Disney, Warner Brothers, Columbia, and Universal, still produce movies, though their ownership is far removed from the original movie moguls who founded them. Gone, too, are the expansive back lots that provided facsimiles of city streets to filmmakers, the star-making machines that turned everyday people into screen idols, and the tight-fisted control studio management once exerted over its product. Hollywood, however, is still America's dream factory.

The Internet, which competes today with earlier forms of popular media, has given birth through podcasting to original audio programs, such as *The Thrilling Adventure Hour* and *Decoder Ring Theater*, that would be right at home with those of radio's golden age, such as *The Shadow* and *Gangbusters*. As for those wonderful old radio shows, they have found new audiences on compact discs, satellite radio, and online. And the three main radio networks that broadcast hits back in the 1930s still provide Americans with free television entertainment, although ABC, CBS, NBC have more competition than their pioneering ancestors could have ever imagined.

Suggested Readings

David Eldridge's *American Culture in the 1930s* (Edinburgh: Edinburgh University Press, 2008) is a comprehensive study of trends in literature, drama, film, photography, music, radio, art, and design, with one chapter wholly devoted to the influence of New Deal programs. William H. Young and Nancy K. Young's *The 1930s* (Westport: Greenwood Press, 2002) provides an even wider overview of American media and culture, from literature, music, and the performing and visual arts, to fashion, leisure activities, and food and drink. For depth in media studies, John Dunning's *On the Air: The Encyclopedia of Old Time Radio* (New York: Oxford University Press, 1998) focuses on the medium of radio. Two studies that look closely at the impact of radio on Americans in the 1930s include Bruce Lenthall's *Radio's America: The Great Depression and the Rise of Modern Mass Culture* (Chicago: University of Chicago Press, 2007), and David Goodman's *Radio's Civic Ambition: American Broadcasting and Democracy in the 1930s* (Oxford: Oxford University Press, 2011). For Hollywood and cinema, Roger Dooley's *From Scarface to Scarlett: American Films in the 1930s* (New York: Harcourt Brace Jovanovich, 1984) provides a detailed overview of popular films of the era. Books that explore other topics of era the include Melvin Patrick Ely, *The Adventures of Amos 'n Andy: A Social History of an American Phenomenon* (New York: Free Press, 1991); Robert Michael Cotter, *A History of the Doc Savage Adventures in Pulps, Paperbacks, Comics, Fanzines, Radio and Film* (Jefferson, NC: McFarland, 2009); Bob Thomas, *Walt Disney: An American Original* (Disney Editions, 1994); Neal Gabler, *Winchell: Gossip, Power, and the Culture of Celebrity* (New York: Knopf, 1994); and Paul Heyer, *The Medium and the Magician: Orson Welles, the Radio Years, 1934–1952* (Oxford: Rowman & Littlefield, 2005).

9

Isolationism Interrupted

"Stormy Weather"
—Harold Arlen and Ted Koehler, 1933

THE 1930S marked a turning point in America's engagement with the rest of the world. On one side of that decade involvement was limited and episodic, and focused on asserting US economic and strategic interests in the Western hemisphere. A swift and decisive victory over the declining Spanish empire in the 1890s provided a brief and dramatic entrance onto the world stage, followed by an equally rapid exit, and only in 1917, as the First World War entered its third year of bloody stalemate, was President Woodrow Wilson able to persuade a reluctant Congress and people to take up arms in a "war to end all wars." Emerging victorious from this conflict, with a wealth of prestige and an abundance of industrial and financial power, America first turned its back on Wilson's dream—the League of Nations, and the global commitments it would entail—and then, during the next decade, it slammed the door on the rest of the world with a restrictive immigration act and a protective tariff. President Warren G. Harding accurately foreshadowed this shortsighted approach with his less than inspiring call for a return to "normalcy." The rise of the Ku Klux Klan with its xenophobic, anti-Catholic, and anti-Semitic agenda and the persistence of two Americas divided along racial lines—with legalized segregation in the South and gross economic disparities nationwide—suggested that Harding's vision was triumphant. Despite the opportunities presented by the postwar world, America's approach to the peoples beyond its shores—and indeed, toward significant elements of its own population—was no more open, generous, or involved than it had been before the United States embarked on Wilson's crusade to "make the world safe for democracy."

Still, as the 1920s unfolded, thoughtful observers began to understand that the quest to restore the prewar status quo, be it a real or imagined vision of the past, was ultimately a fool's errand. Indeed, the very nature of the "new" Ku Klux Klan, with its blatant commercialism and its effort to utilize the mass media to spread its appeal, demonstrated that even the most reactionary of messages could not escape the embrace of modernity. For African Americans, an expanding job market provided an escape from the shackles of Jim Crow, and the ensuing Great Migration weakened the foundations of the agricultural economy of the South, even as it provided a new social and political dynamic in the black communities of the North. A period of unprecedented industrial and financial expansion ushered in a period of prosperity for some, perhaps many, Americans, but it also carried within it the seeds of an economic cataclysm. While the impact of this meltdown would be felt in the household, the community, and the nation, its impact would be global, and its consequences for the relationship of the United States with the rest of the world would be sweeping and transformative.

While Americans are familiar with the images of poverty and misery from the national collective memory, the Great Depression spared no corner of the world. Latin American nations and the European colonies that dominated the maps of Africa and Asia were especially hard hit because their economies were based on the export of agricultural commodities, minerals, and other primary resources. A catastrophic drop in demand for these products resulted when the factories of the industrialized world reduced or suspended their production. The more prosperous industrial nations of the northern hemisphere witnessed the systematic collapse of their "economic miracles," while the more marginal and vulnerable among them were faced with staggering levels of unemployment in addition to public and private debt. Germany's Weimar Republic was just beginning to recover from its postwar political chaos and stagflation when its positive momentum was thrown into reverse. The Soviet Union, whose experiment in socialism was commandeered by Joseph Stalin, rapidly descended into a nightmare of forced labor, agricultural collectivization, and state terror. Italy, having sided with the victors in the First World War, but feeling slighted by its reward from the Conference of Versailles, succumbed to the fascist ideology and absolutist rule of Benito Mussolini. And, on the other side of the world, the emerging power of the Pacific basin, Japan, a nation poor in natural resources but rich in imperial ambition, dreamed of becoming the master of a self-proclaimed "greater East Asian co-prosperity sphere." Ominously, at the dawn of the 1930s, the seductive lure of utopian, racist, and nationalist ideologies—and the reassuring and simplistic worldviews they engendered—had never held a greater attraction in so many parts of the world. As the decade progressed, millions who had been savaged by the Great Depression were willing and anxious to embrace them, both here and abroad.

For the Roosevelt administration and the people who had voted it into office, the overriding priority was economic recovery at home, but as a first term was followed by a second, the world around them provided increasing cause for anxiety. The rise of the Nazi state, with its quest for rearmament and its escalating pattern of diplomatic and military aggression, posed a tangible threat to the European order constructed at Versailles. Civil war in Spain assumed a wider significance as it rapidly evolved into a proxy war between Germany and Italy, on one side, and the Soviet Union, on the other. The Italian invasion of the independent and virtually defenseless African nation of Ethiopia provided a grim addition to the annals of colonial atrocity. The bloody Japanese invasion of China also contributed to the rising tide of violence and reinforced the fear that a future conflict would be truly global in scope. Still, despite these threats on the horizon and after the bloodletting that occurred between 1914 and 1918, most Americans remained determined to stay out of what they perceived to be a collection of unrelated regional conflicts. To many, the proper course was to focus on economic recovery within the imagined security of their oceanic borders.

Though popular, this sentiment was far from universal. Some, driven by political ideology, ethnic identity, or humanitarian concern called for more active, even interventionist, US responses to these crises. As England embarked on its life-and-death struggle against Nazi Germany, the isolationist consensus began to weaken and by the end of the decade the United States was providing Great Britain with all of the economic support and material assistance it could manage short of entering the war. Yet it was not until December 7, 1941, when a Japanese naval task force attacked American installations in Hawaii—"a day that will live in infamy," as President Roosevelt described it—that the United States fully embraced its role and accepted its burden as a global power, and entered the Second World War.

By any standard, the end of the 1930s marked the beginning of a new era in the American experience. In its relationship with the rest of the world, the United States emerged from the throes of depression and the trials of war utterly transformed. With its homeland spared the ravages of combat, with an economic engine fueled by the demands of war, and with unprecedented productivity and power, the United States stood alone as the dominant world power in 1945. Although the Soviet Union was perceived—and indeed, perceived itself—as a legitimate challenger to American global hegemony, recovery from the ravages of the Nazi invasion would be slow, with millions of its people lost to the war and millions more to the dictatorship of Stalin. Except for the Soviet Union's capability to wage a nuclear war—which history has shown to be greatly exaggerated—the Cold War would be an asymmetrical contest that decisively favored the United States.

Clearly, the years between 1939 and 1941 were pivotal in what one author has called America's "rise to globalism." After Pearl Harbor, "isolationism" was no longer a credible option, and in the decades following the Japanese surrender the focus of debate would be whether America's global commitments had become too extensive and should be scaled back and whether the juggernaut of its military-industrial complex should be reduced in size and influence. In fact, until its humbling in the Vietnam War the United States held pride of place on the world stage. Looking backward from these commanding heights, the 1930s can be remembered as the final episode in America's attempt to avoid the risks and rewards of international involvement. This is the decade when, reluctantly, and only after compelled by events, the United States took the first tentative steps on the road that led to its blossoming as a superpower.

Although it was the attack by a renascent Japan that shattered the American dream of remaining at peace, throughout the 1930s the central dramas confronting observers and makers of policy on the western shore of the Atlantic was the rise of Nazi Germany and the Soviet Union, and the threat that they represented to the postwar status quo. There were some insightful

Americans who saw the storm clouds on the horizon, who understood the ambitions of regimes dreaming of a new social order at home and a new imperial order abroad. In November 1933, in the face of strong opposition, President Franklin Roosevelt established diplomatic relations with the Soviet Union. A young diplomat and Russian-language specialist from Milwaukee named George Kennan was assigned to the staff of the new American ambassador, William C. Bullitt. The following spring Kennan revealed his hopes and fears for the Soviet future in a letter to his sister. He wrote that he found himself conflicted, on the one hand, by "sympathy for a nation which, within the limitations of its own character and an imported dogma, is trying to reconstruct its life on a basis finer and sounder than that of any country anywhere," and, on the other hand, by "disgust with the bigotry and arrogance of its leaders, who not only refuse to recognize their own limitations but pretend that they have found the solution of all the problems of the rest of the world in their crude interpretation of a worn-out doctrine." At this stage in his career, Kennan's insights reflected both sides of the raging debate within the American intelligentsia about the essence of the Soviet experiment.

Indeed, when it came to the subject of the Soviet Union, advocacy invariably trumped analysis. On the left, John Reed, the American journalist and committed socialist, had blazed the way for the champions of the revolution with his epic chronicle *Ten Days That Shook the World*, and he was buried in the wall of the Kremlin in recognition of his impassioned partisanship. Lincoln Steffens, the muckraking author who excelled in exposing the dark side of American society, visited the Soviet Union and upon his return famously proclaimed that he had "been to the future, and it works." Even Bullitt, the new US ambassador, arrived with pronounced sympathies for the fledgling regime. He had married and later divorced Louise Bryant, a passionate advocate of the Soviet cause, who was John Reed's widow and fellow traveler in his Russian adventure. By any measure, Bryant was a formidable character and zealous activist in her own right.

This celebratory position did not go uncontested. A host of forces on the right saw the aspirations of the Soviet Union—and indeed, its very existence—as a fundamental threat to Christianity, free-market capitalism, and the American way of life. Organizations and individuals ranging from John

Edgar Hoover and the Federal Bureau of Investigation to the American Legion, a host of Roman Catholic and Protestant clergy, and prominent voices in the Republican Party saw the Bolsheviks as an existential threat that must be opposed, at home and abroad, at all costs. Their critique would reach a new level of intensity (and, in certain cases, irrationality) in the late 1940s and 1950s and persist until the collapse of the Soviet system nearly a half-century later. As for Kennan, the Moscow posting was only the beginning of an illustrious career. He would go on to become the most prominent US diplomat of the twentieth century, and his measured and nuanced interpretation of Soviet realities would, by the end of the Second World War, evolve into a policy of "containment," which would serve as the strategic framework for American conduct during the Cold War.

In the same year that Kennan shared his impressions of the Soviet Union with his sister, a young but seasoned journalist arrived in Berlin. William L. Shirer had much in common with Kennan. They were both thirty-year-old midwesterners fascinated by the wider world and determined to make their mark on it. Born in Chicago, Shirer had graduated from a small college in Iowa before making his reputation as the European correspondent for the *Chicago Tribune* between 1925 and 1932. He expanded his readership with reports from India, where he established a close relationship with Mohandas K. Gandhi, the charismatic leader of the country's ongoing struggle against British colonial rule. In 1934, Shirer accepted the position of Berlin bureau chief for William Randolph Hearst's Universal News Service, and three years later he became the primary European correspondent for CBS radio. Shirer is best remembered for his magisterial narrative of the nightmare of the Hitler years, *The Rise and Fall of the Third Reich* (1960). The less well-known *Berlin Diary* (1940) provided the raw material for this book. More powerful, though less polished than the later work, the *Diary* conveys the sense of moral and political crisis, the relentless march of a nation—indeed, a continent—toward war and holocaust. Some of his entries are terse and cryptic, others reflective and expansive. All document the tragic progress of a nation that was surrendering its soul to a weaver of dreams and delusions, and the arrogance and ugliness that followed.

It did not take long for Shirer to realize that the Germany of his memories was assuming an ominous cast. Arriving on August 25, 1934, he noted the intrusive presence of the secret police. He rapidly became despondent over the loss of "the old Berlin of the Republic" and its "care-free, emancipated, civilized air." He grew tired of "the constant Heil Hitler's, clicking of heels, and brown-shirted storm troopers or black-coated S.S. guards marching up and down the street. . . ." On November 28, he recorded that there was "much talk here that Germany is secretly arming, though it is difficult to get definite dope, and if you did get it and sent it, you'd probably be expelled." Not surprisingly, a year of honest and insightful reporting did nothing to endear him to the Nazi authorities. On January 23, 1936, his companion heard on the radio news "a ringing personal attack on me, implying that I was a dirty Jew. . . ." As the decade progressed and war grew closer, the conditions faced by Shirer and other foreign correspondents, along with those Germans who were not totally compliant with the regime, steadily worsened.

For Shirer, the essential task was to gain an understanding of Hitler and the phenomenon that he represented, and to convey this insight to his audience. Initially, in struggling to get the measure of the man who was the architect of this unfolding nightmare, this American journalist who had, ironically, studied and befriended the fuhrer's polar opposite—Mahatma Gandhi—found himself at something of a loss. In one instance, Hitler arrived at the Nuremberg rally in September 1934 "like a Roman emperor," yet according to Shirer, this aspiring Caesar "fumbled his cap with his left hand as he stood in his car acknowledging the delirious welcome with somewhat feeble Nazi salutes . . . he was clad in a rather worn gabardine trenchcoat, [and] his face had no particular expression at all. . . ." On that occasion, Shirer confessed, "for the life of me I could not quite comprehend what hidden springs he undoubtedly loosed in the hysterical mob which was greeting him so wildly."

By March 1940, with Poland already crushed under a Nazi onslaught and with France soon to follow, Shirer attended Hitler's speech on Germany's memorial day. By this time he had a firmer sense of the dictator's method and appeal. As Hitler spoke at the War Museum, "amidst . . . the arms and weapons Europeans have used to kill one another in all the wars of the past . . . his voice was full of hatred"; and Shirer wondered, "Has the man no other emotion?" Before his final departure from Berlin's Tempelhof field on December 4, 1940, Shirer celebrated the last night he would have to spend in the midst of a literal (and figurative) blackout. He proclaimed in his diary "After tonight the lights . . . and civilization!"

When Shirer reached "civilization," in this case, Lisbon, Portugal, he enjoyed a brief reunion with Edward R. Murrow, the man who had hired him at CBS radio. Four years younger than Kennan and Shirer, Murrow too served as an articulate and influential witness of Europe's descent into dictatorship and war. Born in Polecat Creek, North Carolina, to Quaker parents, Murrow moved with his family to the Pacific Northwest at a young age, where he worked as a lumberjack to help pay for his college education. At Washington State University Murrow went on to distinguish himself as a student and debater. Moving to New York City after graduation, he worked for several humanitarian organizations before joining CBS in 1935. There he made such a strong impression that in 1937 he was posted to London as the network's director of European operations. Like Shirer in Berlin and Kennan in Moscow, Murrow was seated at center stage as the leaders of the Old World, ignoring the failures of the early part of the century, marched resolutely onward toward a new global conflagration.

When the distant war in Poland reached the eastern shores of the Atlantic and Hitler overran the low countries and France before unleashing his Luftwaffe against Britain, it would be Murrow more than anyone else who, with his incisive reporting and signature voice, would bring the conflict (and the existential threat that it represented) into the homes, minds, and hearts of Americans. Night after night, in the late summer and fall of 1940, German bombers launched devastating raids against London and other British cities. Murrow's daily portraits in words made it impossible for his audience at home to view the war as an abstraction. His broadcasts went beyond the arcane particulars of politics and strategy. Instead, through vivid imagery and telling examples, he focused on the common people and their individual and collective struggle to survive. In a report that was emblematic, on London's 9/11—September 11, 1940—as hell rained down from the skies, he captured this spirit of defiance in a sentence that was rife with irony. On that night, Murrow recalled that "walking down the street a few minutes ago, shrapnel stuttered and stammered on the rooftops and from underground came the sound of singing, and the song was 'My Blue Heaven.'"

In reporting on this starkly modern "total war," a struggle in which the line between civilian and combatant had been effectively obliterated and rendered even more terrible by what Winston Churchill called "the lights of perverted science," Murrow went beyond a brute recital of statistics—the number of killed and wounded, the number of buildings destroyed in a particular raid—to the core reality of human suffering and the inspiring story of persistence in the face of adversity that gave it meaning.

In addition to journalists, there were a host of American visitors to Germany in the 1930s who left a chronicle of their impressions. Their reactions ranged from alarm and revulsion to covert or overt enthusiasm. Their writings offer reasoned attempts to understand a social and political phenomenon that was so familiar in some ways, and in others so strikingly unique. None was more thoughtful than a scholar who had lived and studied in Berlin both before the war and during the Weimar Republic. He returned on a fellowship in 1935, a traveler whose identity and experience gave him a special sensitivity to injustice. W. E. B. DuBois, the celebrated author of *The Souls of Black Folk*, had predicted that the "color line" would be the paramount problem of the twentieth century. Ironically, he insisted that during his current five-month visit to the Third Reich, he had been "treated with uniform courtesy and consideration." He also maintained that it was inconceivable to imagine spending "a similarly long time in any part of the United States without some, if not frequent, cases of personal insult or discrimination." He noted that with his own country mired in economic depression, "Germany in overwhelming majority stands back of Adolf Hitler . . . Germany has food and housing, and is, on the whole, contented and prosperous. Unemployment in four years has been reduced from seven to two millions or less. The whole nation is dotted with new homes for the common people, new roads, new public buildings and new public works of all kinds."

Nevertheless, DuBois was quick to stress that this was only part of the story. He cautioned that nine or ten million people lived in poverty, and contended that there had been a steep price to pay for this supposed economic miracle. According to DuBois, Germany was "silent, nervous, suppressed; it speaks in whispers; there is no public opinion, no opposition . . . never any protest of the slightest degree." And, however well he might have been treated as an individual person of color, he fully understood the virulence and significance of the regime's social pathology. In his estimation, "There has been no tragedy of modern times equal in its awful effects to the fight on the Jew in Germany. It is an attack on civilization, comparable only to such horrors as the Spanish Inquisition and the African slave trade. It has set civilization back a hundred years. . . ." Later in life, while in self-imposed exile in the African nation of Ghana, DuBois would write that the "color line" was just one variety of irrational hatred that encompassed the anti-Semitism that had so alarmed him during his return to Berlin. With greater precision than most foreign observers, and well before the tide of murder that was the Holocaust, this African American intellectual had grasped the devil's seed that was at the core of the Third Reich.

The reaction of other American visitors to Hitler's Germany was more cautious and ambiguous. Herbert Hoover, the Republican ex-president who had been absurdly condemned by some for "causing" the Great Depression, and criticized by others—with greater justice—for his inadequate response to this crisis, journeyed to Berlin in March 1938 as part of a ten-nation tour. His timing was not optimal for his hosts, since he arrived in the wake of the Anschluss. He was traveling in an unofficial capacity and only reluctantly agreed to an invitation to meet Hitler. Later, he confided to one interlocutor that during his session with the fuhrer, "a few key words would set Hitler off and 'all of a sudden [he] would jump to his feet and just went to raving talk—tantrums—that showed he was crazy.' Those words were 'Jew,' 'Communist,' and 'democracy.'" Nevertheless, as Andrew Nagorski notes in *Hitlerland: American Eyewitnesses to the Nazi Rise to Power*, this impression did not shake Hoover's central conviction that the United States should go to extraordinary lengths to avoid involvement in another European war. Upon returning to the United States, however, he addressed the Foreign Policy Association in New York and warned that "if the world is to keep the peace, then we must keep peace with dictatorships as well as with popular governments. The forms of governments which other peoples pass through is [*sic*] not our business." As events would prove, Hoover was far from alone in holding these sentiments.

Other Americans who ventured to the German capital in the 1930s were not only openly sympathetic to the Nazi regime but also aided and abetted it in real and concrete ways. A rough index to the more prominent personalities who fit this description is provided by a partial list of the recipients of the Order of the German Eagle, an honorific for foreigners that was first awarded during the latter part of the decade. Among this "elite" company was Henry Ford, the automotive and industrial pioneer, who was greatly admired by Hitler. A dedicated anti-Semite, his *Dearborn Independent* had condemned the "world Jewish conspiracy" even before the Nazis came to power. By this time his company had plants in Berlin and Cologne that produced, among other vehicles, trucks that were essential to the process of German rearmament and the style of blitzkrieg warfare that would follow in its wake. Indeed, Ford's affordable, mass-produced Model-T would become the inspiration for Hitler's Volkswagen.

James Mooney, the overseas director of General Motors, was also decorated with the Golden Eagle; his corporation was equally complicit in the Nazi economic and military renaissance. Thomas J. Watson, the chairman of IBM, was another American recipient of this award: as Edwin Black has documented in *IBM and the Holocaust*, the data processing machines that Watson's company produced would play a key role in the "racial classification" of the German population, an essential step in the nightmare that would follow. To be fair, these American CEOs could not have anticipated the coming Holocaust. By the same token, however, they could have harbored no illusions about the moral character and militaristic intent of the regime that they were enthusiastically and profitably doing business with.

With the possible exception of Ford, the most famous and the most notorious American to be awarded the German Eagle was the renowned aviator Charles Lindbergh, whose solo flight across the Atlantic had elevated him to the status of a national icon. His fame had reached new and tragic heights with the kidnapping and murder of his infant son and the "Trial of the Century" that followed. Often forgotten is the fact that Lindbergh's first visit to Nazi Germany had been arranged by the US military attaché in Berlin. This official was confident that the flyer's celebrity would allow him broad access to aircraft production facilities and provide the embassy with much-needed information on the status and progress of the Luftwaffe. Lindbergh's essential sympathy for the Nazi project would become apparent during subsequent visits, and he would ultimately become the leading spokesman for the isolationist "America First" movement in the months leading up to Pearl

Harbor. Although his defenders, even today, stress his patriotic intent and focus on American interests, Lindbergh's conviction that in the event of war in Europe, "a victory by Germany's European people would be preferable to one by Russia's semi-Asiatic Soviet Union" demonstrated the degree to which he had embraced the Nazi vision of "race" and geopolitics.

Lindbergh was certainly not alone in his belief that the United States should not take sides in the coming European conflict. On the cusp of war, another well-known American, and father of a son who would rise to even greater heights, argued that alliance with, and military support for, Great Britain in its looming conflict with Germany meant that America was casting its lot with the losing side. Joseph P. Kennedy was the US ambassador to Great Britain at its time of ultimate peril, and he won little favor at the Court of St. James. Indeed, no one was surprised when this Irish American Anglophobe retired his position in 1940. During that same year, his second son, John Fitzgerald, saw his analysis of the crisis, *Why England Slept*, published in both the United States and the United Kingdom. This piece was actually the younger Kennedy's Harvard undergraduate thesis. Ironically, it provided a more balanced and analytical look at the roots and impact of appeasement than his father was ever able to provide his superiors in Washington.

Today, there is a tendency to regard figures like Charles Lindbergh and Joseph Kennedy as reactionary voices that lacked a sympathetic and substantial audience on the home front. In fact, nothing could be further from the truth. It is all too easy to forget that persuasive observers and advocates like Shirer, Murrow, and, indeed, President Roosevelt himself faced an uphill struggle to convince Americans of the imminent and deadly threat posed by the Third Reich to not only Europeans but also their own democracy. Moreover, the hope for peace and stability faced another challenge in the form of the very nation (and system) that Hitler and his followers deemed to be their deadly nemesis and archrival for global hegemony.

As with Nazi Germany, the Soviet Union, during its descent into tyranny and terror under Joseph Stalin, did not suffer from a lack of dedicated foreign sympathizers and apologists. In the 1930s, as today, the *New York Times* played a significant role in shaping public opinion. Then, as now, it was widely regarded in the United States as the "newspaper of record." During this decade, the American perspective on "Bolshevik Russia" was influenced to a considerable degree by the work of its Moscow correspondent, an eccentric and enigmatic Englishman named Walter Duranty. This singular figure, who possessed a wooden leg as the result of a train accident in Paris—the city where, as a young man, he had befriended and entered the circle of the satanist Aleister Crowley—would become notorious for his flamboyant lifestyle and his poetic and literary pretensions. Also, as events would prove, his capacity to deceive himself about the state of affairs in the "revolutionary" society and nation that he had been assigned to cover was equaled, if not exceeded, by his capacity to deceive his readers. During his heyday, Duranty was highly regarded. In 1932, he was awarded the Pulitzer Prize for journalism, and that same year presidential candidate Roosevelt invited him to the New York governor's mansion to "talk over the Russian situation."

Duranty tried to present himself as a model of impartiality. In his Pulitzer acceptance speech, he confessed that, initially, he had been "viciously anti-Bolshevik," but he had since "discovered that the Bolsheviks were sincere enthusiasts, trying to regenerate a people that had been shockingly misgoverned, and I decided to give them their fair break." Moreover, he had also come "to respect the Soviet leaders, especially Stalin," whom he considered to have "grown into a really great statesman." Duranty went well beyond giving Stalin and his blood-soaked regime the "fair break" that he had promised until he was released by the *Times* in 1940.

A disturbing case in point is Duranty's reporting on Stalin's terror famine in the Ukraine, a calculated act that killed millions. This issue provided a clear illustration of Duranty's sympathies, not to mention his talent for euphemism. In a representative piece published in the *Times* on March 31, 1933, he acknowledged that the "mismanagement of collective farming" and the disruptive actions of "wreckers" (a favored term of Soviet propagandists) and "spoilers" had affected agricultural production. But, speaking of the regime's determination to modernize this sector of the economy, he explained that "to put it brutally—you can't make an omelet without breaking eggs." In a masterpiece of doublespeak, he also claimed that "there is no actual starvation or deaths from starvation but there is widespread mortality from diseases due to malnutrition, especially in the Ukraine, North Caucasus, and Lower Volga." Later in the decade, Duranty systematically downplayed the extent of Stalin's purges and show trials. After the latest judicial lynching in 1937, he argued in *The New Republic* that the confessions of the accused were genuine and not coerced. Moreover, he proposed that even if these individuals had not actually committed the crimes they were accused of, some mystical dimension of the "Russian soul" had led them to assume guilt, both to spare others and to further the interests of the people as a whole, a bizarre rationalization that was angrily refuted by one of those condemned in absentia, Stalin's nemesis-in-exile, Leon Trotsky.

Surprisingly, this would not be the last chapter in the cautionary saga of Walter Duranty. Suspicions about the veracity of his reporting were rekindled by the wave of revelations that followed the collapse of the Soviet Union. A movement to revoke his Pulitzer Prize, driven in particular by anger over his treatment of the Ukrainian disaster, had gained sufficient momentum by 2003 to prompt the Pulitzer Prize Board to reexamine its 1932 decision. In the end, the board declined to strip Duranty of this recognition because his selection had been based on a set of articles that had not specifically focused on the terror famine. The man of whom the columnist Joseph Alsop had said "lying was his stock in trade" retained journalism's highest honor. Certainly, Duranty's story has wide and persisting implications regarding the ideological turmoil of the 1930s on the character of our modern mass media. Today, in an age when the line between journalism and polemic has become harder and harder to distinguish, the legacy and impact of this period should not be underestimated.

For policymakers charged with navigating the United States through increasingly treacherous waters, the ideological enthusiasms and delusions of a Duranty, and those like him on both the political left and right, were untenable. Painful memories of the First World War and the belated US intervention in that terrible event were fresh in the minds of many Americans who remembered the human cost of involving the nation in the armed pursuit of a distant cause, however compelling it might have seemed at the moment. During the 1930s, most Americans were determined that the United States should not be drawn into another world conflict and convinced that the defense of a higher principle—any higher principle—was not worth its toll in blood and treasure. The issue was not defined so much by which side the United States should support, but by the extent to which it should venture, via trade and diplomacy, to support any side at all. A substantial part of the

Republican Party was fiercely isolationist, and some Democrats shared their resolve to avoid foreign entanglements. As the decade progressed, Western and midwestern Republicans, including senators such as William Borah of Idaho, Hiram Johnson of California, Robert La Follette Jr. of Wisconsin, and Gerald Nye of North Dakota, took the lead in persuading Congress to pass a series of neutrality acts. The primary objective of these measures was to prevent US firms from trading with belligerent nations—irrespective of whether these nations were the aggressors or the victims of aggression.

During the early part of the decade, the lack of enthusiasm for involvement in foreign conflict transcended party lines. For his part, Roosevelt had no desire to insert the nation into the gears of war. As late as 1937, when the economy took another downturn and the wisdom and future of his second New Deal was increasingly being called into question, domestic issues dominated his agenda and shaped his priorities. Still, with a host of regional conflicts adding to the danger posed by a rearming and militant Germany, Roosevelt was fully aware that the United States could not simply walk away from its moral and strategic responsibilities. Driven by the force and logic of events, he began to engage in a running battle with congressional isolationists to provide himself greater freedom to maneuver America's ailing, but still powerful, industrial and commercial engine behind the cause of its friends and allies. Once Austria and Czechoslovakia were absorbed into the Nazi orbit, the pattern was as clear as it was ominous. Although the future of Europe was at stake, Roosevelt's hands were tied, and there was little he could do to provide the endangered nations in Hitler's path with the tools of self-defense.

By 1939, Roosevelt was determined to aid Great Britain by any means short of war when his attempts to gain some flexibility in dealing with this crisis assumed an added urgency. On January 31, he warned members of the Senate Military Affairs Committee that "Hitler was intent on dominating Europe . . . and should he accomplish this, it would imperil the peace and safety of the United States." He continued, pragmatically, "if the Rhine frontiers are threatened the rest of the world is, too. Once they have fallen before Hitler, the German sphere of action will be unlimited." Later that year, with Poland already under Nazi assault and Great Britain at imminent risk from Hitler's legions, Roosevelt was able to win congressional approval for an expansion of his "cash and carry" policy that allowed nations to pay up front and take their purchases away in their own ships. This policy favored the British, who, in geography and naval power, were in a much better position to take advantage of it than the Germans.

Although "cash and carry" helped the British war effort, it was, at best, a partial and inadequate solution. By 1941, England was running perilously short of weaponry and material, not to mention the ability to pay for them. By March of that year, Roosevelt persuaded Congress to agree to his Lend-Lease program, which authorized him "to sell, transfer title to, exchange, lease, lend, or otherwise dispose of . . . any defense article . . . to any country whose defense the President deems vital to the defense of the United States." Repayment could be "in kind or property, or any other direct or indirect benefit" he found acceptable. This language provided the president with the latitude he needed. Lend-Lease would not only bolster the war effort of an increasingly desperate Britain but, in time, it would also provide critical assistance to the USSR, which had been invaded by Germany three months after the measure was passed.

As a final benefit, "cash and carry" provided a means of stiffening Chinese resistance to the Japanese invasion, which was now in its fourth year. In a clear demonstration that profit owes no allegiance, those very American automotive corporations that had willingly traded with the Third Reich went on to provide the trucks and rocket launchers that carried the Red Army to the gates of Berlin. Nine months after Lend-Lease was passed, after the Japanese attack on Pearl Harbor and the ensuing German declaration of war on the United States, the fading hope for peace gave way to the bitter reality of unprovoked aggression. American isolationism, like its British handmaiden, appeasement, was relegated to the graveyard of lost causes.

The specter of a rearmed and imperialistic Germany at the heart of Europe—the primary geopolitical concern of foreign-policy establishments on both sides of the Atlantic during the 1930s—tended then, as it does now, to overshadow other conflicts that provided dire warning of the cataclysm to come. While some considered them peripheral, these were theaters of conflict in which millions suffered the ravages of modern war that would soon descend on millions more. The Italian invasion of Ethiopia in 1935, the outbreak of the Spanish Civil War in 1936, and the ruthless Japanese assault on China in 1937, provided lethal outlets for ideological rivalry, arenas for proxy war, and proving grounds for a devastating new generation of weaponry. However, as much as the US State Department and devout isolationists in and out of government wanted the nation to stay aloof from these distant conflicts, many Americans, driven by intensely felt loyalties and motivations, stepped forward to ensure that their vision of justice would prevail. These Americans came to believe that these struggles, however distant, were inseparable from the ongoing crisis at home, and they were willing to fight for their convictions in the arena of public opinion and, in some cases, on the foreign battlefields themselves.

Italian intentions toward Ethiopia were clear months before the actual invasion was launched. Mussolini's regime visualized this East African nation as a colony where it could resettle its surplus population and create a thriving agricultural economy. It was also driven by a desire to avenge its humiliating defeat in 1896 at the battle of Adowa, when the Ethiopian emperor Menelik annihilated an Italian invasion force. This time, Italy would justify its aggression before the world as a "civilizing mission" designed to stamp out slavery, the slave trade, and cross-border raiding in the southern and southeastern portions of the country. Italian forces won a strategic victory in short order against the forces of Haile Selassie, whose army, despite his efforts to modernize, largely consisted of feudal levies with outdated weaponry. Guerrilla resistance persisted, but by 1936 the emperor had gone into exile in London.

For African Americans, the biblical land of Ethiopia had long stood as a symbol of heritage and pride. Although most traced their origins to the western part of the continent, far from the east African mountains that had been the stronghold of that civilization, the central role played by Christianity and the church in African American communities, both North and South, gave Psalm 68, verse 31, which states that "Ethiopia shall stretch forth her hands unto God," a special power and resonance. In 1935, when Mussolini sent a modern army across its borders, invading one of only two remaining African nations that had not fallen prey to European colonialism, people throughout the African diaspora, in the Caribbean as well as the United States, voiced their outrage and rallied in support of their brethren, stretching forth their hands.

Even before the Italian threat in the 1920s and early 1930s became immediate, the Ethiopian government sent several goodwill delegations to the United States, and their presence attracted black intellectuals to their culture and cause. In 1934, as the situation began to worsen, a small group of American and Ethiopian scholars and students gathered in Washington, DC, and New York City to form the Ethiopian Research Council. The council's purpose went beyond the mere celebration of Ethiopia's past achievements: its mission statement noted that since Ethiopia had become a subject of international attention, the organization would inform the general public about the emerging crisis. After the invasion was launched, a number of prominent individuals and organizations called on black Americans to come to the aid of the beleaguered African nation. The National Association for the Advancement of Colored People (NAACP), in addition to imploring the League of Nations to honor its responsibilities and stand up against aggression, also "lodged protests with Congress and urged its own membership to write to their congressional representatives in opposition to neutrality legislation that it held would benefit Italy."

DuBois, writing in *Foreign Affairs* in 1936, lamented that "race hate will increase" as a result of this aggression, but argued that "Black men and brown men have indeed been aroused as seldom before . . . if there were any chance effectively to recruit men, money, and machines of war among the one hundred millions of Africans outside of Ethiopia, the result would be enormous." Certainly there was significant grassroots support for the besieged nation in African American communities throughout the country. By 1937, an organization calling itself the Ethiopian World Federation had formed and rapidly established branches in a host of cities, including New York, Philadelphia, Buffalo, Baltimore, Nashville, Chicago, St. Louis, and Tulsa.

Nevertheless, while the effort that DuBois called for was widespread, its practical result was partial and disappointing. According to Joseph E. Harris, who has written the definitive study on this subject, "Many blacks contributed to both black and white groups that sent supplies and money to Ethiopia, and there is no way to determine the total amount. Still, the financial assistance . . . from all sources fell far short of what the leaders had expected." Rivalries and conflicting agendas among the various fund-raising groups contributed to this shortcoming, but it should not be forgotten that African American communities, at a clear economic disadvantage before the Great Depression, were particularly hard hit when this crisis reached its full intensity at the time of the Italo-Ethiopian War. Also, while some African Americans expressed a desire to volunteer and fight for the Ethiopian cause, their aspirations were thwarted by a combination of economic constraints and official harassment on the part of the FBI and the State Department. Given the isolationist sentiment at that time, the US government was not enthusiastic about American citizens participating in foreign wars, regardless of their race.

Several aviators managed to make it to Addis Ababa, however. First was the flashy and picaresque Hubert Fauntleroy Julian, the "Black Eagle" or, as some anointed him, the "Negro Lindbergh," and second was John Robinson, the "Brown Condor." Julian was born in Trinidad. He moved to Harlem in the 1920s, where he became an enthusiastic supporter of Marcus Garvey's Pan-African organization, the Universal Negro Improvement Association. In 1931, he went to Ethiopia and won favor with Haile Selassie, an enthusiasm that proved fleeting when, among other incidents, he crashed the emperor's personal plane during a rehearsal of his coronation ceremony. He was asked to leave the country shortly thereafter. Julian returned to Ethiopia at the outbreak of war in 1935, but he seemed to have played no meaningful role in its miniscule air force. Rumors circulated that he was actually an Italian spy, an idea that was given a certain amount of credence the following year when he surfaced in Naples and, according to Harris, "announced . . . that he had become an Italian citizen with the name Huberto Fauntleroyana Juliano." It wasn't long before he discarded this identity and returned to the United States, claiming the switch had merely been a "stratagem . . . to win an audience with Mussolini so he could assassinate him." By contrast, the "Brown Condor," Robinson, would go on to play a far less dramatic but much more substantial role, providing an aerial link between Addis Ababa and the front line during the war and training a cadre of Ethiopian pilots after it.

For African Americans determined to support their Ethiopian compatriots, the Abyssinian highlands were not the only field of battle. A militant segment of the Italian American community also mobilized to support their countrymen, and there were a number of clashes between the impassioned advocates of these rival national causes. Organizations such as the United Italian Association, the Friends of Italy, and the Italian Historical Society served as fund-raisers, political advocates, propagandists, and apologists for the fascist crusade in North Africa. As Harris notes, the situation in the New York City area "where the nation's largest concentrations of African Americans and Italian Americans lived in uneasy proximity" was especially volatile: "physical clashes took place between them in the streets and elementary schools, Italian grocery stores were vandalized, and the heavyweight championship fight of Joe Louis and Primo Carnera became a proxy for frayed relations between the boxers' ethnic constituencies." Not surprisingly, a number of brawls broke out in Brooklyn, Harlem, and Jersey City after Louis knocked out Mussolini's favorite prizefighter in their highly publicized match in Yankee Stadium on June 25, 1935. Unfortunately, the boxing ring was not the only arena in which the partisans of both sides sought to score points. As Harris points out, the popular Italian American mayor of New York City, Fiorello LaGuardia, was widely criticized when he "attended a pro-Italian rally in Madison Square Garden despite pleas from blacks and whites alike not to do so." Predictably, as in other periods of American history when overseas conflict raged, during the 1930s the credo "E Pluribus Unum"—"out of many, one"—was quickly forgotten.

Some Americans proved equally passionate when civil war broke out in Spain in 1936. In this case, ideology rather than racial affinity was the catalyst of outrage and action. Although the concept of the "popular front," an alignment of convenience between elements of the democratic center and the doctrinaire Left on both sides of the Atlantic, provided a wider rallying point for the Republican forces, in the United States both the organizational impulse and the majority of combat volunteers would be supplied by the American Communist Party. In the wake of the devastation left by the Great Depression, the utopian call of communism—in its explanation of the roots of the crisis and in its sweeping vision of social justice—found an increasingly receptive audience throughout the world, and, for this brief time, at least, the cities and farmlands of America provided its dedicated adherents with a fertile recruiting ground.

According to Peter N. Carroll, the first to enlist in this "international" cause were veterans of struggles fought closer to home, committed activists "tried and tested in a variety of campaigns around the country. Their efforts had touched on virtually every radical cause since the beginning of the century: from the labor union organizing drives of the Industrial Workers of the World to unemployment demonstrations . . . from protests against racial injustice to intellectual and ideological polemics." Many came from big cities and, not surprisingly, since the enemy was fascism and its German analog, Nazism, many volunteers were Jews. Hyman Katz, a young Jewish volunteer who defied the wishes of his mother and went to Spain, wrote that "the whole history of our people has taught me to admire the prophets and fighters who died for liberty," and he proudly proclaimed that "I fight against the greatest oppressors of my people." Also, more African Americans served on the battlefields of Spain than made it to Ethiopia. For Americans on the political left, whatever their background, Spain provided an ideal opportunity to match rhetoric with action, a place where "workers of the world" and their ideological allies could take up arms and confront the common enemy.

Predictably, neither the US State Department nor committed isolationists in and out of government were eager to see the Communist Party of the United States of America (CPUSA) and its allies render aid and support, much less a flow of combatants, to one side in a foreign civil war. Although the rebel forces of Francisco Franco were backed by Italy and Nazi Germany, the support of the USSR and "international bolshevism" for the legally constituted Republican government in Madrid did nothing to endear it to the Roosevelt administration or, especially, to its congressional adversaries. As Carroll points out, "although American neutrality laws made no provisions for insurrections and civil wars, Washington ordered a 'moral embargo' against the shipment of war material to either side. . . ." Try as it may, however, it could not prevent US volunteers from traveling to other nations and then to Spain, nor could it deter the CPUSA from doing what it could to back this international crusade against fascism. Within months the first contingents of the Abraham Lincoln Brigade had reached the front, and their doomed crusade would leave a lasting legacy in the memory of the American Left and the history of the tragic decade in which they fought.

As Carroll notes, to one member of the brigade, the conflict in Spain was "a fight to the finish between all that is new and generous and hopeful in the world, and all that is old, cruel, and fetid . . . a clear-cut struggle between the powers of light and the powers of darkness. . . ." In the end, however, the volunteers from the United States and other international detachments had little to celebrate except their own sacrifice and, in some cases, their own heroism. Poorly equipped and often poorly led, usually not by professional officers but by a cadre of amateurs, "the ideology boys," as Ernest Hemingway once described the fighters he would later immortalize in *For Whom the Bell Tolls*, laid down their lives in one ill-conceived attack after another. Outmanned and outgunned, they suffered a litany of defeats ending in a series of "great retreats." Hell often came from the air: the Nazis used the Spanish conflict as a training ground for their new Luftwaffe and the Republican forces had no answer for the German planes that regularly decimated their ranks. If this was not enough, the antifascist crusade also suffered from its own internal divisions and self-inflicted wounds. As one English volunteer, Eric Blair—better known as George Orwell—recounted in *Homage to Catalonia*, the Stalinist commissars did not hesitate to put the anarchist units in their place when they showed too much independence from the "party line." Before it was over in late 1938 with Franco's forces triumphant, nearly one-third of the close to three thousand Americans who served in the Abraham Lincoln Brigade lost their lives. The story did not end there, however. Back home, those who had survived the carnage of the battlefield were faced with the prospect of being hauled before the House Committee on Un-American Activities and interrogated regarding their communist beliefs and associations.

The opening salvoes of global conflict in Africa and Europe were not the only flashpoints that captured the attention of American policymakers and the general public. War, in all its cruel dimensions, would come to Asia four years before Pearl Harbor. After years of sporadic hostilities, Japan launched an all-out invasion of China in July 1937. It was a campaign that would become notorious for the callous disregard of civilian life on the part of the aggressors. Although most Americans viewed China through a complex of patronizing stereotypes, those who paid attention to world affairs acknowledged its innocence and sympathized with the suffering of its people, especially as reports of Japanese atrocities continued to mount. At the beginning of the decade, China was as distant culturally and conceptually as it was geographically. Nevertheless, a novel by a daughter of American missionaries had already succeeded in giving its anonymous millions a more human and familiar face. Pearl Buck, born in West Virginia and raised in China, was awarded a Pulitzer Prize in 1932 and the Nobel Prize for Literature in 1938 for *The Good Earth*, a story of Chinese peasant life focusing on the daily struggles of a single family.

Buck's narrative was deeply informed by the themes of injustice and endurance. Although the novel was dismissed by some as simplistic and sentimental, Buck must ultimately be credited for her uncompromising portrayal of the exploitation of women and her implicit commentary in the tragic odyssey of its central character, Wang Lung, from peasant to landlord, from victim to victimizer. Buck's novel, already widely celebrated, became even more influential when, in a remarkable coincidence of art and event, the MGM film version directed by Sidney Franklin was released in 1937, a month after the Japanese invasion. While the Imperial Army rampaged through the cities of coastal China, American theatergoers were absorbed by the story of Wang Lung, played—in a quintessentially American riot of identities—by Mesheilem Meier Weisenfreund, a Jewish immigrant from the Ukraine better known by his stage name, Paul Muni.

If Buck created an emotional environment that allowed Americans to bond with the cause of the embattled Chinese, another woman would give that generalized sentiment a cutting political edge. Soong May-ling was born on Hainan Island, China, in 1898, and educated in the United States. She was the daughter of Han Chiao-shun, better known as Charlie Soong, a remarkable man who resembled a character in an Asian version of a Charles Dickens novel. An impoverished teenager who made his way to Boston, Soong fell under the influence and sponsorship of Methodist missionaries who would support his education in America and send him back to his homeland to further their cause. In addition to creating the foundation of what would become a vast fortune by printing and selling Bibles in the Chinese language, he became deeply involved in the political currents that led to the overthrow of the last Manchu emperor.

Soong's greatest impact, however, was as the patriarch of a remarkable political family. Among his notable children were daughters Ching-ling, who married Sun Yat-sen, the founder of the Chinese Republic, and May-ling, who married one of Sun's prominent generals, Chiang Kai-shek. As China descended into civil war in the 1920s, the Soong family became a house divided as Ching-ling supported the communists and May-ling became an outspoken advocate for the nationalist and "democratic" army (and party) that was commanded by her husband. After the Japanese invasion had persuaded the warring factions to conclude a truce, "Madame Chiang Kai-shek," as she was known in the West, turned her American experience, fluency in English, and fervent political commitment into a potent public relations weapon. She campaigned relentlessly for the cause of her people and her husband, whom, she hoped, would emerge as the ultimate winner in the struggle for China's future.

Soong May-ling, a graduate of Wellesley College, was a living contradiction to the popular stereotype of the "passive Chinese woman." According to her biographer Hannah Pakula, in 1937 and 1938, "the generalissimo's wife turned out more than a hundred articles, speeches, press dispatches, and statements, not counting interviews and letters, written to be circulated into monied or powerful hands." In a series of three articles in the *New York Times* she denounced the League of Nations for leaving China "frigidly alone . . . to fight as best we can . . . for the principles which the democracies espouse." In addition, she tirelessly argued her cause before missionary groups, women's organizations, and a range of influential forums concerned with US foreign policy.

Her crusade was strengthened by the fact that Henry Luce, the publishing tycoon whose empire included *Time*, *Life*, and *Fortune* magazines, was the son of Chinese missionaries, a friend of the Soong family, and a passionate advocate for a free China under nationalist rule. It was not surprising when, in 1937, *Time* named Generalissimo and Madame Chiang Kai-shek their "Man and Wife of the Year," proclaiming that "no woman in the west holds so great a position as Mme. Chiang Kai-shek holds in China." In the final analysis, all her persistence and eloquence could not persuade the Roosevelt administration to formally enter the war against Japan. Although some credit to purchase war material was forthcoming, a flow that increased after the advent of Lend-Lease, only the bombing of Pearl Harbor was sufficient to change the political calculus in Washington. Nevertheless, her fame continued to grow and her advocacy for her husband only intensified after December 7, 1941, once the United States unleashed its military might against the invaders of her nation.

With Japan defeated, the Chinese civil war resumed with renewed intensity. Following the Communist triumph in 1949, Chiang Kai-shek and his government retreated to the island of Taiwan. Not surprisingly, Madame Chiang went on to become an active participant in the acrimonious American debate over "who lost China" and a significant figure in the anticommunist crusade of the 1950s, always remaining an imperious figure and central personality in a regime that, despite its pretensions, was anything but democratic and notably corrupt. She moved to New York City after her husband's death in 1975 and died in 2003, at the venerable age of 105. Her persona, as well as her politics, is best summed up by an anecdote reported by Eleanor Roosevelt (and recounted by Pakula). At a dinner party, when it was noted that the leader of the United Mine Workers, John L. Lewis, was "acting up," President Roosevelt "turned to Madame Chiang and asked: 'What would you do in China with a labor leader like John Lewis?' She never said a word, but the beautiful, small hand came up and slid across her throat. . . ."

That Soong May-ling could be the epitome of charm when the occasion demanded had been observed by a recently retired US Army Air Corps captain named Claire Chennault when he arrived in Shanghai in June 1937. The cultural contrast must have been a striking one when Chennault, born in Texas and raised in Louisiana, first met Madame Chiang Kai-shek. As he describes it, "a vivacious young girl clad in a modish Paris frock tripped into the room, bubbling with energy and enthusiasm." Chennault had been driven to the French concession in that city to meet his new employer: among her other titles, Madame Chiang was the secretary-general of China's Aeronautical Commission, and Chennault had been hired to conduct a three-month study of the Chinese Air Force. When war with Japan broke out a month later, Chennault's role expanded from consultant to combatant. He was soon engaged in training Chinese pilots, organizing Nanking's air defense, and, at the urging of May-ling, organizing a motley group of foreign pilots known as the Fourteenth Squadron. Daniel Ford describes them as mercenaries who "had more zest for drinking than for fighting [and] Chinese pilots refused to work with them." Even so, the outfit would prove to be the precursor of a far more substantial and effective volunteer air wing.

As China's plight worsened and the Roosevelt administration worked to develop creative ways to assist the victims of aggression short of actually entering the war, the "China lobby" in Washington, led by May-ling's brother, the Harvard-educated, debonair, and extremely wealthy T. V. Soong, redoubled its efforts to secure meaningful military assistance. This effort, in which Chennault himself served as an important advocate, involved the orchestration of a series of financial and organizational maneuvers designed to circumvent the neutrality laws. The end result was the American Volunteer Force, or "Flying Tigers," American pilots flying American planes, an idea that was gradually translated from concept to reality in 1940 and 1941. This unit partially offset the Japanese advantage in the air and, after Pearl Harbor, some of its members were incorporated into the new China Air Task Force of the regular US Army. The exploits of this fighter wing became legendary, and as the war went on it continued to function because of an equally improbable achievement, the airlift over the "hump"—the Himalayas—that helped sustain the Chinese war effort.

Not all of the Americans who stood up for China in its time of trial did so by force of arms. A woman of singular moral courage must be remembered for her nonviolent resistance when Japanese forces entered the republican capital of Nanking in December 1937 and murdered an estimated three hundred thousand people during the six weeks of pillage, sexual assault, and unconstrained carnage known as "the rape of Nanking." Although a small and heroic group of expatriates, including diplomats, medical personnel, and educators, managed to create a "safety zone" and protect many potential victims, they were in no position to stem the onslaught of a military that made no real distinction between civilians and soldiers. Foremost among those humanitarians whose valor and determination stand out was a fifty-one-year-old missionary and teacher from rural Illinois, Wilhelmina ("Minnie") Vautrin. According to Iris Chang, the author of the authoritative study of the Nanking massacre, Vautrin, an administrator at the Ginling Women's Arts and Sciences College, had fallen in love with China, both the land and its people, and she showed no inclination to abandon it in its time of need.

When the Japanese entered the city, she "refused to join the other Americans evacuating Nanking, and . . . the American embassy lent her a new nine-foot American flag to lay flat on the center of the grassy quadrangle . . . to protect the campus against Japanese pilots." The real threat did not come from the air, however. Vautrin and the small band of foreigners she worked with in the safety zone engaged in a constant battle of wits with Japanese officers and civil authorities looking for real and alleged Chinese soldiers to murder and defenseless young women to subject to rape and prostitution. The verbal and, on at least one occasion, physical abuse she suffered would have broken a lesser person. According to Chang, "the sheer number of refugees eventually overwhelmed Vautrin. Hundreds of women crammed themselves into verandas and covered ways head to feet, and many more women slept outside on the grass at night. The attic of Ginling's Science Hall housed more than one thousand women. . . ." Vautrin eventually suffered a nervous breakdown, was evacuated to the United States, and a year after she left the country that she loved, she committed suicide, one more victim of the rape of Nanking and the indiscriminate horror of war.

For those who could see beyond the immediate crisis of economic depression at home and pause and take stock of the world around them—the widening scope of conflict and suffering, of war and rumors of war—there was reason for alarm. This was especially true for America's Jewish population, part of a diaspora whose history gave ample evidence of how rapidly the possibility of persecution, displacement, and violence could become grim reality. Philip Roth, in his dystopian vision entitled *The Plot against America*, provides us with an alternate history in which Charles Lindbergh wins the Republican nomination for the presidency in 1940 and goes on to defeat Roosevelt in the general election. Narrated from the perspective of a Jewish boy growing up in Newark, New Jersey, the Lindbergh administration imposes a regime of reeducation and relocation in an attempt to render America's Jews "truly American." However improbable this scenario may seem today, Jewish Americans in the 1930s had cause for great concern in their own congregations and communities, apart from the unfolding nightmare in Germany. In addition to the "America First" movement, an unlikely coalition that shared the narrow objective of keeping the United States out of another European war, whatever the consequences, there was a declining, but still dangerous, Ku Klux Klan. There was also the erratic, but still formidable, Henry Ford and anti-Semitic demagogues like Father Charles Coughlin, the "radio priest" from Dearborn, Michigan. Perhaps most threatening of all, there was a very small, but highly vocal, minority of German Americans who enthusiastically supported the Nazi project.

By 1936, an organization that was clearly a tool of the Nazi regime, the Friends of New Germany, was disbanded on orders from Berlin. A new party, the Amerikadeutscher Volksbund, or the German American Bund, was organized to replace it. The Bund's leader, a naturalized American citizen named Fritz Kuhn, declared that it would be "as American as apple pie," and proceeded to deliver his inaugural speech on a platform emblazoned with both swastikas and the Stars and Stripes. In its camp in the hills of northern New Jersey, it mimicked the paramilitary posture and hateful rhetoric of its counterpart in the Fatherland, and it more than made up for the modest size of its membership with an aggressive and strident presence. Although in retrospect the threat that the Bund posed may have been exaggerated, American Jews knew from centuries of painful experience that it could be neither dismissed nor ignored.

Once Hitler came to power in January 1933, an anti-Semitic assault in Germany seemed imminent. American Jewish organizations began work to formulate an effective response. Their verdict on a proper course of action was far from unanimous, however. According to Edwin Black, by March the American Jewish Congress was calling for "a national program of highly visible protests, parades, and demonstrations" and the organization the Jewish War Veterans was urging a nationwide boycott of German imports. By contrast, the American Jewish Committee and B'nai B'rith maintained that "the wisest and the most effective policy for the Jews of America is to exercise the same fine patience, fortitude and exemplary conduct that have been shown by the Jews of Germany," insisting that it was not advisable "to inflame already overwrought feelings, but to act wisely, judiciously, and deliberately." Those who called for caution were motivated by fear of retaliation against their coreligionists, a sentiment that was echoed by many German Jews and other Jewish organizations who would be confronted with the real and immediate consequences of Nazi actions. The debate became increasingly contentious as the date approached for the centerpiece of the activists' efforts: a mass rally in New York's Madison Square Garden on March 27, 1933.

Despite a chorus of opposition, the event was not cancelled. In fact, those who hoped for an overwhelming response to their moral call to arms would not be disappointed. Black, who has examined contemporary accounts of this rally, provides a vivid picture of the extent and depth of the support that it generated. On the appointed day, the Garden was packed with twenty thousand people and the surrounding streets were jammed with thousands more who organized their own spontaneous demonstrations. The audience was not limited to New York City. Advances in media allowed the rally to be heard on a national stage. Other gatherings were held at the same time, and at these locations "thousands huddled around loudspeakers waiting for the Garden event, which would be broadcast live via radio relay to two hundred additional cities across the country." A host of religious and political luminaries spoke in the Garden that day. The former New York governor Alfred E. Smith, a Roman Catholic whose bid for the presidency had been broken on the wheel of a parallel form of prejudice, lent his voice to the proceedings. Another key participant, William Green, the president of the American Federation of Labor, proclaimed that "three million American unionists" would "do all that lies within our power" to end "the campaign of persecution against the Jewish people in Germany." The list of other prominent figures who telegraphed their support was a long one.

Ultimately, the most powerful statement that day was made by the driving force behind the organization of the rally and president of the American Jewish Congress, Rabbi Stephen S. Wise, an accomplished speaker who could rivet an audience with his oratory. On that day he made it clear that no American, Jew or Gentile, could draw artificial and arbitrary lines when it came to the struggle against injustice. Noting that Nazi leadership had claimed that its treatment of its Jewish population was a "local German question," Wise invoked the wisdom of Abraham Lincoln: "Defenders of slavery urged and excused slavery on the ground that it was *local.* Lincoln's answer was slavery is local but freedom is *national.*" Wise, a co-founder of the NAACP in 1914, had framed his argument in the words and logic of an American icon and presented it with a conviction and force that made it all but impossible to ignore.

While it is impossible to quantify the impact of the anti-Nazi boycott in the years before Pearl Harbor, it certainly did not help Germany's all-out quest to rearm and prepare for war. As it turned out, economic action was not the only method of resisting the anti-Semitic onslaught at home and abroad. Distinguished and learned individuals such as Rabbi Wise would not be the only variety of American to stand up against the specter of nazism. Indeed, Philip Roth's Newark would become a sort of battleground in this ongoing struggle. As Warren Grover explains in his fascinating study of *Nazis in Newark*, some of the anti-Nazi activism in that city followed predictable paths, including support for the boycott, political petitioning, and collecting charitable donations to assist besieged German Jewry. Other activities were more unconventional, as were the activists in the Jewish community who carried them out.

By 1933, the forerunner of the Bund, the Friends of New Germany, had established a branch in Newark that soon boasted one of its largest memberships in the country. When this organization called for a large-scale meeting on September 21, 1933, writes Grover, "Third Ward Jewish residents and merchants [became] nervous. Signs in German with swastikas on them had been tacked on trees in German areas adjacent to Springfield Avenue, a thoroughfare lined with Jewish businesses." Either on their own initiative or via the prompting of other members of the community, Abner "Longie" Zwillman and his associates decided to involve themselves in the impending crisis. "Zwillman called a meeting of about a dozen of the toughest members of his Third Ward gang, including Hymie 'the Weasel' Kugel, Julius 'Skinny' Markowitz, Harry Green, Harry Sanders, Max Leipzig, 'Primo' Weiner, and the ex-boxers Nat Arno and Abie Bain. A plan was devised to halt the . . . celebration by attacking the attendees."

Zwillman's volunteers came prepared that night, having wrapped pipes in newspapers and hidden them outside the meeting hall. When the ceremony convened, "Arno . . . tossed stench bombs through a second-floor window into the auditorium . . . [and] pandemonium broke loose." Not to be deterred in their crusade for the "master race," the "Friends" called for another meeting on October 16. Heartened by their previous victory, Zwillman's irregulars returned in force. This time, "the fight spread to twelve square blocks" before order was restored. These Jewish defenders would go on to call themselves "the Minutemen." Under the command of the retired prizefighter Arno, they would go on to resist the "Friends," and then the "Bund," until these pro-Nazi organizations were silenced after Pearl Harbor.

In the end, the worst fears of the young Philip Roth would not come to pass. Arno and his Minutemen would not have to face Wehrmacht troops and tanks marching down Springfield Avenue in the same way as an earlier group of Continentals and militia had taken on the Hessians at Princeton and Trenton. Thousands of Americans from places like Newark would fight and die overseas in the war against fascism but, aside from the grieving families of the lost—a pain that should not be casually forgotten, the nightmare of war and Holocaust would not darken the threshold of American homes. The United States would emerge from the trial of economic depression and war as an industrial powerhouse and a global superpower. However, in the ensuing decades, it would go on to learn that prosperity and empire created a new set of challenges for those who followed the "greatest generation."

Suggested Readings

For a cogent introduction to the global crisis of this decade a good place to start is Piers Brandon's *The Dark Valley: A Panorama of the 1930s* (New York: Vintage, 2002). The best single volume treatment of Roosevelt's foreign policy remains Robert Dallek, *Franklin D. Roosevelt and American Foreign Policy, 1932–1945* (New York: Oxford University Press, 1979). Several recent works go into greater depth regarding Roosevelt's foreign-policy struggles and decisions. In *Those Angry Days* (New York: Random House, 2013), Lynne Olson provides an accessible account of the political duel between President Roosevelt and Charles Lindbergh over the American posture toward Nazi Germany. In *Rendezvous with Destiny* (New York: Penguin Press, 2013), Michael Fullilove recounts how the president sent William Donovan, Averell Harriman, Harry Hopkins, Sumner Welles, and Wendell Wilkie to Europe between 1939 and 1941 to provide him with an additional (and personal) source of political insight, which would help him frame an effective response to the emerging conflict.

Several biographies illuminate the lives and contributions of significant American actors in this drama. Particularly impressive is John Lewis Gaddis, *George F. Kennan: An American Life* (New York: Penguin Press, 2011), a detailed and definitive account of an influential diplomatic career that stretched from the crucible of the 1930s to the advent of the Cold War. Steve Wick provides an engaging account of the journalist who warned America about the real and present danger at the heart of Europe in *The Long Night: William L. Shirer and the Rise and Fall of the Third Reich* (New York: Palgrave Macmillan, 2011), a work that provides a valuable supplement to Shirer's own *Berlin Diary.* Mark Bernstein and Alex Lubertozzi offer a valuable resource and commentary in *World War II on the Air: Edward R. Murrow and the Broadcasts That Riveted a Nation* (Napierville, IL: Sourcebooks, 2003). Max Wallace explores the attitudes and impact of some of the more famous defenders of the rising Third Reich in *The American Axis* (New York: St. Martin's Press, 2003). Andrew Nagorski, *Hitlerland: American Eyewitnesses to the Nazi Rise to Power* (New York: Simon & Schuster, 2012), provides a valuable window on the viewpoints of Americans who experienced the Third Reich firsthand. Oliver Lubrich has edited a valuable collection of travelers' accounts—including the piece by W. E. B. DuBois, "What of the Color-Line?—in *Travels in the Reich, 1933–1945: Foreign Authors Report from Germany* (Chicago: University of Chicago Press, 2010). Edwin Black provides a controversial account of the difficult choices faced by the American—and world—Jewish community during this decade in *The Transfer Agreement: The Dramatic Story of the Pact between the Third Reich and Jewish Palestine* (Washington, DC: Dialogue Press, 2009).

The following works should be consulted by readers interested in exploring these specific subjects in greater depth; they served as valuable resources in the creation of this chapter. S. J. Taylor, in *Stalin's Apologist* (New York: Oxford University Press, 1990), provides a disturbing portrait of Walter Duranty, little known today but a highly influential English journalist who played a key role in shaping American opinion on the Soviet Union during the 1930s. For a recent biography of the woman who brought the plight of the Chinese peasantry to the attention of the American people during this era, see Hilary Spurling, *Pearl Buck in China: Journey to the Good Earth* (New York: Simon & Schuster, 2010). Hannah Pakula has written a detailed biography of one of the more interesting (and enigmatic) figures of this decade, *The Last Empress: Madame Chiang Kai-shek and the Birth of Modern China* (New York: Simon & Schuster, 2009). For an engaging history of the American pilots who came to the defense of China in the early stages of the war, see Daniel Ford, *Flying Tigers: Claire Chennault and His American Volunteers, 1941–1942* (New York: Harper/Smithsonian Books, 2007).

The often neglected (and sometimes heroic) story of the response of individual Americans to the regional conflicts of the 1930s is ably told by Peter N. Carroll in *The Odyssey of the Abraham Lincoln Brigade: Americans in the Spanish Civil War* (Stanford: Stanford University Press, 1994); Iris Chang, *The Rape of Nanking* (New

York: Basic Books, 1997); and Joseph E. Harris, *African-American Reactions to the War in Ethiopia, 1936–1941* (Baton Rouge: LSU Press, 1994). The short and inglorious story of the Nazi movement in America is recounted by Arnie Bernstein in *Swastika Nation: Fritz Kuhn and the Rise of the German-American Bund* (New York: St. Martin's Press, 2013). Warren Grover's *Nazis in Newark* (New Brunswick, NJ: Transaction Publishers, 2003) is a gem of local history that recounts the resistance of an American Jewish community to the belligerent supporters of the Third Reich. The celebrated American author Philip Roth provides an intriguing exercise in counterfactual history in *The Plot against America* (New York: Vintage, 2005).

Conclusion

"Goodnight, Sweetheart"
—Ray Noble, Jimmy Campbell, and Reg Connelly, 1931

IN 1998, *NBC Nightly News* journalist Tom Brokaw penned *The Greatest Generation*, a book that chronicles the lives of forty-seven individuals who came of age in the 1930s. For Brokaw, what distinguished this group as the "greatest generation" was their extraordinary perseverance and dedication in the face of extreme hardship. Coming of age during the Great Depression, they overcame the hardships and dislocations produced by America's greatest economic catastrophe and worst ecological crisis. They then gloriously served the nation as it confronted one of the world's most preeminent military crises, winning World War II and defeating the ruthless, totalitarian dictatorships of Adolph Hitler, Benito Mussolini, and Hideki Tojo. When the war ended, they quietly returned to their unassuming lives, built a safe, stable, and prosperous postwar nation, and laid the foundation that allowed America to become a world economic superpower and beacon for democracy. For these reasons, Brokaw concluded this was a generation whose accomplishments and exploits were on par with those who endured the American Revolution and the Civil War. As he eloquently explained, "At every stage of their lives they were part of historic challenges and achievements of a magnitude the world had never witnessed before."

Brokaw's term "the greatest generation" has become ensconced in the American lexicon, synonymous with the exploits of those that endured the Great Depression and triumphed during World War II. But it is not so much the term itself as it is the high-minded idealism and extraordinary tenacity against the longest of odds that drives Americans' understanding of what defines the greatest generation. The popularity of recent films such as *Seabiscuit* (2003) and *Cinderella Man* (2005) both attest to contemporary society's reverence for Depression Era America. The films, set against the backdrop of the 1930s, are classic tales of underdogs persevering to find redemption and eventually success in the face of enormous challenges and often utter hopelessness. But the films also speak to the ongoing fascination and reverence the public holds for the 1930s. Whether it is an undersized and run-of-the-mill stallion reaching the pinnacles of racing fame or a worn-out Irish American boxer rising from the humiliation of the unemployment lines to become heavyweight champion of the world, the films speak to America's ability to find success in the worst of times. As in Brokaw's book, emphasis is not so much on the miserable conditions and hardships of the era as it is on the ability to triumph over the decade's adversity.

Looking at the 1930s from the vantage point of today, it is certainly understandable why society focuses on the heroic underdogs that came from the era. Over seventy years have passed since the end of the Great Depression, and nearly eighty-four since the crisis began. The sights, sounds, and experiences—the very immediacy of the era—are in effect lost when we selectively view this historic decade through a modern lens. Today, we know the outcome of the Great Depression just as we know the results of other great epochs in American history such as the American Revolution and the Civil War. Gone is the overwhelming sense of uncertainty and helplessness of not knowing whether the nation would endure the unprecedented crisis of the 1930s. As the collective national psyche becomes further removed from the experiences of the Great Depression, it is hard not to craft a simple narrative in which the emphasis is on America's certain ability to overcome the catastrophe. The unfortunate result is a misleading historical narrative that, while acknowledging the struggle, places greater emphasis on the outcome. The adversity of the decade is simply a means to a triumphant end.

To Americans living through the 1930s, it is doubtful that many at that juncture would have looked around and seen themselves living in the midst of greatness. Rather, the decade was a tumultuous period, marked for most by pronounced struggle, chaos, uncertainty, and at times utter hopelessness. Unemployment levels soared to unthinkable numbers. Many Americans found themselves homeless, forced to live in the countless Hoovervilles popping up in abandoned fields and along the nation's railway tracks. Hunger became commonplace, leading many to stand for hours in breadlines that stretched across city blocks. Poverty became a way of life. Labor strikes and protests occurred with growing frequency as frustrations boiled over and people became increasingly angry by the lack of resolution to the economic crisis. Racism and nativism rose as people trying to make sense of their dismal times lashed out against African Americans, ethnic Americans, and immigrants, convinced that these "strangers" were somehow responsible for their problems. Political demagogues and radical ideologies seized on the national angst, offering extreme remedies and shady nostrums to weary listeners looking for quick fixes to ease the suffering. As war raged in Europe and the Pacific, Americans remained resolute in their determination not to get involved in the international conflicts. Instead they remained consumed by national self-interest, intently focused on more pressing domestic economic issues. Far from great, to many Americans living in the 1930s there existed an overwhelming sense of national decline, a feeling that the United States had lost its moral compass in the midst of the profound economic crisis.

How contemporary America views the legacies of the 1930s is equally curious and similarly contradictory. Just as society lauds the exploits of the greatest generation, many of the policies, programs, and institutions that emerged from the era are currently under assault. Social Security, a defining feature of Franklin Roosevelt's New Deal, faces constant attacks by conservative politicians and political pundits calling for the government to get out of the pension business and set in motion plans to privatize the program. The National Labor Relations Board, established with the Wagner Act in 1935, finds itself handcuffed as Republican and conservative politicians refuse to process President Barrack Obama's appointees, claiming they and the administration are overly pro-labor. The labor movement meanwhile finds itself in retreat. Forced to battle corporate outsourcing, hostile employers, and worker apathy, by 2010 union membership stood at 11.4 percent of the workforce nationwide, its lowest levels since the start of the Great Depression.

Symbolic of organized labor's shifting fate is the battle that raged in Wisconsin in 2011 when Republican Governor Scott Walker signed a budget repair bill drastically cutting wages and benefits for state and local government workers, restricting their ability to engage in collective bargaining and hindering their ability to organize. Walker's policies stand in stark contrast to the 1930s, when federal and state governments encouraged collective bargaining as a means to address the economic problems confronting the working class. Unemployment insurance is under similar attack, condemned as socialistic and a drag on America's work ethic, and politicians are calling for the enactment of means testing, drug screenings, and most recently in Florida, a skills test that would require applicants to answer a series of basic math and reading questions before their claims can be processed. In early 2013, calls to increase the minimum wage faced quick rebuke, with leading critics labeling the idea a "jobs killer." Some politicians have gone so far as to advocate abolishing the minimum wage law altogether, a policy once seen by the greatest generation as vitally necessary to improving the standard of living of America's working class when it was created in 1938. Even as the most recent great recession played out in 2008, although Americans turned to Washington for action much like citizens in the 1930s looked to Roosevelt, the public criticized the use of federal funds to bailout banks and critical businesses and decried the growing size of the federal government. Both strategies served as key philosophical elements guiding the New Deal years. In a strange irony, while contemporary Americans celebrate the achievements of the "greatest generation," they are quick to find fault and attack many of the programs and solutions they created in combating the Great Depression.

In March 2013 in an editorial appearing in *USA Today*, the leading conservative critic Jonah Goldberg, discussing the "greatest generation," declared, "as Washington grapples with the legacy costs of the 'greatest generation'—including the unsustainable burden of paying the retirement bills for the GIs' supremely entitled children, the Baby Boomers—perhaps it is at least worth recognizing that the government and the culture designed to benefit one generation has come at the cost of those that come after it." As

Goldberg's comments attest, the battle over the legacy of the 1930s endures. The interesting fact is that the present-day political debates—both domestic and foreign—are still framed largely by events of the 1930s. More than most, the legacy of the 1930s continues to endure well into the twenty-first century. Whether the decade produced the "greatest generation" is debatable. However, there is little doubt that it was a decade that had among the greatest of influences in shaping America today.

Index

Abraham Lincoln Brigade, 243
Addis Ababa (Ethiopia), 263
Adowa, battle of, 261
Aeronautical Workers Union (AWU), 149
Africa, 261–63
African Americans: and the arts, 117–18; civil rights, 86–91; conditions in North, 80–81, 246; conditions in South, 103–4, 123, 245, 246; effects of Depression on, 97–98; migration, 79–80; under New Deal, 98, 103–4, 123; overseas conflicts, 261–64; women, 178
Agee, James, 117
Agricultural Adjustment Act (AAA) (1933), 45, 103, 104, 105, 122, 126
Agricultural Adjustment Act (AAA) (1938), 122, 131
agriculture, 13, 44–45, 58; economy, 67, 246; farming practices, 51, 55; innovations, 52; problems in, 13, 44–45, 51, 52, 55
Allen, Gracie, 217
Alsop, Joseph, 358
Amalgamated Clothing Workers of America, 141, 152
America First, 255, 271
American Association for the Advancement of Science, 69
American Birth Control League, 182–83
American Federation of Labor (AFL), 134–36, 141–44, 149, 154, 155, 159, 164, 175, 273; craft unionism, 134–35, 142, 150, 151, 152, 155, 160, 174; expulsion of CIO unions, 153; organizing in Depression, 141–44, 149, 151–52; strikes and protests, 145, 149–50
American Jewish Committee, 272
American Jewish Congress, 272, 273
American Legion, 250
American Liberty League, 3, 105–6, 118, 148
American Mercury, The (magazine), 59, 173
"American Plan," 138
American Workers' Party, 150
Amos 'n Andy (radio show), 217–19
Amsberry, Lavina, 177
anarchists (Spain), 266
Anderson, Marian, 209
Andrew, Charles, 1
Andy Hardy (film), 188
Anschluss, 254
anti-Catholicism, 245

anti-Nazism, 272–75; "Minutemen" (Newark), 275
anti-Semitism, 108, 245, 254, 271–75
Apparel Arts (magazine), 196
appeasement, 260
Arno, Nat, 274
Associated Press, 53
Association for Scientific Workers, 69
Astaire, Fred, 195–96, 197, 209, 214
Atlantic Monthly (magazine), 71
atomic age, 65
Austria, 259
automobile, 8, 19, 64, 85, 225
Autry, Gene, 192
Avery, Sewell, 106
aviation, 54, 211, 235
Awful Truth, The (film), 3, 199

Bain, Abie, 274
Banking Act (1933), 47, 103, 112
bank crisis, 13–19, 20, 23, 39–41; bank holiday, 40, 208; problems, 14–15, 39–41
Bankhead, John, 123
Bank of the United States, 14–15
Ballantine, Arthur, 40
Barrymore, John, 199, 209
Barrymore, Lionel, 85, 209
Basie, William "Count," 95, 240, 242
Beer–Wine Revenue Act, 42
Bell, Thomas, 163, 164
Bellow, Saul, 117
Bennett, Constance, 199
Bennett, Hugh Hammond, 62
Bergen, Edgar, 216, 217
Berkeley, Busby, 213
Berle, Adolph, 38
Berlin, 77, 251–55, 260
Berlin, Irving, 78, 94, 214
Berlin Diary (book), 250
Bethune, Mary McLeod, 178
Black, Edwin, 255, 272–73
Black, Hugo, 119
Bloor, Ella Reeve "Mother," 177
B'nai B'rith, 272
Boas, Franz, 69
Bolsheviks (and Bolshevism), 138, 250, 256, 257, 265
Bontemps, Arna, 84, 91, 92, 94
Bonus Expeditionary Force (Bonus Army), 24–26, 33, 42
Borah, William, 259
boycott, anti-Nazi (1933), 272–73
Breen, Joseph I., 228–29, 230
Bride of Frankenstein (film), 230
Bridges, Harry, 150
Broadway, 184
Brokaw, Tom, 275, 278–79
Brooklyn (New York City), 15, 116, 162, 264
Bryant, Louise, 249
Buck, Pearl, 267
Bullitt, William C., 249
Burnett, Ollie, 123
Butler, Pierce, 113

Cagney, James, 191, 226
Cantor, Eddie, 217
Cantril, Hadley, 216
Capone, Al, 193, 227–28
Capra, Frank, 185
Carnegie, Andrew, 153, 194
Carnegie Hall, 242
Carnera, Primo, 264
Carroll, Peter N., 264–65
Carson, Rachel, 3, 69–72, 74, 75
"cash and carry," 260
Catholic Legion of Decency, 228

CBS (Columbia Broadcasting System), 214, 217, 234, 243, 250, 252
Central Republic Bank of Chicago, 22–23
Cermak, Anton, 23
Chang, Iris, 270–71
Chaplin, Charlie, 9, 173, 210, 211, 212
Chase and Sanborn Hour, The (radio show), 204, 216
Chatterton, Ruth, 225
Cheever, John, 117
Chennault, Claire, 269–70
Chiang Kai-shek, 267
Chicago Tribune (newspaper), 102, 237, 250
China, 247, 260, 266–71
"China Lobby," 270
Chinese Air Force ("Fourteenth Squadron"), 269
Chinese civil war, 269
Christianity, 108, 249, 264
Churchill, Winston, 253
City Lights (film), 211
Civilian Conservation Corps (CCC), 42–43, 48, 98, 103, 181
Civil Works Administration (CWA), 49, 181
Clark, Bennett Champ, 141
Clements, Earl, 107
Colbert, Claudette, 199
Cold War, 248
colonial economies, 246
Committee for Industrial Organizations. *See* Congress of Industrial Organizations
Communist League of America, 150
Communist Party of the USA (CPUSA), 150, 264, 265
company unionism, 139, 146, 148, 153
Comstock, William, 39
Congress of Industrial Organizations (CIO), 2, 136, 151, 152–54, 160, 164, 175, 176; automobile industry, 8, 154–58; origins, 136, 151–53; steel industry, 153–54, 158, 159; strategy, 153
Connolly, Walter, 185
conservationism, 42–43
"containment." *See* Kennan, George
convenience foods, 187
Coolidge, Calvin, 1–2, 5, 7–8, 22, 24, 33, 36, 131
Correll, Charles, 218
Cotton Club, 95–97
Coughlin, Father Charles, 107–8, 115, 125, 272
Cousins, Norman, 171
Couzens, Frank, 175
Cox, Father James, 25
craft unionism, 134–36, 142–43, 149, 150, 155, 160
Crawford, Joan, 184, 209
Crowley, Aleister, 257
Cukor, George, 184, 185
Cullen, Countee, 83, 84, 91, 92, 94
cult of domesticity, 182
Cummings, Homer, 127–28
Cyr, Paul, 11
Czechoslovakia, 259

Dames (film), 213
Davidson, Donald, 66
Davis, Bette, 184, 209
Davis, John, 28
Dawes, Charles, 22, 23
Dearborn Independent (newspaper), 255
Democratic Party, 28, 29, 33, 34, 106, 110, 259; in 1928, 10, 28; in 1932, 25, 33–36; in 1936, 101–2, 112, 125–26; New Deal Coalition, 42, 102, 130, 131–32

Dent, Lester (Kenneth Robeson), 235
Depp, Johnny, 199
Detroit Federation of Labor, 175
Dewson, Molly, 178
Dick Tracy, 217, 237, 238
Dillinger, John, 192–95
Dobbs, Farrell, 150
Doc Savage, 231, 232, 233, 234–37, 243
Domestic Allotment Act, 122
Don Juan (film), 210
Dos Passos, John, 196
Douglas, Aaron, 83
Dracula (1931) (film), 230
Dubinsky, David, 152
DuBois, W. E. B., 82–83, 253–54, 262
Du Pont, 63, 106
Dunne, Irene, 199
Dunne brothers, 150
Duranty, Walter, 257–58
Dust Bowl, xi, xii, 2, 19, 51–63, 65, 74, 75, 122

Earhart, Amelia, 54, 166–67
Economy Act (1933), 42, 171
Edison, Thomas, 210
Einstein, Albert, 65, 66
Eisenhower, Dwight D., 25
elections: of 1920, 5, 32; of 1928, 9–10, 28–29; of 1932, 22, 32, 33, 35–37, 208; of 1936, 101–2, 112, 125–26
Ellington, Duke, 96–97, 242
Ellison, Ralph, 117
Emergency Banking Relief Act, 40–42, 46, 103
Emergency Committee for Employment, 18, 20
Emergency Farm Mortgage Act, 44, 48
Emergency Relief Appropriation Act, 116
Emergency Relief Committee in New York, 174
Emergency Work Bureau in New York, 174
environmental ethic, 58, 72, 73
Equal Rights Amendment (ERA), 179, 183
Esquire (magazine), 94, 196
Ethiopian Research Council, 262
Ethiopian World Federation, 262
Evans, Walker, 117

Fairbanks, Douglas, 8–9
Fair Labor Standards Act, 119, 130
farmers, xii, 2, 13, 51, 52, 122–24, 177; farm protests and strikes, 21, 177–78; federal entitlements, 62; hardships, 3, 16, 17, 19, 44, 122; sharecroppers, 79, 83, 97, 122–23, 176; tenant, 21, 54, 176
Farmer's Holiday Association (FHA), 177–78
Farmer's Wife, The (magazine), 177
Farm Settlement Administration, 123
Farm Tenancy Act, 123, 124, 131
Farrell, Glenda, 185–86
Fauset, Jesse Redmond, 83
Faust, Frederick Schiller, 188
Federal Bureau of Investigation (FBI), 189, 194, 207, 263
Federal Deposit Insurance Corporation (FDIC), 47, 48
Federal Economy Act, 171
Federal Emergency Relief Act (FERA), 44, 49, 60, 103, 116, 174
Federal Labor Unions, 143–44, 149–50, 154. *See also* American Federation of Labor
Federal Securities Act, 47
Federal Theater Project (FTP), 117

Federal Writers' Project (FWP), 59, 117–18
Female (film), 225
feminism, 172, 179, 182, 183, 200
Fischer, James, 207
Fitzgerald, F. Scott, 196, 232
Flint Sit-Down Strike, 156–58, 174
Flusser, Alan, 195
Flying Tigers (American Volunteer Force), 270
Ford, Daniel, 269
Ford, Henry, 8, 19, 141, 255, 272
Ford Motor Company, 20, 154
Foreign Affairs (magazine), 262
Foreign Policy Association, 254
Fortune (magazine), 268
42nd Street (film), 213
France, 26, 87, 251, 252
Franco, Francisco, 265
Franklin, Sidney, 267
Frazier, E. Franklin, 92, 94
Free Employment Agency in New York, 171
Fremming, Harvey, 152
Friends of Italy, 264
Friends of New Germany, 272, 274
Fuller, Meta Warrick, 82

Gable, Clark, 85, 199
Gaines, Lloyd, 90
Gandhi, Mohandas K., 250, 251
Gangbusters (radio show), 190–91, 243
Garbo, Greta, 184, 209
Garvey, Marcus, 263
Geiger, Robert, 53
gender, xii, 2, 66, 136, 160, 161, 164, 167, 170, 176, 183, 185, 186, 198, 199, 200, 204. *See also* men; women
General Electric, 11, 63, 156
General Motors, 106, 154, 155, 156–58, 174, 255
Gentlemen's Quarterly (*GQ*) (magazine), 196
German American Bund (Amerika-deutscher Volksbund), 272, 274
German Americans, 272–74
Germany, 77, 212, 246, 247, 248, 250–51, 253–54, 255, 256, 259, 260, 265, 266, 272–74
Gershwin, George, 213, 242
Gershwin, Ira, 213
Getty, J. Paul, 192
Gibson, Walter B., 233, 234, 236
Gila National Forest, 73
Gingrich, Arnold, 196
Ginling Women's Arts and Sciences College (Nanking), 270–71
Girdler, Tom, 159
Ghana, 254
G-Men (film), 191
Goddard, Paulette, 173
Goldberg, Jonah, 281–82
Goldman, Emma, 173
Gompers, Samuel, 142
Gone with the Wind (film), 85
Good Earth, The (book and film), 267
Goodman, Benny, 95, 240, 241, 242, 243
Good News, (film), 200
Gorn, Elliot J., 194
Gosden, Freeman, 218
Gould, Chester, 238
Gould, Jay, 194
Grand Hotel (film), 209
Grant, Cary, 195–96, 199, 243
Great Britain (England/United Kingdom), 220, 247, 252, 256, 259–60
Great Dictator, The (film), 212
"greater East Asian co-prosperity sphere," 247

"greatest generation," 246, 278–79
Great Migration, 81, 83, 95, 99, 217, 246
great recession (2007–2009), 168, 281
Green, Harry, 274
Green, William, 142–44, 149–50, 152, 154–55, 273
Grimke, Angelina Welde, 84
Grover, Warren, 274
Guthrie, Woody, 3, 60–61

Hack, Richard, 191
Hahn, Emily, 172
Haile Selassie (Emperor), 261, 263
Hall, Maurice C., 68
Hall, Mordaunt, 227
Hallquist, Josie, 177–78
Harding, Warren, 5, 6–7, 36, 131, 223, 245
Harlem, 92, 94–97, 218, 263–64
Harlem Renaissance, 81–84, 91–92, 93, 94, 217
Harlem riot (1935), 97
Harlow, Jean, 85, 86
Harris, Joseph E., 262–64
Harvard University, 30, 87, 256
Hauptmann, Bruno Richard, 190, 205, 206, 207
Hays, Will, 223, 228
Hearst, William Randolph, 105, 124, 190, 250
Hell's Angels (film), 211
Hemingway, Ernest, 196, 266
Hepburn, Katherine, 199
Hillman, Sidney, 152
Hitler, Adolph, 77, 78, 251, 253–56, 259, 272, 278
H. J. Heinz, 170
Hogue, Alexandre, 57–59
Holocaust, 255, 275
Home Owners' Loan Act, 44
Hoover, Herbert, 1, 2, 7, 11, 17–19, 23, 140, 189, 190; Bonus Army and, 24–26; early career, 4–5; election of 1928, 4, 5, 9–10; election of 1932, 32–33, 35–38; impact on New Deal, 26, 40, 41, 46, 48; post-presidency, 254; public views of, 22, 33, 36, 111; views on relief, 20, 43
Hoover, J. Edgar, 189, 191
Hopkins, Harry, 38, 44, 116, 174
Horner, Henry, 40
Hotel Employees and Restaurant Employees (HERE), 175
House Committee on Un-American Activities, 266
Housewives' Leagues, 186
Houston, Charles, 87–90
Howard, Charles, 152
Howe, Louis, 37–38
Hughes, Charles Evans, 38, 113, 114, 129
Hughes, Howard, 192, 211, 227
Hughes, Langston, 83, 92–93, 94
Hurston, Zora Neale, 92, 93–94, 117
Hutchinson, Bill, 135, 152

I Am a Fugitive from a Chain Gang (film), 214
IBM (International Business Machines), 255
India, 250
Industrial Workers of the World (IWW), 150, 156, 265
industrial unionism, 136, 143, 151, 153, 155
International Ladies' Garment Workers' Union, 141–42, 152, 176
International News Service, 190
International Pecan Sellers Union, 176

isolationism, 248, 256, 258–59, 260–61
Italian Americans, 263–64
Italian Historical Society, 264
Italo-Ethiopian War, 247, 260, 261–64, 265
Italy, 246, 247
It Happened One Night (film), 199

Japan, 54, 247, 248, 260, 266–71
Jazz Singer, The (film), 211
Jeffries, Herb, 84
Jewel Robbery (film), 225
Jewish Americans, 14, 15, 265, 271–75
Jewish War Veterans, 272
Johnson, Hiram, 259
Johnson, Hugh, 38, 104–5
Johnson, Jack, 96
Johnson, James Weldon, 91, 92
Jolson, Al, 211
Jones, Marvin, 123
Journal of Forestry (magazine), 73
journalism: newspapers, 205, 206, 216, 221, 238; radio, 206, 208, 216; tabloid, 204–5; "Trial of the Century" coverage, 205–7
Judge Priest (film), 84, 85
Judicial Procedures Reform Bill, 127, 129
Julian, Hubert Fauntleroy, 263

Kalil, Susie, 57
Katz, Hyman, 265
Keighly, William, 191
Kennan, George, 249, 250, 252
Kennedy, John F., 256
Kennedy, Joseph P., 256
King Kong (film), 173
Kjorstad, Effie, 177–78
Kline, Benjamin, 76
Krycki, Leo, 175
Kugel, Hymie ("the Weasel"), 274
Kuhn, Fritz, 272
Ku Klux Klan, 245, 246, 272

La Cron, James, 56
Lady for a Day (film), 185–86
La Follette, Robert, 160, 259
LaGuardia, Fiorello, 97, 264
Landon, Alf, 101, 125–26
Lange, Dorothea, 55
Larson, Nella, 84
Latin America, 246
League of Nations, 245, 262, 268
Lear, Linda, 72
Lehman, Herbert, 39
Leipzig, Max, 274
"Lend-Lease," 132, 260
Leopold, Aldo, 72–75
LeRoy, Mervyn, 226
Le Sueur, Meridel, 59–60, 173
Let's Dance (radio show), 241
Lewis, David, 120
Lewis, John L., 134–36, 150–54, 157, 158, 159, 269
Lewton, Val, 172
Life (magazine), 57, 268
Lima County News (newspaper), 194
Lindbergh, Anne Morrow, 189, 205, 206
Lindbergh, Charles, 54, 189–90, 205, 206, 207, 255, 256, 271, 275
Lindbergh, Charles, Jr., 189, 205, 207
Lippmann, Walter, 37, 107
Literary Digest (magazine), 101–2
Little Caesar (film), 226, 227
Little Orphan Annie, 204, 217
Little Princess, The (film), 220
Little Steel Strike, 159–60
Lloyd, Harold, 9
Lombard, Carole, 199

Lone Ranger (radio show) 188, 243
Long, Huey, 108–13, 115, 125; background, 109–10; opposition to Roosevelt, 3, 111–13; "Share Our Wealth," 112–13
Lord, Daniel, 225
Lorentz, Pare, 55–57
Louis, Joe, xi, 264
Luce, Clare Boothe, 184
Luce, Henry, 268
Luftwaffe, 252, 255, 266
Lundeen, Ernest, 120
Lynd, Robert and Helen, 169
Lytle, Andrew, 66

Madden, Owen, 96–97
Madison Square Garden, 264, 273
Manchu Dynasty, 267
Marcus, Bernard, 14–15
Marcus, Joseph, 14–15
Margold Report, 88, 89
Markowitz, Julius ("Skinny"), 274
Marshall, Thurgood, 88, 89
Martel, Frank, 175
Marx Brothers, 202, 203, 217
McArthur, Douglas, 25
McCarthy, Charlie, 216
McDaniel, Hattie, 85–86, 91
McGroarty, John, 120
McKay, Claude, 83, 84
McMahon, Thomas, 152
McReynolds, James, 113, 114, 127
Mellon, Andrew, 7, 11–12, 17, 25
men: changing social roles, 2, 167, 168, 187–88, 200; fashion, 195–97; fathers, 167, 187–90; in home, 168–69
Mencken, H. L., 37, 206
Menelik (Emperor), 261
Mercury Theater, 214, 215, 216, 234
Mercury Theater on the Air (radio show), 214–15
military–industrial complex, 132, 248
missionaries (China), 267–68
Mitchell, Margaret, 85
Mitchell, Wesley C., 69
Model-T, 8, 255
modernism, 54, 58, 67
Modern Times (film), 173, 211
Moley, Raymond, 38
Mooney, James, 255
More the Merrier, The (film), 200
Mortimer, Wyndham, 154–55
Motion Picture Producers and Distributors of America (MPPDA), 223
Motion Picture Production Code, 225
motion pictures: in 1920s, 8–9, 204; in 1930s, 84, 85, 91, 203, 209, 219–20; attendance, 221–22, 229, 232; audience appeal, 2, 3, 209, 212–14, 226; censorship of, 222–26, 228–29; economic impact, 221–22, 228; gangster, 191, 213, 225–28, 238; greatest year (1939), 209; horror, 230; musicals, 212–14; sound, 9, 203, 210–12, 221
motion picture studios, 212, 213, 221, 222, 223, 225, 228, 229, 243; Columbia, 198, 222, 243; Disney, 243; Fox, 85, 221; Metro–Goldwyn–Meyer (MGM), 213, 222, 267; Paramount, 221; RKO, 198, 213, 221; United Artists, 222; Universal, 221, 230, 243; Warner Brothers, 191, 211, 213, 214, 222, 226, 227, 243
Muni, Paul (Mesheilem Meier Weisenfreund), 214, 226, 227, 267
Murphy, Frank, 175
Murray, Donald, 89
Murray, Phillip, 154
Murray, Will, 232

Murrow, Edward R., 252–53, 256
Mussolini, Benito, 247, 261, 278
Muste, A. J., 150
"My Blue Heaven" (song), 252
My Man Godfrey (film), 199

Nagorski, Andrew, 254
Nanking (massacre/"rape of"), 270–71
Nanovic, John L., 232, 235
National Association for the Advancement of Colored People (NAACP), 82, 86–87, 88–91, 92, 262, 273
National Association of Manufacturers (NAM), 138, 141
National Association of Merchant Tailors, 197
National Consumer League, 179
National Industrial Recovery Act (NIRA), 45–46, 103–6, 112–15, 118, 140–41, 144, 145, 149; goals, 45–46, 104–5, 140; problems, 104–5, 112–15, 140–41, 144–47; Section 7(a) and, 141–42, 144, 146
nationalism, 247
National Labor Relations Act (NLRA), 146–48, 159, 178; hostility, 148, 159, 160, 280; legality, 148, 152; origins, 147
National Labor Relations Board (NLRB), 148, 159, 280
National Recovery Administration (NRA), 45–46, 48, 104–5, 115, 178, 181
National War Labor Board (World War I), 136
National Youth Association, Negro Council, 178
Nazism, 59, 78, 247, 256, 265–66, 272, 274
neutrality acts, 259, 270
Newark (New Jersey), 271, 274–75
New Deal, xii, 3, 6, 26, 36–49, 63, 65, 101–33, 134, 143, 160; brain trust (advisers), 38, 43, 47, 49, 103, 122; criticism of, 104–5, 106–13, 115, 125, 130, 135, 145–46; philosophy, 3, 38–39, 42, 43–49, 102–3, 115–16, 119, 121–23, 131–33; political impact, 102–3, 125–26, 131; problems, 98, 103–5, 132–33, 149; relief programs, 43, 44, 56, 98, 116–18, 121, 130–31; Second, 101–33, 259
New Republic (magazine), 172, 209, 258
Newseum, 190
New York City, xii, 14, 21, 32, 35, 39, 78, 80, 81, 82, 92, 93, 95, 96, 117, 205, 215, 217, 242, 264, 296, 273
New York Philharmonic, 57
New York Times (newspaper), 207, 208, 227, 256–57, 268
Night at the Opera, A (film), 60
Nobel Prize, 59, 267
Norris, George, 141
Nowak, Stanley, 175
Nuremburg (rallies), 251
Nye, Gerald, 259

Old Age Revolving Pension Plan, 107
One Man's Family (radio show), 188
Order of the German Eagle, 255
Orwell, George (Eric Blair), 266
Out of This Furnace (book), 163–64
Owens, Jesse, 77–79
Owsley, Frank Lawrence, 66

Pakula, Hannah, 268–69
Parker, Jean, 185
patriarchy, 187

Patton, George, 25
Paul, Alice, 183
Pearl Harbor (attack), 248, 255, 260, 266, 268, 270, 274, 275
Pearson, Edith, 177–78
Pepper, Claude, 119
Perkins, Frances, 38, 45, 120, 178
Perry, Lincoln Theodore Monroe Andrew (Stepin' Fetchit), 84–85, 86, 91
Petrified Forest (film), 209
Pew, James, 106
P. H. Haines Knitting Company, 170
Planned Parenthood Federation of America, 183
Plessy v. Ferguson, 88–89, 90
Poland, 251, 252, 259
"Popular Front," 264
Pound, Ezra, 196
Powell, William, 199, 225
Production Code Administration (PCA), 227, 229
progressivism/Progressive Era, 6–7, 30, 62, 70, 71, 82, 87, 125, 179; influence on Hoover, 5, 17, 20; influence on Roosevelt, 30, 48, 119, 124
Prohibition (and repeal), 33, 34, 42, 193
Public Enemy, The (film), 226–27
Public Works Administration (PWA), 45, 63, 103
Pulitzer Prize, 53, 117, 257–58, 267
pulp magazines/novels, 231–33, 234, 235, 236–37
Pyle, Ernie, 53–55

Quigley, Martin, 225

race, xii, 2, 66, 69, 77, 80, 81–82, 91–95, 110, 120, 136, 160, 176, 181, 196, 204, 217, 218–19, 223, 224, 242, 256, 262, 263, 274
radicalism, 66, 138, 150, 173, 177
radio, 8, 97, 188, 190, 205, 206, 207, 208, 221, 231, 243; genres on, 204, 217, 233, 238; popularity of, 204; popular performers on, 217; power of, 204, 215–16, 241; rise of importance of, 216
Radio City Music Hall, 214
Railroad Pension Act, 114
Ransom, John Crowe, 66
Raskob, John Jacob, 106
realism, 54, 58, 59
Reconstruction Finance Corporation (RFC), 22–23, 36, 44
Reed, John, 249
reportage writing, 59, 173
Republican Party, 38, 250, 254, 259, 271; in 1920s, 5, 7, 8, 11, 12; in 1928, 5, 9; in 1932, 22, 23, 32–36; in 1936, 101–2, 112, 125–26; opposition to New Deal, 280
Resettlement Administration, 56
Reuther, Walter, 156, 175
Revenue Act of 1935, 124–25
Roach, Hal, 106
Roberts, Owen, 113, 114, 127, 129
Robinson, Bill, 84, 91
Robinson, Edward G., 226
Robinson, John ("the Brown Condor"), 263
Robson, May, 185
Rockefeller, John D., 7, 194
Rogers, Ginger, 209, 213, 214
Rogers, Will, 84, 85
Rooney, Mickey, 188
Roosevelt, Eleanor, 31–32, 53, 166, 178–80, 269; newspaper columns, 179, 208–9; relationship with Franklin

Roosevelt, 26, 31, 179; social worker, 32; use of radio, 207, 208
Roosevelt, Franklin Delano, 2, 6, 16, 23, 24, 26, 28–49, 57, 78–79, 98, 140, 142, 151, 165, 177, 187; advisers, 37–38, 43, 47, 49, 103, 122; childhood, 30; Democratic National Convention (1928), 28–29; election of 1932, 3, 33, 257; election of 1936, 125–26; fireside chats, 41, 208; foreign relations, 247, 248, 249, 256, 259, 268, 270; inauguration (1932), 38–39; polio, 28, 32; political philosophy, 32, 48–49, 124, 132–33, 281; relationship with Eleanor Roosevelt, 31; relationship with Teddy Roosevelt, 29, 30; views on labor, 134, 144, 269; use of media, 64, 205, 207–8
Roosevelt, James, 30
Roosevelt, Sara Delano, 30–31
Roosevelt, Theodore (Teddy), 5, 6, 29, 30–31, 48, 110, 125
Roosevelt Recession of 1937, 132–33
Ross, Nellie Tayloe, 178
Ross, Sam, 117
Roth, Philip, 271, 274, 275
Rural Electrification Act (REA), 63
Ruth, Babe, 192
Rybicki, Edward C., 171

Sanders, Harry, 274
Sanger, Margaret, 182–83
Sarris, Andrew, 199
Savoy Ballroom, 95
Scarface (1932) (film), 226, 227
Scarface (1983) (film), 228
Schechter Brothers, 65, 114–15
Schoen, Max, 68
science, 63–76; applied, 67; Enlightenment, 65; inventions and innovations, 63, 64; scientific humanism, 68, 70; scientists, 63, 64; in society, 65–69;
Science Advisory Board, 65
Scottsboro Boys, 98–99
screwball comedies, 198–200, 203, 212
Securities Exchange Commission, 47–48
Selznick, David O., 85
Senate Military Affairs Committee, 259
Shadow, The, 204, 231–34
Shanghai, 269
Share Our Wealth, 112–13
Shearer, Norma, 184, 222
Sheridan, John, 152
Siebolds, Geraldine "Jerry," 53
Shirer, William L., 250–52, 256
Singer, Saul, 15
Sino–Japanese War (1937–45), 261, 266–71
Sloan, Alfred, 106
Smith, Al (Alfred E.), 10, 28, 29, 33, 34, 35, 106, 273
Smoot-Hawley Tariff (1930), 19–20
social class, 9, 92, 93, 160, 198, 204, 212; middle, 9, 75, 87, 136, 161, 166, 195, 196, 212, 231, 232, 239; working, 96, 134, 136, 139, 141, 142, 147, 149, 158, 160, 161–65, 173, 195, 231, 232, 281; upper, 2, 29–31, 97, 179–80, 198, 203, 231, 242
social justice, 60, 87, 105, 108, 176, 264
Social Security Act, 119–22, 124, 125, 126, 128, 130, 131, 147, 178, 280
Society of American Foresters, 73
Soil Conservation (magazine), 57
Soil Conservation Act (SCA), 122
Soil Conservation Service (SCS), 62
Soong, "Charlie" (Han Chiao-shun), 267
Soong, Ching-ling, 267

Soong, May-ling (Madame Chiang Kai-shek), 267–69
Soong, T. V., 270
Southern Agrarian movement, 66–68
Southern Tenant Farmers Union, 176
Soviet Union, 246–49, 256–58, 260, 266
Spain, 247, 264–66
Spanish-American War, 245, 247
Spanish Civil War, 247, 260, 264–66
Stalin, Joseph, 246, 256, 257–58
Steel Workers' Organizing Committee (SWOC), 154, 158; Little Steel Strike, 159–60; steel industry conditions, 158
Steffens, Lincoln, 249
Steinbeck, John, xii, 59
Steinberg, Neil, 197
Stepin' Fetchit. *See* Perry, Lincoln Theodore Monroe Andrew
Stewart, Jimmy, 85
stock market crash, xi, 2, 10–11, 16, 19, 20, 47, 71, 129, 140, 168, 170, 174, 187, 203, 238, 241; Black Tuesday, xi, 10–11, 19; origins of, 10–12, 14, 17–18; Roosevelt and regulation, 47–48
Stone, Lewis, 188
Stork Club, 205
Street & Smith, 231, 232, 234, 235
Sun Yat-sen, 267
Superman, 217, 233, 237
supermarkets, 187
Sutherland, George, 113
Swing era, 235, 240, 242; dances of, 94, 240; popular bands of, 95, 96, 240, 241, 242
Swing Time (film), 214

Taiwan, 269
Tarzan, 188, 222, 235
Tate, Allen, 66
Taylor, Myron, 158–59
teenagers, 238–41
Temple, Shirley, 85, 91, 219–21
Tenayuca, Emma, 176–77, 178
Tennessee Valley Authority (TVA), 48, 63
Third Ward gang (Newark), 274
Thomasi, Mari, 117
Thompson, Virgil, 57
Time (Magazine), 239, 268
Tolstoy, Leo, 176
Toomer, Jean, 82, 84
Top Hat (film), 214
Topper (film), 199
Townsend, Francis, 106–7, 115, 119, 120, 125
Trading with the Enemy Act of 1917, 40
"Trial of the Century." *See* Lindbergh, Charles
Trotsky, Leon, 258
Tugwell, Rexford, 38, 56
Turkel, Studs, 117
Turner, Daniel, 21
Twentieth Amendment, 37

Ukraine (terror famine), 257–58
United Automobile Workers' Union (UAW), 154–58, 175
United Cannery and Agricultural Packing and Allied Workers of America (UCAPAWA), 176
United Italian Association, 264
United Mine Workers of America (UMW), 134, 141, 142, 151, 152, 154
United States Bureau of Fisheries, 71
United States Department of Agriculture (USDA), 56, 57, 62
United States Department of State, 261, 263, 265
United States Forest Service, 73
United States Mint, 178

United States Navy, 192
United States Steel Corporation, 11, 154, 158, 159
United States Supreme Court, 88, 89–90, 99, 113–15, 126–29, 152, 223; Agricultural Adjustment Act, 122, 126; Court Packing Plan, 127–29, 130; "Four Horsemen," 113, 114, 127, 128; *NLRB v. Jones & Laughlin Steel Corp.*, 148; *Schechter Poultry v. US* (1935), 114–15, 126, 146
Universal Negro Improvement Association, 263
Universal News Service, 250
utopianism, 247, 264

Vanderbilt University, 66
Van Devanter, Willis, 113, 128
Van Meter, Homer, 194
vaudeville, 84, 217
Vautrin, Wilhelmina ("Minnie"), 270–71
Versailles Conference, 247
Victorian era, 167, 182, 204, 220
Vitaphone, 211
Volkswagen, 255
volunteerism, 6, 18, 19, 22, 23, 26, 140

Wagner, Robert, 118, 120, 141, 146–47
Wagner Act. *See* National Labor Relations Act
Walker, Scott, 281
Wallace, Henry, 104
Wall Street Journal (newspaper), 192
Wang Lung, 267
Warburg, James, 38
Ware, Susan, 172
War Industries Board (World War I), 45, 48, 105, 140
War of the Worlds, The (radio show), 214–16, 234
Warren, Robert Penn, 66
Waters, Walter, 24
Watson, Thomas J., 255
Webb, Chick, 95, 242
Wehrmacht, 275
Weimar Republic, 246, 253
Weiner, "Primo," 274
Weir, Ernest, 106
Weissmuller, Johnny, 188, 222
welfare capitalism, 139
Welles, Orson, 117, 214, 215, 216, 234, 244
West, Mae, 184
Whiteman, Paul, 239
Wilder, Thornton, 117
William, Warren, 185
Wilson, Woodrow, 45, 47, 48, 86, 110, 127, 136, 140, 143, 245
Winchell, Walter, 205, 244
Wise, Rabbi Stephen S., 273–74
women: as consumers, 186–87; discrimination against, 170–71, 178, 181; married, 171, 180; motherhood, 181–82; rural, 175–77; single, 171–74; and unemployment, 98, 169, 170; working, 169, 171, 174, 175, 181, 200, 205
Woods, Colonel Arthur, 20
Woodward, Ellen Sullivan, 178
Woolworth's, 158, 175
workers, 2, 18, 20, 93, 116, 119, 165, 281; economic conditions, 12, 20, 105, 119, 130, 132–33, 137; employer hostility, 16, 138, 147, 155, 160; ethnic divisions, 98, 161–64; migrant, 3, 80, 81; militancy (strikes), 2, 18, 134, 138, 144–45, 149–50, 154, 156–58, 159–60, 163, 174–78, 280; skilled, 67, 143; union membership, 46, 118–19,

workers (*cont.*)
136, 137, 138, 141–42, 144, 146, 160, 280–81; unskilled, 38, 67, 96, 135, 139, 142, 143, 149, 151, 160; women, 98, 168–71, 174–77; World War I, 136, 137, 138, 143
Works Progress Administration (WPA), 116–18, 124, 131, 132, 178, 181
World's Fair (1939), xxi, 64
World War I (Great War), 6, 7, 12, 13, 18, 24, 26, 45, 52, 54, 65, 79, 87, 105, 140, 186, 199, 245, 247, 258
World War II, 53, 63, 68, 99, 132, 160, 165, 199, 237, 248, 250, 258, 278–79
Wray, Fay, 173
Wright, Richard, xi, 93, 117
Wyatt, Walter, 40

Yale Forest School, 73

Zaritsky, Max, 152
Zwillman, Abner ("Longie"), 274